KU-530-601

German Culture and Society
The Essential Glossary

Edited by Holger Briel

Department of Linguistic and International Studies
University of Surrey

A member of the Hodder Headline Group
LONDON

Distributed in the United States of America by
Oxford University Press Inc., New York

First published in Great Britain in 2002 by
Arnold, a member of the Hodder Headline Group,
338 Euston Road, London NW1 3BH

http://www.arnoldpublishers.com

Distributed in the United States of America by
Oxford University Press Inc.,
198 Madison Avenue, New York, NY10016

© 2002 Arnold

All rights reserved. No part of this publication may be reproduced or
transmitted in any form or by any means, electronically or mechanically,
including photocopying, recording or any information storage or retrieval
system, without either prior permission in writing from the publisher or a
licence permitting restricted copying. In the United Kingdom such licences
are issued by the Copyright Licensing Agency: 90 Tottenham Court Road,
London W1P 0LP.

The advice and information in this book are believed to be true and
accurate at the date of going to press, but neither the authors nor the publisher
can accept any legal responsibility or liability for any errors or omissions.

British Library Cataloguing in Publication Data
A catalogue record for this book is available from the British Library

Library of Congress Cataloging-in-Publication Data
A catalog record for this book is available from the Library of Congress

ISBN 0 340 76394 9 (hb)
ISBN 0 340 76395 7 (pb)

1 2 3 4 5 6 7 8 9 10

Production Editor: Rada Radojicic
Production Controller: Martin Kerans
Cover Design: Terry Griffiths

Typeset in 10/12pt Minion by Phoenix Photosetting, Chatham, Kent
Printed and bound in Great Britain by MPG Books Ltd, Bodmin, Cornwall

What do you think about this book? Or any other Arnold title?
Please send your comments to feedback.arnold@hodder.co.uk

Contents

Preface

In many ways, this book is an impossible undertaking. How can one attempt to comprise a (cultural) history of a country within a few hundred pages, even if the chronological starting point is set as recently as 1920? How to do justice to the manifold forces and events shaping the German-speaking world? Indeed, how to delineate what is German, and what are culture and society?

In putting this volume together, I endeavoured to include entries concentrating on major social, political and cultural events of the last 80 years or so, giving much consideration to changes in attitudes, geographies and political systems. This volume aims to be a comparative cultural history, rather than positive historiography. While not wishing to enter into the emotional discussions on what constitutes 'culture', if nothing else, it is constantly changing, and a text on culture and society must account for these changes. It has become commonplace to broaden definitions as to what should be included in such a cultural history; history as 'the history of what great men did' has long since disappeared as the 'proper' way of looking into 'our' past. So has the Structuralist approach of assigning a-personal forces sole agency in the historical processes. And rightly so. Cultural history today is viewed as an assemblage of forces and people(s) interacting in certain ways under certain conditions, with the outcome of these interactions not prescribed by a teleological Hegelian world spirit, but rather viewed as an open-ended process reaching both into the past and the future in order to come about. Furthermore, each period has its own way of dealing with its past(s) and future(s). And as the philosopher Adorno reminds us, even truth has its time limit, its sell-by date. Which, however, does not absolve one from attempting the project of truth, but rather forces one to reflect upon the process of truth-finding (and, one might add, truth-making) as one goes along.

Covering the most important historical events, many of the entries then deal with more recent events, which might be of the most interest to many readers. Furthermore, while Austria, Switzerland and Liechtenstein do figure, they do not do so in a central capacity; readers would want to consider more country-specific readers for further information on those countries.

Indeed, the selection of entries was perhaps the most challenging aspect of the project.

Preface

I attempted to involve as many people as possible in it in order to assure a broad consensus as to what should be included. Sometimes I begged to differ with my colleagues, but most of the time I gladly accepted their advice. Still, there will be omissions. At best, this text can only aim to be a dense patchwork account of events, similar to what the anthropologist Clifford Geertz calls a 'thick description' of events. But most of all, I attempted to make this book a practical and useful guide for those seeking information about a particular issue dealing with Germany, its peoples and its cultures. This book is conceived as an introduction, and comprehensiveness cannot be its goal; rather, readers are provided with introductory information on subjects, and then pointed in the direction where they will be able to find more profound and detailed discussions on the subjects in question. To that effect, the Further Reading sections at the end of most entries and the Bibliography at the back of the volume should prove helpful.

Finally, I would like to thank all the contributors without whose thorough work and sometimes insistent questioning of methods and topics this project would not have come to fruition; Susan Tebbutt, who through our theoretical discussions helped me to see the selection process more clearly; all my colleagues at the University of Surrey who had to put up with me during my involvement in this project; furthermore, Herbert and Anneliese Briel, who provided invaluable insight when my historical range and recollection failed me; Yvonne Hau who went out of her way to help me with the initial and final editing process; and last but not least the editorial team at Arnold, and especially Eva Martinez, who was a great help in making me adhere to deadlines and in preparing the final document. Of course, all mistakes, omissions and such are my own.

Holger Briel
London
February 2002

Notes on contributors

Dieter Aichele studied and trained to be a librarian in Frankfurt/Main, Germany. He has an MA in German Studies and Computational Linguistics from Trier, Germany, and Orono, Maine (USA). He works in library and IT-related positions in Germany and the UK.

Peter Arnds is Associate Professor of German and Italian at Kansas State University, and studied at Munich, Colby College, Maine, and Toronto. He has published a book on Wilhelm Raabe and Charles Dickens as well as numerous articles on contemporary German literature. He is presently finishing a book-length manuscript entitled 'Grass and Nazi Genocide: The Politics of Popular Culture in *The Tin Drum*'.

Katya Bargna is a Postdoctoral Fellow in the Department of Germanic Studies at Trinity College, Dublin, having previously worked in the Department of Drama at the University of Hull. She has published articles and presented conference papers on contemporary German theatre, GDR theatre, *Tanztheater*, and postmodernism. She is currently working on a book entitled '*Das erste gesamtdeutsche Theater': The Rise and Rise of the Berliner Volksbühne, 1992–2002*.

Claudia A. Becker has been Assistant Professor of Writing/Literary Theory and Criticism at Loyola University Chicago, USA, since 1998. She is an Applied Linguist by training. Prior to her appointment at Loyola, she taught classes in German language, culture, business, and film at the University of Illinois at Chicago, UCLA, and Pepperdine University. Her research areas are writing and reading strategies, writing in the foreign language, creative writing, classroom assessment, and teaching methodology. In 2001, she was awarded the Robert L. Kahn Poetry Prize by SCALG (= Society for Contemporary American Literature in German) for her poems: 'Beobachtungen einer Buchenwald-Besucherin im Jahre 1998'.

Notes on contributors

Hendrik Berth was a research assistant at the University of Leipzig, and since 2000 he has been a research assistant at the Universitätsklinikum Dresden. Webmaster of www.wiedervereinigung.de, his research interests are German reunification, content analysis, psychoncology, and genetics.

Martin Brady is an independent scholar of German literature, film and musicology. He has published widely on all of the above. In addition, he has organized several film festivals in the London area.

Holger Briel is Lecturer in German and Cultural Studies at the University of Surrey. His research interests include contemporary German society, new media and philosophy. He is the author of *Adorno und Derrida, oder wo liegt das Ende der Moderne?* (1991), and co-editor of *In Practice: Adorno, Critical Theory and Cultural Studies* (2001). In addition, he has written numerous articles on contemporary German language, literature, philosophy and media.

Paul Cooke is Lecturer in German Studies at the University of Wales Aberystwyth. He has published on German literature, film and politics, including the book *Speaking the Taboo: A Study of the Work of Wolfgang Hilbig* (Amsterdam/Atlanta: Rodopi, 2000). He is currently writing a book on East German cultural identity since 1990.

Winifred Davies is Senior Lecturer in German at the University of Wales Aberystwyth. Her research interests are in the field of German sociolinguistics, especially standardization processes and language in education. Her publications include *Linguistic Variation and Language Attitudes in Mannheim Neckarau*.

Helke Dreier has an MA in History and Political Science from the University of Kassel. In 2001, she was made a Fellow at the Institute for Peace and Democracy at the Fernuniversität Hagen, where she is finishing her PhD thesis on 'Separate Courts – Common Government? Landgräfin Caroline of Hesse-Darmstadt and her Political Ability to act'. Her research area is the eighteenth century with a special focus on gender research.

Sabine Eggers is Lecturer in German at Mary Immaculate College, University of Limerick. She is presently completing her doctorate at the Humboldt-University of Berlin on historical discourse and images of the 'Other' in the poetry of Johannes Bobrowski and Peter Huchel. She has published articles on East German poetry and on aspects of East German culture.

Christian J. Emden is a Research Fellow at Sidney Sussex College, Cambridge, and teaches German intellectual history from 1750 onwards. His main research interests are the history of knowledge in the eighteenth and nineteenth centuries, and the philosophy of culture in early twentieth-century Germany. He is currently completing a book-length study on language and culture in Nietzsche's philological writings.

Chris Flockton is Professor of European Economic Studies at the University of Surrey, where he teaches and researches on the German and French economies and on EU economic integration. He has published widely in these areas of study but has, over the past twelve years, focused primarily on the economics of German unification, with a particular interest in economic transformation in the new *Bundesländer*.

Hugo Frey is a Lecturer in History at University College, Chichester. His research areas are modern European and French history.

Lothar Funk obtained his PhD in Economics in 1996 from the University of Trier. He was seconded to the Institute for German Studies at the University of Birmingham, where he was German Academic Exchange Service (DAAD) Senior Fellow in Economics and Director of Economic Research. Currently, he is Senior Lecturer in Economics at the University of Trier and Visiting Fellow at the Institute for German Studies, European Research Institute, University of Birmingham.

Manuel Gull is working on his PhD thesis, 'German National Identity, Berlin and the Holocaust Memorial' at Nottingham Trent University. Recently, he has been engaged in fieldwork in Berlin.

Markus Hallensleben is Lecturer at the University of Tokyo (Graduate School, Department of German). He is the author of *Else Lasker-Schüler: Avantgardismus und Kunstinzenierung* (Tübingen, 2000), and has published articles on Heine, Hauptmann, Lasker-Schüler, Peter Hille, Robert Schindel, Bodo Hell, Botho Strauss and Martin Walser, as well as on the early twentieth-century avant-garde's influence on new media. His current research interest includes the metaphor of body in art and sciences.

Stefan Hauser is currently undertaking research at the University of Innsbruck. Until 2000, he was Austrian Lektor at the University of Surrey. His research areas are Austrian culture and linguistics.

Anselm Heinrich graduated from the University of Münster and is currently working on his PhD at the University of Hull. In his thesis he examines the programmes of provincial theatres in Britain and Germany during the Second World War. Anselm is teaching theatre history and modern German theatre in the Drama Department of the University of Hull. He is also a freelance translator and works as a Foreign Language Assistant.

Corinna J. Heipcke is DAAD-Lektorin at the University of Surrey. She wrote her PhD thesis on the genderization of authorship in late eighteenth-century German-language literature. She has published on twentieth-century women's mystery novels, Elfriede Jelinek and Karen Duve. Her most recent research project investigates the Letters of Caroline of Hesse-Darmstadt (1721–74) with the aim of broadening the definition of the genre 'letter'.

Gisela Holfter is Head of German at the University of Limerick and Co-Director of the Centre for Irish–German Studies. Her research interests are German–Irish relations (in the eighteenth to twentieth centuries); travel literature; Heinrich Böll; cross-cultural communication; languages for specific purposes. Her teaching interests are German literature of the nineteenth and twentieth centuries; business German; and German as a foreign language.

Enida Ighodaro is a German and Law graduate of the University of Surrey and is the author of a dissertation entitled 'Does the German universal service legislation hinder the development of the telecommunications market in Germany?' Her interest in telecommmunications was enhanced while working at the German telecommunications company Viag Interkom GmbH shortly after the German telecommunications market had been deregulated. She is currently undertaking the Postgraduate Diploma in Legal Practice.

Matthew Jefferies is Lecturer in German History at the University of Manchester, and a visiting lecturer at the Northern Institute of Technology, Hamburg-Harburg. He is the author of *Politics and Culture in Wilhelmine Germany. The Case of Industrial Architecture* (Oxford: Berg, 1995) and many articles on nineteeth- and twentieth-century German history. His interest in the *Neue Deutsche Welle* was first aroused while writing for *New Musical Express* in the 1980s.

Britta Kallin is Assistant Professor of German at the Georgia Institute of Technology, Atlanta. She has published on Brecht, Grass, Schaedlich, Wolf, Streeruwitz, and Jelinek. Her research focuses on post-war German and Austrian drama, fiction, and film; particularly women's writing, gender theories, minority literature, and national identities.

Hermann Christoph Kühn completed his legal studies at the universities of Augsburg, Göttingen, London (King's College) and Rouen/France, and has taught law and politics at the University of Augsburg, Germany and the University of Sheffield. His research interests are international criminal law and comparative criminal law.

Astrid Küllmann-Lee was Coordinator for German and other languages at the LSE Language Centre from 1992, and is the author of HUGO's *German for Business* (1992). She has been the Secretary of the Association for Modern German Studies (AMGS) since 1998.

Jörn Leonhard studied Modern History, Political Sciences and German Literature at Oxford and Heidelberg. He completed his Doctorate at Heidelberg University in 1998. Since 1998 he has been Fellow and Tutor in Modern History and Fachlektor of the German Academic Exchange Service (DAAD) for Modern German and European History at Wadham College, University of Oxford.

Stefan Manz is DAAD-Lektor for German language and *Landeskunde* (History, Politics, Culture) at Durham University. His research and teaching interests include post-war Germany, the Anglo-German relationship as well as migratory movements in history.

Graham Martin is Honorary Research Fellow (retired Senior Lecturer) in German, University of Strathclyde. He studied languages at Cambridge, comparative education at Trinity College, Dublin, is a frequent visitor to Switzerland and Liechtenstein. He has several publications on aspects of these countries to his name.

Benjamin Noys is Lecturer in English Literature at University College, Chichester.

Andrew Otto is Lecturer in Law at the University of Warwick and DAAD Fachlektor for German Law. He lectures on German constitutional law, German private law and comparative criminal justice. His research interests are in comparative law and legal history.

Stuart Parkes is Emeritus Professor of Contemporary German Studies at the University of Sunderland. He is the author of *Writers and Politics in West Germany* (1986) and *Understanding Contemporary Germany* (1997). He is also the co-editor, with Arthur Williams *et al.*, of several volumes of essays on contemporary German literature.

Rajeev S. Patke teaches at the National University of Singapore. His publications include *The Long Poems of Wallace Stevens* (Cambridge, 1996), (ed.) *Institutions in Cultures* (Rodopi, 1996), and an essay on Benjamin (Diacritics, 2002).

Barbara Rassi studied History and English at Vienna University. She is currently working as Austrian Lektor at the University of Surrey. Additionally, she is a radio correspondent for *orange 94.0*, an independent radio station in Vienna.

Amresh Sinha teaches in the Department of Film, Video and Broadcasting at New York University and at the School of Visual Arts. His articles have appeared in *Connecticut Review, Spectacular Optical, Sign Processes in Complex Systems, In Practice: Adorno, Critical Theory and Cultural Studies, Patriot,* and *The Making of Modern Bihar, Alphabet City: Lost in the Archives* (forthcoming). He is currently working on a book: *Memory, Mimesis, Film: Readings in Adorno, Benjamin and Alexander Kluge.* He is also editing a book, entitled *Memory and History in Film/Literature.*

Jeff Schutts is an historian of Modern Europe with research interests in German–American relations, consumer culture, and the peace movement. He is working on his PhD thesis on the history of Coca-Cola in Germany at Georgetown University. He is employed as a lecturer at the University of British Columbia and other schools in Vancouver, Canada.

Markus Oliver Spitz studied German, English, Education and Sociology in Bochum and Bonn. His Master's thesis dealt with Friedrich Dürrenmatt's theory of comedy as exemplified by the late plays *Der Mitmacher* and *Achterloo.* He is completing his PhD thesis at the University of Exeter analysing Christoph Ransmayr's novels.

Bernd Carsten Stahl studied industrial engineering, economics, and philosophy in Hamburg, Hagen, Bordeaux, and Witten. After spending 10 years as an officer in the German armed forces he worked as a research assistant at the University Witten/Herdecke in Germany. Since September 2000 he has been working as Lecturer in the Department of Management Information Systems of University College Dublin, Ireland. His research interests are business ethics and normative questions of information systems.

Inge Strüder is Visiting Research Associate at the Gender Institute at the London School of Economics. She has published widely on gender issues.

John Taylor is Lecturer in German History and Economics at the University of Surrey. His research interests include German economic history and the history of the FRG.

Alfred D. White is Reader in the School of European Studies, Cardiff University, where he has lectured since 1966; author of books on Brecht, Frisch, Storm, and the use of German novels for the study of social history; and of articles on language in German periodicals, literary periods, documentary literature, and expressionist and modern authors.

Abitur   (from Latin, *abire*, 'to exit') Comparable to the English A-levels, or the American High School diploma, the German *Abitur* (in Austrian German, *Matura*) consists of a series of written and/or oral final examinations – including an optional research project in one of the *Leistungskurse* (literally: 'achievement courses') – in the second semester of grade 13 of an academic high school (*Gymnasium*) or its equivalent; a passing score needs to be achieved with a satisfactory grade; *Abitur* is the basic requirement for admission to a university; any holder of an *Abitur* is theoretically eligible to apply for any field of studies. (**Claudia A. Becker**)

Further reading

Ardagh (1991, pp. 240, 244, 248–51, 500); Steiner (1996).

Abstrakte Poesie   Kinds of poetry in which the aim of creating sense by verbal means is abandoned or modified. The text may be reduced to unarticulated series of words, arranged for visual or typographic effect, or written for reading aloud for purely acoustic effect. In the pure form, all metaphorical ambiguity is avoided in the pursuit of a pure play with the potential of words as material, favoured by the *Wiener Gruppe*. Most abstract of all are computer-generated texts (Bense). Nonsense verse qualifies, though not the philosophical subtleties of a Morgenstern; much Dadaist writing (Arp, Tzara, Schwitters) qualifies here, and a vein of nonsense poetry runs through twentieth-century literature, as in E. Jandl's celebrated *Ottos Mops*, a poem using no vowel but o. Some would reckon poetry with a core of meaning which is reduced by paring away the language to keywords often incomprehensible without prior knowledge as abstract work (Stramm, Celan). In concrete poetry (see Konkrete Poesie) with its characteristic typographical experiments, also generally counted as abstract, the meaning of the words also frequently retains a residual value. Widespread doubts about the usefulness of poetic expression after 1945 fuel the advance of abstract poetry. (**Alfred D. White**)

Further reading

Weiss (1986). Covers, tangentially, various aspects of abstraction.

Adenauer, Konrad   1876 Cologne–1967 Bad Honnef. Statesman. *Oberbürgermeister* (Mayor) of Cologne 1917–33; leanings to Rhineland separatism; chased from office by the Nazis, briefly reinstated 1945. Chair of the CDU successively in the British zone and at federal level 1946–66; made it a mass party with wide appeal, excluding extremists. President of the *Parlamentarischer Rat*, the group which wrote the *Grundgesetz*, 1948–49; first *Bundeskanzler* (Chancellor) heading a shifting coalition 1949–63. Strove to emphasize West Germany's reliability in the western bloc by joining European economic and political institutions and rejecting Soviet overtures. Fostered close relations with France. All this would have happened without Adenauer, but his leadership ensured clear-cut decisions – at the cost of polarizing internal politics – and gained respect in western capitals. (**Alfred D. White**)

Further reading

Köhler (1994). Authoritative treatment. Schwarz (1995–97). The fullest work in English.

Adorno, Theodor   1903 Frankfurt–1969 Brig, Switzerland. Cultural critic and philosopher of music, whose work is characterized by uncompromising rigour and density of argument. Supported literary MODERNISM and the composers of the Second Viennese School. Resisted modern developments in the field of politics (ANTI-SEMITISM), philosophy (Kierkegaard, Husserl, HEIDEGGER), and, in more provocatively mandarin terms, jazz and the music of Stravinsky. His most notable influence takes the form of an alertly negative reaction to the ramified effects of the Culture Industry on art and society.

Born in Frankfurt into a family of assimilated Jewish origins. Studied philosophy. Wrote dissertations on Husserl (1924) and Kierkegaard (1931–33). Studied composition briefly with Alban Berg in Vienna. Associated with Max HORKHEIMER's Institute of Social Research. Forced out of a post in the University of Frankfurt in 1933. Worked briefly on Husserl at Oxford under Gilbert Ryle (*Against Epistemology*, 1956). In 1938 joined Horkheimer's Institute, which had moved to New York in 1935. Followed him to California in 1941, where they wrote *The Dialectic of Enlightenment* (1944). The American decade also produced *Composing for the Films* with Hans Eisler (1947), *The Philosophy of Modern Music* (1948) and parts of *The Authoritarian Personality* (1950). Returned to the University of Frankfurt in 1949 for two decades of prolific activity, overshadowed in 1969 by on-campus confrontations with student protestors. Books: *In Search of Wagner* (1952), *Prisms* (1955), *Notes to Literature* (1956–65), *Mahler* (1960), *Introduction to the Sociology of Music* (1962), *Quasi una fantasia* (1963), *Hegel* (1963), *The Jargon of Authenticity* (1965), *Negative Dialectics* (1966), *Aesthetic Theory* (1970). Bibliography: Joan Nordquist (1988). German edition: *Gesammelte Schriften* (1970–86, 20 vols). Translations: *The Culture Industry* (1991), *Alban Berg* (1991), *The Stars Down To Earth* (1994), *Critical Models* (1998), *Beethoven* (1998), *Sound Figures* (1999), *Metaphysics: Concepts and Problems* (2000), *Problems of Moral Philosophy* (2000), and *The Psychological Technique of Martin Luther Thomas' Radio Addresses* (2000). (**Rajeev S. Patke**)

Further reading

Cook (1996); Hohendahl (1995); Jameson (1990); Jarvis (1998); Jay (1984); O'Conner (2000); Rose (1978).

Advertising   In terms of advertising spending, Germany represents one-quarter of the European market and has a world market share of 7.2 per cent. The advertising industry and its market have developed rapidly from the late 1980s, with an expansion by more than 50 per cent to 2000. The industry comprises approximately 3000 advertising agencies and communications companies and is very fragmented. Advertising agencies are represented nationally by the Association of Advertising Agencies (Gesamtverband der Werbeagenturen, GWA), there is self-regulation of the industry through the German Advertising Council (Deutscher Werberat) and the industry's lobbying association is the Central Association for the Advertising Industry (Zentralverband der Werbewirtschaft). Structural changes among the media have raised the share of broadcast advertising, but Germany remains exceptional in the strength of its print media as an advertising form. Thus, for example, back in 1984, when commercial broadcasting was only just beginning in the FRG, print media represented 70 per cent of the total advertising market. By 2000, this share had fallen to 52 per cent, with daily newspapers accounting for 28 per cent. Broadcasting's share had risen to 23 per cent, with, in particular, commercial broadcasting expanding strongly. The *Staatsvertrag zur Neuordnung des Rundfunkwesens* of 1987 set down advertising laws favourable to commercial broadcasters. In public service TELEVISION, there is an early evening advertising zone, the *Werberahmenprogramm* of a maximum 20 minutes daily, while in the commercial sector advertising content must not exceed 20 per cent of broadcast time. This is often grouped as a *Werbeblock* in the early evening. Car, telecoms and media programme advertising predominate. The industry is highly competitive, although the ten biggest advertising companies dominate and consolidation continues with integration of advertising, PR and communications companies. Present and future challenges are tobacco advertising bans, the Internet as a medium and the ageing of the population, bringing changing CONSUMPTION patterns. (**Chris Flockton**)

Further reading

Kellner *et al.* (1995).

Agriculture   Farming represents only 0.9 per cent of the German gross domestic product and employs fewer than 3 per cent of the workforce. In both West and East Germany it has undergone radical changes since 1945, although of fundamentally different kinds. The decline in the farm labour force in the west was accompanied by a continuing amalgamation of farms and a rise in labour productivity. The number of farms fell by about 1 million to 429 000 holdings larger than 2 ha in agricultural area by 1999, while the 3.9 million family workers in the sector in 1950 had shrunk to 1.43 million by 1999. Of these, only 27 per cent worked full-time, while 52 per cent were part-time employed and the remainder worked seasonally in the sector. The average west German farm remains small, at 29 ha, although farms worked full-time were

42 ha in size. It is the multitude of small, part-time farms run by worker-peasants, of average size 10 ha, which is such a particularly west German feature. Overall, labour productivity growth has averaged approximately 5 per cent annually but this has been wholly insufficient to close the income gap with the non-farm sectors. Income variations within farming are large, reflecting farm size, natural conditions and the associated production type – the many livestock farms of the hill areas have notably lower incomes than the large grain and sugar-beet farms of the *Börde* areas or the intensively farmed vineyard or fruit farms of the Rhine and Main valleys. In contrast, East Germany suffered the cruel, forced collectivization of the *Bodenreform*, which in the period 1952–60 had replaced the 600 000 holdings by approximately 4700 collective and state farms. Collective farms in principle were co-operatives, whereby farmers retained title to the land, although machinery was pooled. These giant farms, of 4500 ha in size for arable farms, were transformed into registered co-operative societies, partnerships or incorporated companies. Since 1990, over 750 000 workers, or three-quarters, have had to leave the land, but large arable farms have a favourable future. (**Chris Flockton**)

Further reading

Bundesministerium für Verbraucherschutz, Landwirtschaft, Ernährung und Forsten, *Grüner Bericht*, biennial.

Americanization 'The Yanks have colonized our subconscious', observed Wim WENDERS in a film from 1976. From chewing gum to Coca-Cola, from Fordism to rock-and-roll, for over a century Germans have been concerned about the 'Americanization' of their culture. However, as publisher Rudolf Kayser noted of 'Americanism' in 1925, 'It suffers the usual fate of catchwords: the more it is used, the less one knows what it means.'

Even in the nineteenth century German immigrants to the United States lamented 'Americanization' as they struggled to maintain their cultural IDENTITY. The phenomena soon transcended the New World. In 1902, a British book translated and published in Berlin announced, *The Americanization of the World, or the Trend of the Twentieth Century*. Nonetheless, before the First World War, most Germans remained confident of the supremacy of KULTUR over the shallow materialism of 'civilization' American-style. This changed when the United States emerged from the war as the dominant power, flooding Europe with tourists, consumer products, and investment dollars. '*Amerikanismus*' became controversial in the WEIMAR REPUBLIC as industrialists 'rationalized' production, and INTELLECTUALS debated jazz, Hollywood films, *Girlkultur*, and other manifestations of modern life. The anti-Americanism marking this discourse continued in the THIRD REICH. After the Second World War, the Cold War 'Westernization' of the Federal Republic, and the consumerism of its economic miracle, made West Germans seem the 'most Americanized' of Europeans.

Nonetheless, the continued ambiguity of Americanization was evident when a US Army officer suggested that the post-1968 peace movement protesting US policy demonstrated the success of American efforts to democratize Germany.

Scholars of Americanization have discounted conceptions simply equating it with either modernization or cultural imperialism. Although American economic, cultural and political influence on Germany was significant, the Americanization controversy is considered a discursive field where Germans addressed their economic development, technological change, and evolving social roles. (**Jeff Schutts**)

Further reading

Ermarth (1993); Lüdtke *et al.* (1996); Jarausch and Siegrist (1997); Nolan (1994); Poiger (2000); Wagnleitner (1994); Willett (1989).

Anti-Semitism   Anti-Semitism has been a transhistoric and transregional fact, culminating in the HOLOCAUST or Shoah during the Nazi regime. According to *Brockhaus Encyclopaedia*, 'Antisemitismus' is '[ein] seit etwa um 1880 verbreiteter politisch-ideologischer Begriff' ('a political and ideological term that has been used since around 1880'). This term denotes 'sowohl die Abneigung oder Feindseligkeit gegen Juden' ('the dislike of as well as the discord against Jews'). Starting in the 1980s, the relationships between Germans and Jews have been researched in various studies at German universities, taking a multitude of approaches into consideration: historical, social, cultural, religious, criminological, and/or psychological. The situation, however, has not significantly changed over the years. The latest comparative pilot study on anti-Semitism was conducted by Sturzbecher and Freytag in 1999. The investigators interviewed 4500 young adults in the federal states of Brandenburg and North-Rhine Westphalia. The findings revealed that 29.5 per cent, i.e. more than one in five Brandenburg subjects, had an anti-Semitic attitude; in North-Rhine Westphalia, 11 per cent, i.e. more than one in ten subjects displayed an attitude that indicated anti-Semitism. In this recent pilot, Freytag and Sturzbecher found evidence that in Brandenburg in contrast to North-Rhine Westphalia, anti-Semitism was not passed on from parents or grandparents. The researchers found wide-spread Jew-hatred which could not be explained. 'Unwissenheit und Fremdheits-Erleben' ('lack of knowledge and an experience of alienation') toward the Jewish culture were cited as the causes for this phenomenon there. The American Jewish Committee (AJC) has conducted several pilot studies on German attitudes towards Jews including a representative sample of the German population in the past ten years. The following issues in the German context were the foci of this organization's analysis: 'Is contemporary anti-Semitism a direct continuation of the Jew-hatred of the past, or is it in some sense a new phenomenon? Has the Holocaust finally delegitimated anti-Semitism, or has it merely driven it underground? What are the images of Jews that currently circulate in society? Are there any population subgroups that are especially susceptible to

5

anti-Semitism? How has the reality of the State of Israel affected expressions of anti-Semitism?' The study revealed that more than one in five Germans surveyed expressed negative feelings towards Jews. Furthermore, more than one in three Germans surveyed failed to show interest in maintaining the memory of the Holocaust. In particular, 22 per cent of Germans surveyed 'preferred not' to have Jews as neighbours, 28 per cent of Germans surveyed 'disapproved' of a Jew being nominated as a candidate for president of Germany, 20 per cent of subjects believed that Jews had 'too much influence', 31 per cent of Germans surveyed thought that Jews exerted 'too much influence on world events', and 39 per cent of Germans surveyed were of the opinion that 'Jews [were] exploiting the Holocaust for their own purposes'. In conclusion, all pilot studies indicate that everybody needs to start early to solve this unsettling hostile situation in the German context. Sturzbecher, the Director of the Institut für angewandte Jugendforschung at the University of Potsdam, proposed a 'Zehn-Punkte-Katalog' that can be used by students and teachers when studying the topic of 'Jüdische Geschicht und Kultur'. (**Claudia A. Becker**)

Further reading

Golub (1991); Golub (1994); Silbermann (1982); Silbermann and Schoeps (1986); Sturzbecher and Freytag (2000).

Arbeiterliteratur   Workers' literature depends on a literate working class with a little leisure and some self-awareness as workers. As such, it emerged in the late nineteenth century. Enjoyment of high literature was furthered by attempts at educational self-help associated with social democracy, trade unions, and later communism. On the creative side, Max Kretzer in the 1880s wrote novels with socialist lessons; worker-poets who came to prominence during the First World War aimed to express the contents of workers' life with the quality associated with mainstream lyric poetry. What party and union periodicals published, though, is writing by and for workers (female workers specifically included): short biographies and workplace reports intended to enhance solidarity. This operative writing developed to the fact-based industrial novels of Reger and others in the 1920s. At the same time the *Bund proletarisch-revolutionärer Schriftsteller* (League of proletarian-revolutionary authors) concentrated on radical formal as well as political innovation. The National Socialist period, with its enforced alliance of workers and employers in the *Arbeitsfront*, was a dead period, but after 1945 a fresh workers' literature was propounded in the *Dortmunder Gruppe* 61 (Dortmund Group 61), best known for the novels of ex-miner Max von der Grün. Harder-hitting was the work of Günter WALLRAFF, who moved between various manual jobs in order to write about working conditions. In East Germany, the idea of the worker as writer was fostered by the *Bitterfelder Weg*. But much good writing about the world of work came from more educated authors for whom industry was incidental to their life-experience (Christa WOLF). Growing affluence, the decline of heavy industry and the consensus view of modern Germany as a classless society militate against workers' literature today. (**Alfred D. White**)

Further reading

Promies (1986). Authoritative introduction to *Gruppe 61* and related authors. Jahn *et al.* (1994). Survey aimed at German school teachers.

Architecture Since the early Middle Ages, German architecture has been divided between its south, whose architecture was influenced by the architecture (and know-how) of the northern Italian city-states, and the north, influenced by the architecture of the Flemish cities. In the nineteenth century, with its national and imperial aspirations also seeking manifestations in brick and stone, German architecture revelled in neo-Renaissance and neo-Gothic styles. Beginning with the *Deutscher Werkbund* in 1907, a new thinking began to permeate architecture in Germany. Functionalism and aesthetics were to be fused, with technology playing a major part. Glass and metal became the most important stylistic elements of what would become the *Neues Bauen* (new building). This movement in turn was to influence the Weimar BAUHAUS. Located first in Weimar, then in Dessau, it was to produce and influence artists such Ludwig MIES VAN DER ROHE, Walter GROPIUS and Hans Scharoun. Interior design became part of the programme as well. The influence of Bauhaus was to end abruptly with HITLER's ascent to power, but would live on in the country of its exile, in the USA, and would return to Germany after the war. Hitler's architectural vision was on the one hand the re-discovery of more regional styles, such as 'alpine' in the south and coastal in the north, and on the other the megalomaniac visions of the dictator of the '1000-year Reich', as embodied by Albert Speer's plans for Berlin. The only building erected on the basis of this plan, though, was the Berlin Olympic stadium dating from 1936. After 1945, different needs would influence German architecture once again. Germany needed to be rebuilt, as quickly as possible, and functional and easily erected structures would dominate the German cityscapes. While some mostly southern cities opted for rebuilding in the traditional southern style, other cities such as Frankfurt and Hamburg opted for new design. Notable structures of the last few decades are the Berliner Philharmonie (Scharoun 1963), the Olympiastadium in Munich, with its tent-like roof (Behnisch 1972), the Stuttgarter Staatsgalerie (Sterling 1982), and, since unification, the re-building of the Reichstag (Sterling) and the whole of the Potsdamer Platz in Berlin. Another important square in Berlin, Alexanderplatz, its heart during the WEIMAR REPUBLIC, is still awaiting its re-building. (**Holger Briel**)

Further reading

Tafel (1996). Good overview of German architecture.

ARD (*Arbeitsgemeinschaft der öffentlich-rechtlichen Rundfunkanstalten Deutschlands*) Starting in 1954, the local *Länder*-run TV-stations began co-operating in the airing of each other's programmes and in co-producing programmes. This was done through the ARD, which is also known as *Das Erste* (the first TV station). The federal structure of German broadcasting was introduced in order not to repeat the mistakes of the THIRD REICH, where GOEBBELS' *Reichspropaganda-ministerium* was able to completely dominate and prescribe all broadcasting (in the GDR, a centralized broadcasting structure according to the Russian model was used). Generally, this co-operation has worked very well, with a station only very rarely refusing to broadcast joint programmes, mostly due to political considerations. The ARD is run by the Rundfunkrat (Broadcasting Council), which consists of members of the public at large, representatives of political parties, churches, technicians and members of the clergy. As the ZDF, the ARD came under pressure as private stations, such as *SAT1, PRO7* and *RTL* were licensed in the 1980s and has steadily lost audience percentile points; a noteworthy exception is the *Tagesschau* (*Looking at Today*), its prime time news show, which still enjoys the highest audience rating and is generally regarded to be the most trustworthy of all German news programmes. (**Holger Briel**)

Further reading

Humphreys (1994). Well-researched and comprehensive account of German media. Kreuzer and Thomson (1993–94). Extensive study of German TELEVISION.

Arendt, Hannah   1906 Hannover–1975 New York. Hannah Arendt is considered to be one of the most important twentieth-century German philosophers. Her thinking was strongly influenced by German philosophy, especially by her academic teachers HEIDEGGER and JASPERS, but also by Kant and Nietzsche. A second influence on her writings is her experiences as Jewish woman and victim of National Socialist persecution.

In her works, Hannah Arendt investigates totalitarianism and the possibility of a Jewish existence, which – as she states in her biography of Rahel Varnhagen – seems only possible as a 'Pariah' or 'Parvenu'. Her main work, *The Origins of Totalitarianism*, focuses on the analysis of Imperialism, ANTI-SEMITISM and totalitarian rule, the main elements of National Socialist dictatorship. Based on this analysis, Hannah Arendt developed a model of totalitarianism to which she later added an investigation of Stalinist rule in the Soviet Union.

In her theoretical works, Hannah Arendt explored the character and significance of politics, which to her mean a sphere of freedom. In this sphere, man as *zóon politikón* enacts human dignity in the exchange with others and in concrete actions. According to Hannah Arendt, man has to find his place in the world and go through the process of living his life. By doing so he acts freely and thus politically. The consequences of politics that derive their sources from philosophical theory rather than from human interaction and discussion are worldlessness, ideology and totalitarianism. In her political and philosophical writings *The Human Condition, On Violence*, and *The Life of the Mind* she distinguishes between free political action, on the one hand, and life-sustaining work and mere production, on the other. She also draws a distinction between power as a communicative political event and control used as an instrument. Arendt emphasizes that spontaneous action cannot be derived from theoretical constructs. This is only possible in a 'thinking without banisters', i.e. without the ficticious security of given political ideologies. (**Helke Dreier, trans. Corinna J. Heipcke**)

Further reading

Arendt (1951); Canovan (1992).

Arp, Hans (Jean) 1887 Strasbourg–1966 Basel. Sculptor, painter and poet. Co-founder of Dada (1916), Arp pioneered chance procedures and collage techniques in visual and literary media. (**Martin Brady**)

Further reading

Gaßner (1994).

Art While much painting and sculpture was in a neo-classical mode in the nineteenth century, German art came into its own in the early twentieth century. German *Jugendstil*, the *Brücke* and the *Blaue Reiter* were all movements which would influence the art scene way beyond German borders. Expressionism in particular would hold sway throughout the 1920s, with artists such as Max Beckmann, George Grosz, and others leading the way. Another influence on WEIMAR REPUBLIC art was Dadaism, a movement founded by Hugo Ball in 1916 in Zurich. Several members of the movement were subsequently living in Berlin. Dadaism, in its anarchic and 'anti'-stances exposed the brittleness of society after the First World War, with much of the old certainties having been swept away by the brutality of the first fully mechanized war. Another response to this new world was the *Neue Sachlichkeit* (New Sobriety), a movement attempting a clinical look at a society in flux; Otto Dix's paintings of street scenes in Berlin and the photo-montages of John Heartfield would come to represent much of the atmosphere of those days. Several of the artists who had already participated in the movements of the 1910s, such as Paul Klee and Lionel Feininger, would associate themselves with the BAUHAUS movement (Walter GROPIUS; Ludwig MIES VAN DER ROHE, *et al.*), which attempted the *Gesamtkunstwerk* (complete art environment), including ARCHITECTURE, interior design, everyday utensils, and 'proper' art. During the THIRD REICH, most important artists left Germany very early on. Very few stayed behind; one of them was Emil NOLDE, but he eventually went into 'inner emigration' and was certainly not among the nomenclature's favourites. In 1935 the Nazis mounted an exhibition entitled 'Degenerate Art' in Munich, which included most of the important painters of the early twentieth century. Contrary to the hopes of Nazi officials, the show prompted huge public interest, whereas an exhibition of officially sanctioned art (mostly neo-classical art and socialist realism-like art) just down the road was virtually ignored. After 1945, the tradition of socialist realism continued in the GDR, whereas West Germany would look west for its inspiration. The *documenta*, held for the first time in 1956 in Kassel, arguably became the best-known new art festival in West Germany, drawing huge crowds and AVANT-GARDE international and national artists. Important artists associated with the festival were Joseph BEUYS, and later on, members of the *Jungen Wilden*, such as Anselm KIEFER and Georg Baselitz. Beuys's influence is still felt throughout the international art world, and many of his students at Düsseldorf, such as Jörg Immendorf, Markus Lüpertz and Anselm Kiefer are still very much active today. Other artists coming into prominence from the 1980s onwards include the painters A.R. Penck, Gerhard RICHTER, H.A. Schult, and the video artist Rebecca Horn. After unification, the art scene became even more diverse, with galleries as far away as New York taking an interest in new East German painting. The by far most important artistic 'happening' of the 1990s, however, has to be attributed to Christo and his 1995 wrapping of the Berlin Reichstag to huge public acclaim. Throughout the last decades, funding for the arts has remained relatively high with major new museums built in Stuttgart, Frankfurt and Berlin (see also MUSEUMS); other major artistic endeavours include the Villa Massimo in Rome and the upkeep of the artists' colony in Worpswede. (**Holger Briel**)

Further reading

Damus (1995). Good overview of the West German art scene. Rogoff (1991). An assessment of German art in relation to international movements.

Austrian German   There is almost general agreement among linguists (and indeed Austrians) that the language spoken by 98 per cent of native Austrians is a form of German, not a language in its own right. This fact is recognized by the Austrian Constitution, which in Article 8 states that 'the German language is the official language of the Republic'. However, there is little doubt that the German used in Austria differs in many respects from the German in other German-speaking countries. This is true of all forms and 'levels' of the language, ranging from local DIALECTS to the standard form. MINORITIES and immigrant languages add an additional layer of complexity.

Most Austrians are able to vary the 'register' (i.e. the form and usage of language) according to situation, degree of intimacy or public presence, addressee, etc. Many will speak 'dialect' at home or with close friends, shifting 'upwards' in pronunciation, lexicon, and style in more official situations. Ideally, they are able to move relatively freely in a continuum between the two extremes, local dialect and Austrian Standard German (ASG), with the so-called *Umgangssprache* (colloquial language) in between (in contrast to the situation in Switzerland or northern Germany). This linguistic flexibility makes communication more difficult for non-native speakers. Since the 1980s, most linguists regard German as a 'pluricentric' language, i.e. a language which not only exists in a single form but in several standard forms or national varieties, with 'standard' being a widely accepted, codified form taught at schools and used in official situations and the media. ASG differs in many ways from German (especially northern German) Standard German (GSG) sometimes referred to as *Binnendeutsch* or *deutsches Deutsch*; differences can be found in the lexicon, in plural forms, in morphology, and in pronunciation, e.g. [ch] at the beginning of foreign words pronounced as [k]: *China, Chemie*; weak or no aspiration with *p,t,k* (GSG: mostly like *p-h, t-h, k-h*), this makes ASG sound less 'harsh'. It is important to remember that there is some variation even within Austria (e.g. *Fleischhauer* in eastern regions, *Metzger* in western regions, for butcher) and that Switzerland and/or southern Germany share some of these features with Austria, even if they may not be regarded as standard there (e.g. in Bavaria).

These differences can be explained by the political and cultural developments in Austria over the past centuries and its links to Eastern and South Eastern European cultures (cf. the many Slavonic terms in the field of FOOD AND DRINK). Given the significance of language for the concept of nationhood and the historically very complex relation between Austria and Germany, it is hardly surprising that Austrians often use language as a means to emphasize their distinctiveness. Having said that, language is constantly changing, and it is not rare among younger Austrians to say *tschüs* (goodbye), which older Austrians would regard as (northern) German and therefore not acceptable. (**Stefan Hauser**)

Further reading

Clyne (1995). Good introduction and comparison to Germany, but not all examples totally correct. Ammon (1995).

Austrian literature   Much earlier literature was produced on what was later Austrian soil, but the history of Austrian literature proper begins with the Austro-Hungarian Empire (1806). Awareness of the continuity of the Habsburg dynasty brought fondness for subjects from Spanish culture or history (Grillparzer, Hofmannsthal) and from the non-German-speaking parts of the Empire (Stifter, Saiko); and after 1871 a feeling of being the senior Germany, wiser and more peaceable than the upstart empire in Berlin.

From the nineteenth century we remember Lenau's and Platen's poetry, Grillparzer with his alternately painfully introverted and poetically patriotic dramas, and Stifter's novellas. Though north German, Hebbel wrote plays for the Vienna BURGTHEATER, an institution which still provides a benchmark of quality for German-language THEATRE. Around 1890 MODERNISM flourished with the Viennese coffee-house literary school, orchestrated by Bahr, giving us Schnitzler's psychological narratives and melancholy dramas (*Reigen*, the original of the Ophul's film *La Ronde*), and the exquisite poems and poetic dramas of Hofmannsthal (often libretti for Richard Strauss). There follow the first publications of Robert MUSIL, chronicler of the decline of the Empire, and

Karl KRAUS, practitioner of satirical *Sprachkritik* (linguistic criticism). Literature was close to philosophy, psychology, MUSIC, painting, ARCHITECTURE, and applied arts in Vienna in the early twentieth century (Loos, Freud, Kokoschka are recognized writers). The German-language writers of Prague (Kafka, Brod) formed their own school, open to the Czech surroundings.

In 1919 the Empire died, mourned in Joseph Roth's novels, and today's smaller Austria arose. The globe-trotting reporter Kisch wrote volumes of travel reportage glorifying communism. After 1945 lyric poetry developed with Ilse Aichinger, Ingeborg BACHMANN and CELAN – the latter a Jew from the eastern end of the old Empire. Other experimental directions were taken by the *Wiener Gruppe*, the writers around the Graz periodical *Manuskripte*, and the obsessive autobiographer and manic playwright Thomas Bernhard. (**Alfred D. White**)

Further reading

Watanabe-O'Kelly (1997). Short treatments; further bibliography (p. 581). Yates (1992). Authoritative treatment of its subject.

Automobile industry   The Germans continue their post-war love affair with the car although new registrations domestically fluctuate sharply around 3.8 million, with a consequent impact on an industry which, including automotive supply, accounts for 17 per cent of German industrial output and employed 392 500 workers domestically. At the end of 1999, there were 42.5 million registered cars and 4 million commercial vehicles on the roads: at such high levels of car ownership, the proportion of households having two cars has reached 28 per cent. The German auto industry is the third largest in the world and if domestic and foreign production of German brands are grouped together with German firms' joint ventures with other car-makers, then output reaches 23 per cent of global vehicle production. DaimlerChrysler and Volkswagen rank within the world's five largest auto manufacturers. Domestic car production reached 5.3 million units in 1999, compared with 3 million in the mid-1980s, while 3.5 million are produced at foreign sites by German car-makers. Additionally, two-thirds of German output is exported, primarily to western Europe, although the USA is the largest market, taking 14 per cent of German auto exports. Conversely, foreign manufacturers supply 34 per cent of the home market, with cars primarily from France, Italy and Japan. Of domestic producers, the most favoured suppliers are Volkswagen, Opel and Ford, with market shares of 23 per cent, 18 per cent and 10 per cent, respectively. Under strong international competition, there have been intense pressures for rationalization, merger and joint ventures among vehicle assemblers and parts suppliers, alike. Over the longer period, German manufacturers have sought greater efficiency by sharply reducing the number of underlying platforms in their model range and by involving sub-assembly suppliers and parts suppliers very closely in their product development and factory operations.

Competitiveness has been maintained, in spite of high hourly wage costs by excellent engineering, fuel efficiency, a focus on diesel engines, and a quality image. Challenges are the EU directives on fuel emissions, recycling of scrapped vehicles and a single EU delivery price level. (**Chris Flockton**)

Further reading

Wirtschaft und Statistik, monthly. *Wirtschaftswoche*, weekly.

Avant-garde   The term avant-garde defines either an innovative aesthetics of arts, or a sub-culture within bourgeois society. The aesthetics of the German avant-garde is based on the European avant-garde movements within the Romance MODERNIST era of the late nineteenth and early twentieth century (symbolism, futurism, Dada, constructivism, cubism, surrealism), and became important in Germany after 1910 as well as in Austrian, Swiss, and German arts and literature after 1945 (Vienna Group, KONKRETE POESIE (Concrete Poetry), Fluxus). Whereas the European avant-garde movements tried to overcome the borders of nations and classes, politics and society, life and art, genre and work, the German avant-garde was more concise in creating certain styles. It utilized the same techniques, such as fragmentation, defamiliarization, collage and montage, but focused either on expressing an inner movement (expressionism) or representing reality as mechanistic and materialistic (New Objectivity). With the earlier movements of the European avant-garde, it had one common goal – to reject traditional aesthetics, which focused on content-based ideals and the autonomy of the artist, and, instead, to show the making of artwork as a functional process of art production. Enzensberger (1962) complained that the avant-gardist idea of invention within arts and of a socialist revolution through art had never been really successful and therefore could be seen as an anachronism. (See Enzensberger, 1997.) Since then the term has lost its political implication. Its synonymy for modernity still applies to the German neo-avant-garde (New German Cinema, Pop Art) and POSTMODERNISM, which referred to the avant-garde as a historic movement and kept its aesthetics alive, rather than enforced them politically. Nowadays, avant-garde as a term often describes nothing else than a certain bohemian-like life-style, something new or advanced, and is not limited to the arts. Likewise, the criterion 'avant-garde' has mostly been used by critics and scholars, rather than by the artists themselves. (**Markus Hallensleben**)

Further reading

Bürger (1984). A classic in aesthetics, using theories from the Frankfurt School. Chapters II.2–III.5 are the easiest to read. Enzensberger (1997). Includes 'The Aporias of the Avant-Garde' (1962). Murphy (1999). Revision of Bürger's theory, dealing with DÖBLIN, BENN, Kafka, expressionist drama, and FILM.

B

Bachmann, Ingeborg 1926 Klagenfurt, Austria–1973 Rome, Italy. Author. Bachmann wrote poems, short stories, essays, novels, libretti and radio dramas. In her works she portrays people's inability to fulfil their visions of a new reality. She also focuses on relationships between women and men, especially highlighting a woman's experience in a traditional society. Bachmann influenced authors like Max FRISCH, Günter GRASS and Christa WOLF. Her works include volumes of poetry, *Das dreißigste Jahr* (*The thirtieth year*), *Malina* and *Der gute Gott von Manhattan* (*The Good God of Manhattan*). (**Barbara Rassi**)

Further reading

Bachmann (1995). Collection of seven stories with a very good introduction.

Balance of payments West Germany has traditionally enjoyed trade and current account surpluses for most of the years since the mid-1950s, but unification in 1990 marked something of a break. As a highly open economy, with a pronounced export dependency, the FRG grew with an important contribution being made by foreign demand. This reflected, in part, only moderate domestic CONSUMPTION growth and lower-than-world INFLATION, which helped to sustain a DM which was undervalued in real terms for many of those years. More recently, the limited domestic sources of growth have brought economic stagnation in years of poor global demand. High goods trade surpluses meant that Germany achieved the record world exports position at the end of the 1980s and end of the 1990s. In 1989, its current account surplus of DM107.5 bn represented 4.5 per cent of GDP: this changed dramatically into deficit in 1990 and in later years to mid-decade, as German production of investment and consumer goods was re-directed to the new *Länder*. More recent improvements have, nevertheless, been heavily influenced by European and US demand fluctuations and by the emerging markets and Russian debt crises. While large trade surpluses continue to be earned, these are more than compensated by losses on the invisibles account – chiefly, growing deficits on the travel and tourism account, increasing net payments to the EU budget and continuing transfer of savings abroad by foreign workers. Some 55 per cent of Germany's trade is with the EU area, although the USA is the second trade partner after France. Machinery and transport equipment make up 50 per cent of German exports. These also make up 37 per cent on its imports, which otherwise reflect a heavy raw material dependency. Foreign direct investment and portfolio capital flows are large and growing and Germany-based financial institutions have become the channel for foreign investments into the EURO area. (**Chris Flockton**)

Further reading

Owen Smith (1994). Deutsche Bundesbank, *Monatsbericht*, monthly.

Banking and the Deutsche Bundesbank   Having 3675 banks, Germany is an over-banked country and consolidation pressures remain acute to raise efficiency and profitability. A traditional threefold distinction is made between the private and the public commercial banks and the co-operative sector. However, all but the specialist banks are universal banks in character, offering a full range of services from payments and lending to bond and share underwriting and corporate consultancy. The so-called 'big three' (the *Deutsche, Dresdner* and *Commerzbank*, although after a 1998 merger the *Bayerische HypoVereinsbank* is now third in size) date from the *Gründerzeit* years of rapid industrialization in the late nineteenth century, and were very closely involved in funding the establishment and expansion of enterprises of the period, such as Siemens. They have remained housebanks to the firms, holding minority share participations, giving credit facilities and exercising a voice on their supervisory boards. In the public sector, there are 607 savings banks, often owned by municipalities, and their umbrella banks, the 13 *Landesbanken*, which act as giro banks for the system and as housebank and development bank for the *Länder*. The *Landesbanken* are under threat from EU competition authorities, as they have increasingly come to compete with private banks. The *Deutsche Genossenschaftsbank* takes overall charge of the 2504 co-operative banks, which comprise *Volksbanken* in municipalities and *Raiffeisenbanken* in rural areas. These have mutual status, with capital provided by members. In recent years, bank consolidation and merger have come to involve the major insurance and reinsurance companies to produce huge banking and insurance conglomerates. Their direct influence over enterprises may weaken as a result of the 1999 tax reform, which weakens the attraction of direct industrial participations.

The Deutsche Bundesbank, as central bank and note-issuing bank responsible for monetary policy and the stability of the price level, was established by law in 1957, building on the *Bank deutscher Länder*, which dated back to 1948. The independence of the central bank was renowned, as was its commitment to price stability. The 17-member central council, including presidents of the *Landesbanken*, made interest rate decisions using traditional instruments of monetary control and pursued monetary targeting from 1974 onwards. Its successor from 1999, the ECB, was modelled directly on the Bundesbank. (**Chris Flockton**)

Further reading

Owen Smith (1994).

Bauhaus   School of Art, Design and Architecture. Founded in Weimar in 1919 by Walter Gropius, and closed in 1933 by its last director Mies van der Rohe, the Bauhaus was the most influential school of ART, design and ARCHITECTURE in the twentieth century. Its legacy is present today in areas as diverse as furniture design and typography. It employed AVANT-GARDE artists (including Wassily KANDINSKY and Paul Klee) as teachers across a wide range of subjects (from painting, sculpture and theatre to ceramics, metalwork and photography). Marcel Breuer's steel tubular chairs (1925 onwards) are perhaps its most recognizable icons. (**Martin Brady**)

Bausch, Pina Born 1940 Solingen. Choreographer, dancer and film-maker. Internationally influential choreographer of modern dance and founder of Tanztheater Wuppertal. *Cafe Müller* (1978), typically, portrays human relationships as ritualized conflict. (**Martin Brady**)

Beckenbauer, Franz Born 1945 Munich. One of the most important, successful and popular figures in German FOOTBALL today. Often referred to as 'Kaiser Franz' or just 'The Kaiser' ('Emperor') Beckenbauer became famous as one of the world's best ever sweepers and the only man to have won the World Cup both as a player and as a manager (1974 and 1990). His most important contribution to world football is his invention of the attacking sweeper. Beckenbauer started his career in Munich where he quickly established himself as one of the key players. He led Bayern Munich to three successive European Cups, the European Cup Winners' Cup and several Bundesliga championships. He was capped 103 times for Germany, scored 14 goals and was captain of the 1974 German international side. Beckenbauer also played several successful seasons for New York Cosmos. After his retirement as an active player in 1984 he became manager of the German international side before coaching Olympique Marseille from 1990. In 1994 he moved back to Munich and became Bayern's club president. Although he is one of the most influential figures in German football today, he declined to become president of the German Football Association (DFB) in 2001. In his long career as a player Beckenbauer impressed not only through his successes and the unique roll of honour but also because of his style and genius. There was an elegance and arrogance in his play which suggested that he was always in command – the 'Kaiser'. (**Anselm Heinrich**)

Further reading

www.ifhof.com/hof/beckenbauer.asp
www.worldarchive.com/LEGENDS/beckbaur.html

Benjamin, Walter 1892 Berlin–1940 Port Bou, Spain. Philosopher, literary critic, cultural historian, writer and translator. A contemporary of the Jewish scholar G. Scholem and the philosopher Theodor W. ADORNO, Benjamin is one of the most important writers during the time of the WEIMAR REPUBLIC and the 1930s. In *Ursprung des deutschen Trauerspiels* (1928), he examines the 'idea' of the baroque, i.e. its intellectual consciousness and historical self-perception. *Das Kunstwerk im Zeitalter seiner* *technischen Reproduzierbarkeit* (1936) focuses on a cultural theory of photography and FILM and investigates the aestheticization of politics in the twentieth century. It continues to be highly influential in contemporary film theory. Other important writings include *Der Begriff der Kunstkritik in der deutschen Romantik* (1919), *Goethes Wahlverwandtschaften* (1924–25), *Berliner Kindheit um Neunzehnhundert* (1932–33), *Über den Begriff der Geschichte* (1940), and the so-called *Passagen-Werk*, several volumes of notes, excerpts, quotations and reflections on the origin of modernity in nineteenth-century Paris. He also published a wide range of essays on literary theory, surrealism and Kafka and translated works by Proust and Baudelaire. (**Christian J. Emden**)

Further reading

Benjamin (1996ff.). After several English translations of varying quality, the most accessible edition. Includes commentary and well-written introductions. The first volume contains a selection from 1913–26, the second volume a selection from 1927–34. A third volume is in preparation. Benjamin (1998). A very solid and affordable translation of *Ursprung des deutschen Trauerspiels*, but without a critical commentary. Benjamin (1999). The only translation of the so-called *Passagen-Werk*. While the German edition stretches over two volumes, this translation consists of one volume, but it inevitably contains less background material and commentary. McCole (1993). A comprehensive account of Benjamin's intellectual development, which outlines the major themes of his work and pays special attention to his understanding of history. Buck-Morss (1991). Probably the most detailed and informative study of the *Passagen-Werk* and Benjamin's cultural theory. Also includes much material on Benjamin's other writings. Witte (1985). A short and informative introduction to the major themes of Benjamin's work, with an overview of his life and career. Includes many photographs.

Benn, Gottfried   1886 Mansfeld–1956 Berlin. Writer and medical doctor. Benn studied theology, philosophy in Marburg and then medicine in Berlin. In 1911 he began practising as a military doctor, in 1912 he moved to Berlin, working as pathologist and serologist. In the same year, a volume of poetry, *Morgue,* was published to great acclaim. With its relentless description of the morbidness of human existence, Benn's work was able to tap into the expressionist atmosphere of his time. During the First World War, Benn worked as a doctor in Brussels and continued writing. 1917 saw the publication of the prose text *Gehirne* (*Brains*) and a volume of poems entitled *Fleisch* (*Flesh*). In the 1920s, Benn would slowly move away from his expressionist style and concentrate on essays about nihilism and cultural history. In 1932 he was elected member of the *Preußische Akademie der Künste*. After HITLER had come to power, Benn remained convinced that this new rule would strengthen the German spirit and create new German art. He (in)famously defended his views in radio addresses such as *Der neue Staat und die Intellektuellen* (The new state and the intellectuals) and *Antwort an die literarischen Emigranten* (Answer to the literary emigrants). But in 1936, he ran into trouble with the Nazis, and in 1938 was thrown out of the *Reichsschriftumskammer* (Writer's Association of the Reich) and moved into 'inner emigration', into an autonomous '*Reich des Geistes*' (realm of the spirit). In 1948 his *Statische Gedichte* (*Static Poems*) were published in Switzerland, immediately creating a huge (and positive) media buzz, which would only become louder with further publications in 1949. While some of his returning colleagues would not forgive him his erstwhile closeness to the Nazi regime and thought, the newer generation of writers did admire the stringency and expressiveness of his texts. In 1951 Benn received the Büchner Prize. (**Holger Briel**)

Further reading

Lenning (1962).

Beuys, Joseph   1921 Krefeld–1986 Düsseldorf. Painter, sculptor and performance artist. West Germany's pre-eminent post-war artist renowned for his philosophy 'Everyone is an artist' and use of commonplace materials including fat and felt in his sculptures and performances. A prolific multi-talent, Beuys's early work includes delicate drawings, oils and watercolours suffused with natural symbolism. From 1960 he increasingly used sculpture, performance and public debate to address political and environmental issues. Actively engaged with the Greens (see GRÜNEN), his last major project, *7000 Eichen* (7000 Oaks, completed 1987), celebrated 'Stadtverwaldung statt Stadtverwaltung' ('Green the Cities – Cut Red Tape'). (**Martin Brady**)

Beyer, Frank   Born 1932 Nobitz. Director. Beyer was one of the most famous directors in the GDR. He directed such classics as *Spur der Steine* (1966) and *Jakob der Lügner* (1974, *Jakob the Liar*). His relationship with the authorities was a difficult one. While he had received much applause for his anti-fascist first film, *Nackt unter Wölfen* (1963, *Naked among Wolves*) he had his next film, *Spur der Steine* premiered, but it was taken off the shelves immediately afterwards. Its subject matter, the rifts between various leading party members, and told via the simile of construction work on a house, was deemed too controversial to give it more screenings. His vindication took until 1974, when his film *Jakob der Lügner* came out. It told the story of Jacob inventing radio broadcasts to keep inhabitants of the Jewish ghetto hopeful and it won Beyer great acclaim on both sides of the German border. However, his relationship with the party censors deteriorated once again when he protested against the expatriation of Wolf BIERMANN. In 1980 Beyer was thrown out of the SED, further hampering his career. After unification, he was finally able to work unimpeded by ideological strictures, and films such as *Nikoleikirche* and *Abgehauen* vindicate him as one of the most important chroniclers of the GDR. (**Holger Briel**)

Further reading

Beyer (2001).

Biermann, Wolf   Born 1936 Hamburg. Singer-songwriter and poet. Political singer and guitarist influenced by Heine and BRECHT. His ballads and records earned him devoted fans and deportation from the GDR (1976), an event which caused many GDR INTELLECTUALS to protest and bemoan the apparent inability of the system to reform. (**Martin Brady**)

Further reading

Biermann and Pleitgen (2001).

Bloch, Ernst   1885 Ludwigshafen–1977 Tübingen. Philosopher. In 1908, Bloch received a PhD in philosophy from the University of Würzburg and then went on to work in Heidelberg as a publisher and teacher. During the First World War, he protested against German politics and moved to Switzerland because of his pacifist philosophy. In 1918, his first main text was published, *Geist der Utopie*. Upon his return to Germany he joined the Communist Party of Germany. As the Nazi movement became a relevant force, Bloch increased his criticism of its goals. In 1933, Bloch emigrated again to Switzerland, then moved to Paris, then to Prague and in 1938 to New York. There he began work on his main philosophical text, *Das Prinzip Hoffnung*, stating that humans will eventually overcome the estrangement between nature and society by living on the principle of hope. In 1948, he accepted a professorship at Leipzig and from 1954 to 1959 the 3 volumes of *Das Prinzip Hoffnung* were published. Increasing differences with and repression from the GDR government convinced him in 1961 to accept a professorship at Tübingen in West Germany. He protested against the Vietnam War and became a leading figure in the student movement. In 1967 he received the *Friedenspreis des Deutschen Buchhandels*. (**Holger Briel**)

Böll, Heinrich   1917 Cologne–1985 Langenbroich. He was one of the principal German writers during the four decades after the Second World War and embodied for many people outside his home country 'the other Germany', one that people could trust again after Fascism. He was seen as the literary conscience of the Federal Republic of Germany, someone for whom morality and aesthetics were congruent. His literary works include novels, short stories and radio plays. In his first book of short stories *Wanderer, kommst du nach Spa …* (1950; *Traveller, If You Come to Spa …*) he wrote against the inhumanity of war. He became well known and turned to full-time writing after he received the prize of the GRUPPE *47* in 1951 for his satirical short story 'Die schwarzen Schafe' ('Black sheep'). Among his novels in the following years were *Wo warst du, Adam?* (1951; *Adam, Where Art Thou?*), *Und sagte kein einziges Wort* (1953; *Acquainted with the Night*), *Haus ohne Hüter* (1954; *Tomorrow and Yesterday*) and *Billard um halb zehn* (1959; *Billiards at Half Past Nine*). In nearly all of Böll's works one can find a strong element of religion, however, he became increasingly critical of the CATHOLIC Church in Germany, particularly in *Ansichten eines Clowns* (1963; *The Clown*). Most of his works deal with contemporary German issues important at the time of publication and therefore give a guide to contemporary

German history, with critical reflections on German politics and society. Böll also had a strong relationship with Ireland and published his impressions of the country in *Irisches Tagebuch* (1957; *Irish Journal*). In 1972 he was awarded the Nobel Prize for Literature. Later works included *Die verlorene Ehre der Katharina Blum* (1974; *The Lost Honour of Katharina Blum*), which attacked tabloid journalism and *Frauen vor Flußlandschaft* (1985; *Women in a River Landscape*) and, posthumously, formerly unpublished early stories *Der blasse Hund* (1995; *The Mad Dog*). (**Gisela Holfter**)

Further reading

Balzer (1997); Butler (1994); Vormweg (2000).
www.heinrich-boell.de/index1.shtml

Borchert, Wolfgang   1921 Hamburg–1947 Basel. Writer. Borchert's part autobiographical play *Draußen vor der Tür* (*The Man Outside*, 1947) portrays the tragic return home of a wounded soldier. It was one the earliest literary attempts to work through the horrific effects of the THIRD REICH and went on to become one of the most important literary texts for the post-war generation. (**Martin Brady**)

Böttcher, Jürgen, a.k.a. Strawalde   Born 1931 Frankenberg. Film-maker and painter. The GDR's most innovative film-maker, whose only feature film, *Born in '45* (*Jahrgang 45*, 1966) was banned. Shot his first of 40 documentaries in 1957. Experimental in form and indebted to *cinéma-vérité*, they deal with topics as diverse as furnace builders, the East Berlin Zoo, artists and everyday life in the GDR. *Martha* (1978) is a sparse and moving portrait of a rubble woman on her last working day and *Shunters* (*Rangierer*, 1984) is a brilliant Kafkaesque study of men at work. From 1990 mainly active as a painter. (**Martin Brady**)

Brandt, Willy   1913 Lübeck–1992 Unkel. Statesman. Brandt was born as Herbert Frahm. Politically active in a number of socialist organizations since his early youth he had to flee Nazi Germany in 1933 because of his political activities. He went into exile to Scandinavia. It was during his years of emigration that he took on the name of Willy Brandt. Upon his return to Berlin in 1947 Brandt became engaged in the Social Democratic Party of Germany (SPD), the party he had joined in 1944. His vision of a peaceful German nation at the heart of a unified European continent soon captured his party fellows and Brandt became a leading figure in the post-war SPD.

He was Governing Mayor of Berlin (1957–66) at the time the Wall between East and West Germany was built in 1961. When the SPD became the junior partner in a coalition with the conservative Christian Democrats (CDU) at the federal level in 1966, Willy Brandt was made Vice-Chancellor of West Germany and Foreign Secretary. In 1969 Brandt was elected Chancellor of West Germany, the first Social Democratic chancellor of the post-war era. During his years in government Willy Brandt developed his famous *Ostpolitik*, a new approach to the West German relationship with the

Eastern Communist bloc. The *Ostpolitik* is regarded as Brandt's most significant achievement and earned him the Nobel Peace Prize in 1971. In brief, it called for a Cold War rapprochement between the Western and the Eastern bloc, without, however, weakening West Germany's link with its Western allies. In 1974 Brandt was forced to resign from his post because his close associate Günter Guillaume was found to have spied for the German Democratic Republic. Brandt continued as chairman of the SPD until 1987. (**Manuel Gull**)

Further reading

Brandt (1997); P. Koch (1989).

Braun, Volker   Born 1939 Dresden. Author. Braun is at home in many genres; he has published poems, plays and prose texts. Unwilling to give up his notion of private life and happiness to the greater good of all, Braun always had a difficult relationship with the GDR censors. Things came to a head with his *Unvollendete Geschichte* (*Unfinished Story*, 1975 in *Sinn und Form*, a literary journal; 1977 as book). It is the story of a girl in the GDR, whose father prohibits her seeing a boy who might try to go west and thereby commit a crime according to GDR law (*Republikflucht*). Feeling left alone, the boy tries to commit suicide and is rescued at the last minute. Braun then keeps the ending deliberately open. In his vehement assertion of individual happiness, Braun became a mouthpiece for the younger GDR generation's critique of the system, a position he shared with Ulrich PLENZDORF. (**Holger Briel**)

Brecht, Eugen Berthold Friedrich   1898 Augsburg–1956 East Berlin. Brecht's experimental plays, as well as his theory of 'epic' theatre, have exerted a decisive influence on the development of twentieth-century theatre. Primarily known for his dramatic work, Brecht is also one of the most important German poets of the century. His work is informed by his determination to unsettle his audience and by his view of literature as an instrument of social change. Born to middle-class parents in Augsburg, Brecht moved to Berlin in 1924 where he developed a keen interest in Marxist theory and socialist art. His plays of the 1920s, such as *Die Dreigroschenoper* (*The Threepenny Opera, 1928*), and particularly his 1930s 'learning plays', criticize capitalism from a socialist perspective. They are manifestations of his theory of 'epic' theatre, formulated in detail in *Kleines Organon für das Theater* (*Short Organum for the Theatre*, 1949). Unlike traditional, 'Aristotelian' theatre, Brecht's epic theatre did not seek to appeal to the audience's feelings, but rather to their reason, encouraging them by means of *Verfremdungseffekte* (distancing/estrangement effects) to reflect critically on the social forces behind the events on stage, and to apply their analysis to their own social situation. When the Nazis came to power in 1933, Brecht went into exile to Switzerland and Denmark – where he wrote *Svendborger Gedichte* (*Svendborg Poems*, 1939), containing the famous poem 'An die Nachgeborenen' – and finally to the USA, where he produced his major plays, such as *Mutter Courage und ihre Kinder* (*Mother Courage and Her Children*, 1941) and *Galileo* (*The Life of Galileo*, 1943). In 1948 he returned to East Berlin. He was fêted by the East German government and given control of a theatre, the Berliner Ensemble, but most of his writing during his last years fell short of the quality of the work produced under the pressures of exile. In the 1950s his writing was attacked by party functionaries because its rational approach was diametrically opposed to the focus on empathy demanded by the pre-scriptive theory of 'socialist realism'. The ambivalence of Brecht's relationship to com-munism informs his most significant publication of the late period: *Buckower Elegien* (*Buckow Elegies*, 1953), is a collection of 'minimal' poems which contrast communist aims with the shortcomings of East German reality. (**Sabine Eggers**)

Further reading

Giles and Livings (1998). A collection of recent essays discussing specific aspects of Brecht's writing for the theatre, focusing particularly on his aesthetics, his cultural politics and the cultural and political contexts of his work. Thomson and Sacks (1994). A readable introduction to various aspects of Brecht's work and life. Most chapters are concerned with his dramatic work, including interpretations of his major plays, his use of music, and his legacy for twentieth-century drama, dramatic theory and acting styles. Chapter 15 focuses on his poetry.

Broch, Hermann   1886 Vienna–1951 New Haven, Connecticut. Author. Born into a wealthy Jewish textile family, Broch was slated to take over his father's company, when he decided in 1928 to study humanities. Because of his heritage, he was forced to emi-grate in 1938 to the USA, where he would research mass psychology, get involved in pol-itics and accept a professorship at Yale University. Already in 1931 and 1932 he had published the first two parts of a novel, *Die Schlafwandler* (*The sleepwalkers*) to wide acclaim. The third part would follow posthumously in 1964. On the way to a new mythol-ogy (which would not lend itself to Nazi propaganda) and influenced by James Joyce, Broch attempts to give an account of the demise of three different characters in three dif-ferent epochs (1888, 1903 and 1918). The text which would establish his fame, though, was *Der Tod des Vergil* (*Virgil's Death*, 1945), in which he lets the dying poet reflect upon the breaking up of the/his world, a topic close to Broch's heart. (**Holger Briel**)

Further reading

Lützeler (1987).

Bundeswehr   *Bundeswehr* is the proper name of the German armed forces, literally meaning 'federal defence'. After the Second World War it was initially planned to keep Germany demilitarized forever. The outbreak of the Cold War and more specifically of the Korean War led to a reconsideration of this position by the Western allies and eventually to Germany's rearmament and the commission of the *Bundeswehr* in 1955. The purpose of the *Bundeswehr* was to support NATO against a potential attack by the Warsaw Pact for which the West German territory would have been the battleground.

For this purpose, the *Bundeswehr* was structured into the *Luftwaffe* (air force), the *Marine* (navy), and the *Heer* (army) with a strength of 500 000 soldiers. Most of the *Bundeswehr* troops were under permanent direct NATO command. From the beginning the *Bundeswehr* was conceived as a conscription army with every male German having to serve for 10 to 18 months. The alternative was conscientious objection resulting in compulsory social service which lasted slightly longer.

The most serious test for the *Bundeswehr* so far has been German reunification. East and West German armed forces (former enemies) were merged and according to the reunification treaty had to be reduced in strength from almost 700 000 to 340 000. Additionally, Germany regained its full sovereignty and thus the ability to deploy armed forces according to political will. This led to a first political crisis during the second Gulf War when Germany decided not to send any soldiers. A decision by the German Supreme Court clarified that the Bundestag is free to deploy the *Bundeswehr* according to its political will. This has led to the necessity of completely restructuring the *Bundeswehr* which was conceived for heavy warfare in Germany and now has to fulfil different tasks in Serbia, Kosovo, and other places.

Serious problems facing the *Bundeswehr* right now are the chronic lack of finance; the resulting discussion of the final strength of the *Bundeswehr*; and the future of conscription. (**Bernd Carsten Stahl**)

Further reading

www.bundeswehr.de

Burgtheater   Situated in Vienna, the *Burgtheater* is the most important Austrian theatre and one of the leading German-speaking THEATRES. In 1776 Emperor Joseph II declared the existing *Theater nächst der Burg* (Theatre next to the Imperial Palace) the official *Teutsches Hof- und Nationaltheater*, instructing it to perform 'good German originals and fine translations'. The *Burgtheater* reached a peak under H. Laube (1849–67) who developed a demanding repertoire of plays performed by the theatre's famous ensemble. In 1888 it moved to the newly erected building in the Ringstrasse. Since the 1890s, it has incorporated Austrian (Nestroy, Raimund, Schnitzler) and international (Ibsen) playwrights into the repertoire to counterbalance classical plays. During the Nazi period, the emigration of many of its artists left it with a falling reputation. It was heavily damaged in a bomb raid in 1945 and the reconstructed theatre re-opened in 1955. Among the older, more conventional audience, the traditional *Burgtheater* was famous for its characteristic style in both performance and speech (so-called '*Burgtheaterdeutsch*'). However, theatre-managers in the 1970s and especially C. Peymann in the 1980s broke away from the tradition by opening the *Burgtheater* to modern, often highly controversial performances, e.g. the premiere of Thomas Bernhard's *Heldenplatz*, causing a national discussion and thereby demonstrating the special position of the *Burgtheater* as an Austrian cultural institution. In 1999 K. Bachler was appointed theatre-manager. (**Stefan Hauser**)

Canetti, Elias   1905 Rustschuk, Bulgaria–1994 Zurich. Author. Canetti grew up in England, Austria, Switzerland and Germany. German was only his fourth language, but he made it his writing language. He studied natural sciences in Vienna and received his doctorate in 1929. In 1936, his novel *Die Blendung* (*Auto da Fé*) was published to wide acclaim. The novel tells the story of Peter Kien, a Sinologist, whose attempt at keeping a chaotic world at bay via his studies, is brutally negated, leading him on to the road of self-destruction. In his later life, Canetti would continue to write unconventional pieces, such as his study on masses and power (*Masse und Macht*, *Crowds and Power*, 1960), travel writings, aphorisms and his three volumes of autobiography. He received the Nobel Prize for Literature in 1981. (**Holger Briel**)

Further reading

Lawson (1991).

Catholicism   Christianity in the area of present-day Germany starts with St Boniface, an Anglo-Saxon missionary, instrumental in founding the still-important monastery at Fulda (744). A strong monastic tradition was established; the earliest German culture arose within it – mysticism (Hildegard of Bingen, Master Eckhart), literature, imposing churches and fine religious artefacts. Martin Luther's protest at the sale of indulgences (1517) set off the Reformation; much of the north and south-west was lost to the Catholic cause. The disastrous Thirty Years' War (1618–48) harmed Catholicism. The Counter-Reformation, however, brought stress on sensual elements: dramatic liturgy and baroque churches. Prussia and the Second Reich viewed Catholicism as an alien force, and were attacked in Bismarck's *Kulturkampf* (cultural struggle) during the 1870s. The Catholic political party, the *Zentrum*, long influential, was abandoned by the Vatican when a Concordat with HITLER (1933) gave the Church guarantees concerning education and established an official church tax collected by the state (making the German Church, for a time, enviably rich). Under Hitler, individual churchmen protested about totalitarianism, official anti-religious attitudes, euthanasia and the persecution of Jews, but the official Church refused to oppose the regime in order not to intensify the conflicts of conscience for individuals. In divided Germany, few Catholics lived in the East; in West Germany population movements loosened traditional geographical religious divides. The *Zentrum* was subsumed in the ecumenical CDU (in Bavaria, CSU). The Church gained support temporarily and continued strong in the Rhineland and Bavaria. It took a hard line in the Cold War, but was fairly liberal on social matters.

In reunited Germany it has 27 dioceses; about 100 lay organizations form a steering group (*Zentralkommittee der deutschen Katholiken*). Secularization has reduced numbers. The relationship of the German hierarchy with the Vatican can be tense, as in recent controversy over whether church social bodies may participate in the state procedure for advising women who are considering abortion. (**Alfred D. White**)

Further reading

Meyers Grosses Universal-Lexikon (1981–86). Article 'Katholische Kirche'. Survey of history and organization of German Catholicism in the context of the wider church and belief.

katholische-kirche.de (website, German language only, with current press releases, features, links to Bishops' Conference and dioceses)

CDU (*Christlich Demokratische Union Deutschlands*) The CDU was the largest conservative party in West Germany and remains so in unified Germany. In Bavaria, its sister party is the CSU (*Christlich-Sozial Union*, Christian Social Union). Immediately after the Second World War, the CDU moved into government, with Konrad ADENAUER as Chancellor. It retained its power until the late 1960s when it was first forced to become part of a *Große Koalition* with the SPD, and then forced into the opposition by Willy BRANDT's SPD. In 1982 Helmut KOHL managed to revive its fortunes to become Chancellor. He in turn was defeated in the 1998 ELECTIONS by Gerhard SCHRÖDER, again from the SPD. (**Holger Briel**)

Further reading

Dalton (1993).

Celan, Paul 1920 Tschernowitz–1970 Paris. One of the most celebrated German poets of the post-war era, Celan was greatly influenced by Symbolism and Surrealism. His abstract poems, which contain an array of metaphors, are composed in a way that haunts the reader: 'Mohn und Gedächtnis' (1952: 'Poppies and Memory'), 'Sprachgitter' (1959: 'Language Constraints') and 'Die Niemandsrose' (1963: 'Nobody's Rose') are some of his most famous poems. His writing is often characterized as 'Kriegsdichtung' or VERGANGENHEITSBEWÄLTIGUNG ('War Poetry' and 'Coming to terms with the Past'). The artistic impact of Celan's poems have been compared to fanciful mosaics, stained-glass windows or modern abstract paintings, often of a dreamlike or cold artistic nature. On the other hand, the strangely chiselled patterns of his images and similes are imprinted onto our memories; the musically contrastive construction of some poems highlighting the fate of the Jewish people, 'Die Todesfuge' being the best known. (**Astrid Küllmann-Lee**)

Further reading

Celan (1995, 1996 and 1999). Emmerich (2001).

Collective bargaining and employee participation The West German industrial relations system dates back to the period of allied occupation and has retained its key characteristics. It is marked by neo-corporatism, where large industry-based unions negotiate with central employer federations. The ensuing agreements have a wide application across Germany and firms in a sector. It was this system which was applied unchanged to the east in 1990. In 1945, the Allies, particularly the British, favoured industry-based unions to overcome the previous fragmentation and rivalries and 16 trade unions (later, 17) were largely organized on this basis, grouped under the umbrella of the DGB (Deutscher Gewerkschaftsbund) trade union confederation, which itself was formed in 1949. Exceptions were the DAG (Deutsche Angestellten Gewerkschaft) white-collar union, which broke away in 1947 so as to recruit across sectors, the Deutscher Beamtenbund, which sought to recruit civil servants and the Christlicher Gewerkschaftsbund Deutschlands, which broke away in 1955 and has a Christian Democrat (CDU) orientation. Trade union density has been falling particularly sharply over the 1990s, partly as a result of loss of members in the east, and now stands at 33 per cent in the DGB branches and 70 per cent in the public sector. Partly in response, there has been a recent concentration to produce 11 DGB-affiliated unions: IG Metall has absorbed small unions and Verdi, the new white-collar union, groups five predecessor unions including the DAG. Typical of the system is its high level of juridification, such that wage contracts must expire before a strike. There is a *Friedenspflicht* (duty to reach agreement and a cooling-off period is required after a strike ballot), elaborate conciliation and arbitration arrangements and strong centralization in the system, such that agreements apply to all employers in the employers' federation. Employee participation arrangements cover a requirement for elections to work councils in all but the smallest companies, as well as employee representation on supervisory boards of joint-stock companies. In coal and steel there is parity representation of capital and labour. (**Chris Flockton**)

Further reading

K. Koch (1989).

Commemoration Commemoration is a term used to describe instances of remembrance. What events are being commemorated and the manner in which they are commemorated are the result of a complex interaction between IDENTITY and memory. Acts of commemoration are shaped both by the historic event to which they refer and the self-image a nation or a group of people has of itself in the present. They are acted out at the intersection between the public and the private spheres. Very often the public memory of history is in contrast to the private recollection of individuals.

In Germany, this conflict is very apparent in the commemoration of the Second World War and the HOLOCAUST. Unlike the victorious allied nations of the Second World War (the USA, the Soviet Union, the United Kingdom and France), Germans are prevented from commemorating their fallen soldiers as heroes. The lost war and the memory of the Holocaust, an unprecedented event in its barbarity and scale, leave little room for mourning dead German soldiers. So each year in November on *Volkstrauertag* (People's Mourning Day), Germans get together to remember 'the victims of war and tyranny' (as inscribed in Germany's Central War Memorial in Berlin). They remember all those who died, both their own soldiers and those of the allied nations, and also those that fell victim to the Nazi annihilation policy. This practice is highly controversial and many Germans argue strongly for more differentiation in remembrance. In addition to *Volkstrauertag*, a number of commemorative acts throughout the year are dedicated specifically to victims of the Holocaust, mostly to the Jewish victims but increasingly to other groups of victims, such as the handicapped and Sinti and Roma, as well. (**Manuel Gull**)

Further reading

Evans and Lunn (1997); Gillis (1994); Reichel (1999).

Consumption   Material progress in the early years of the Federal Republic was frequently described in terms of patterns of consumption. After the 'eating wave' (*Fresswelle*), when people were again able to eat their fill, there followed the clothes wave (*Kleiderwelle*) and the travel wave (*Reisewelle*). By the 1960s, the country was seen by many socio-critical writers and commentators as an archetypal consumer society (*Konsumgesellschaft*) based on the American model. By contrast, the GDR was rarely if ever able to satisfy its population's demand for consumer goods and this failure must be regarded as a major reason for that state's downfall.

Patterns of consumption in contemporary Germany follow those one would expect in an advanced and generally prosperous society. Expenditure on food as a percentage of household expenditure is declining: from 18.5 per cent in 1991 to 16 per cent in 1998, while expenditure on health care is increasing: from 3.2. to 4.5 per cent over the same period. At the same time, there are differences between the Federal Republic and other countries that render its simple classification as a 'consumer society' somewhat problematic. Despite recent liberalization, laws restricting shop-opening hours, especially on Saturday afternoons and Sundays, remain much stricter than in, for example, Britain and the USA. On average, Germans also save a high proportion of their incomes, with this tendency more pronounced in the east. Households with monthly incomes of more than DM6275 in the east saved 18.8 per cent of this amount in 1997, while those in the west with more than DM9008 only saved 13.8 per cent. Even pensioner households with incomes generally well under DM4000 managed to save something: 8.4 per cent in the west and 9.3 per cent in the east. (**Stuart Parkes**)

Further reading

König (2000); Wildt (1996).

DAAD The German Academic Exchange Service (Deutscher Akademischer Austauschdienst/DAAD) was founded in 1925 as a private student initiative. Before it was monopolized by the Nazi regime in 1934, it had established contacts with ten countries. Since its re-foundation in 1950, it has supported higher education institutions and student bodies with an increasing number of exchange students world-wide and a largely government-funded budget (DM422.3 million in 1999). In 1987 it became the national agency for EU higher education programmes. Since 1989 it has expanded its activities to cover countries of Central and Eastern Europe, and in 1999 took on the role of higher education marketing (international advice centres, trade fairs and exhibitions, information events). Numerous programmes are open to all countries and disciplines. They range from language courses and work placements to semester- and one-year fellowships for students and graduates, and from shorter research and teaching visits to guest lecturerships for academic staff. Women took a 44 per cent share (1999) across more than 100 programmes, involving short- and long-term scholarships, study visits, lecturers abroad, and scientific collaborations between German and foreign higher education institutions. As of 2001, over 64 000 people have been supported, of which roughly 26 000 were foreigners. The DAAD's core mission is to promote exchange in word and deed, by means of financial support and political action. It reaches out not only to science and education, but also to business and industry. Furthermore, it understands itself as an intermediary for the implementation of foreign cultural and academic policy as well as for the educational co-operation with developing countries. With a total of 15 offices world-wide (including the head office in Bonn), it provides information on education and higher education in the Federal Republic of Germany, on higher education and degree courses abroad, and on sources of funding and scholarships. (**Markus Hallensleben**)

Further reading

DAAD (2000a). Flyer with short outline. DAAD (2000b). Helpful brochure. DAAD (2001–2). Booklet includes information on other organizations as well.
www.daad.de.

DEFA The DEFA (Deutsche Film AG) is the East German successor of the UFA. In October 1945, the Soviets decided to sequester the German FILM companies in the Soviet zone and order a group of reliable German communists to form a committee that would prepare German film production. This committee moved into the old UFA headquarters at Berlin. They called themselves 'Filmaktiv'. In May 1946, Filmaktiv received the licence for a film production company and renamed itself DEFA. Only days later, the DEFA started producing its first film, *Die Mörder sind unter uns*, with Hildegard Knef.

In contrast to film companies in the western sectors and later in West Germany, the DEFA was a monopoly and entirely financed by the state. Even producers, directors and actors were fully employed and did not have to fear for their jobs if a film was not successful.

These seemingly heavenly conditions were hampered by censorship, though. In June 1951 after having successfully drawn the crowds for a month, Falk Harnack's DEFA-film *Das Beil von Wandsbeck* was silently taken off the market because of 'political errors'. The unaltered, full-length version could only be shown in 1981. After the death of Stalin the close adherence to late Stalinist aesthetics was loosened and the East German film industry opened its gates to western artists. Jean-Paul Sartre produced *Die Hexen von Salem* at Babelsberg, Jean Gabin *Die Elenden* and Gérard Philippe *Till Ulenspiegel*. This was not a permanent development, though. Every time the GDR political elite feared change, it increased pressure. In 1965, after the fall of Khrushchev, the Central Committee banned 12 DEFA-films and official debarments were pronounced.

Only after the Wall was torn down, could an independent DEFA film production become possible. After reunification, though, the German government decided to sell DEFA. The *Treuhand* liquidated DEFA in 1990–92. (**Corinna J. Heipcke**)

Further reading

Heimann (1994). Heimann's work gives insight into post-war politics and their role in shaping DEFA. Filmmuseum Potsdam (1994). This richly illustrated catalogue gives an overview of the films produced by DEFA from its beginnings to its sale by the *Treuhand*.

Deutsche Mark   From 1948, the DM became synonymous with a price stable currency and became the world's second reserve currency. The currency reform of 1948 replaced the Reichsmark, of which there were vast, worthless holdings by the DM giving a collapse in black-market prices. Cash and bank holdings of Reichsmark were exchanged at 10: 1 for the new currency (although finally, only 6.5 per cent not 10 per cent was paid). Individuals also received their first DM60 at parity with their RM. The new currency firmed progressively over the 1950s as German export surpluses accumulated and as the German central bank pursued low INFLATION. The DM became seriously undervalued and a target for speculators. During much of the 1950s and 1960s, the rise in the DM money stock reflected the external component of DM monetary creation, namely, the exchange at fixed exchange rates of trade surpluses and capital inflows attracted primarily for speculative reasons. Though revalued in 1961, 1969 and 1971 (Smithsonian Agreement), the DM had become the polar opposite to the US dollar in the Bretton-Woods System: the late DM revaluations put the dollar under great strain. With the Bretton-Woods collapse in 1973, the DM floated against

29

non-European currencies (EU currencies joined the 'Snake' as satellites to the DM), and the Bundesbank (see BANKING AND THE DEUTSCHE BUNDESBANK) could operate monetary policy relatively freely. The DM soared by 39 per cent in the 1973–79 period, weakening with the second oil shock. From 1979 the DM was linked in the European Monetary System to EU currencies and the EMS operated as a DM block. The Maastricht Treaty of 1991 provided for a single currency, the EURO, in three stages, and the institutions and monetary policy are those of a 'super-Bundesbank'. The DM was linked irrevocably in January 1999 to the Euro at DM1.95583, with notes and coins appearing in January 2002. (**Chris Flockton**)

Further reading

Deutsche Bundesbank (1998).

Dialects   The German term 'Dialekt' is normally used by specialists for a variety which is geographically and socially restricted in usage. Linguistically it is characterized by grammar, vocabulary and pronunciation that are as non-standard or local as possible, i.e. a variety that is either at the extreme end of a continuum between standard and non-standard speech (e.g. in Hessen), or so different from standard that some people might consider it a separate language (e.g. in Switzerland). Lay people, on the other hand, often use 'Dialekt' to refer also to varieties which are closer to standard and consequently not as restricted geographically or socially. These new dialects have replaced traditional local dialects in many communities, especially urban ones, and can still be quite distinct from standard. Recent research suggests there has been no general shift towards standard German at the expense of the dialects (understood as regional rather than local dialects) and attitudes towards these new dialects are relatively positive, reflecting the continuing importance of regionalism in German society.

The German-speaking territory has traditionally been divided into three major dialect areas – Low, Central and Upper German. The major linguistic and social division is between LOW GERMAN in the north, and High – Central and Upper – German roughly south of Düsseldorf. As well as being linguistically very distinct, the two dialect areas are characterized by different linguistic value systems: regional non-standard varieties are more stigmatized in the north than in the south. (**Winifred Davies**)

Further reading

Barbour and Stevenson (1990). Chapters 3–6 provide a description of the major German dialects as well as a discussion of the social significance of linguistic variation in Germany. Clyne (1995). Chapters 4–5 are an accessible and readable account of regional and social differences in modern German.

Dietrich, Marlene   1901 Berlin–1992 Paris. Actress and chanteuse. Icon of screen and stage in Germany (until 1930) and Hollywood. Films include *The Blue Angel* (1930), *Shanghai Express* (1932). (**Martin Brady**)

Further reading

Bach (2000).

Döblin, Alfred   1878 Stettin–1957 Emmendingen. Author and psychiatrist. Döblin studied medicine at Berlin but began writing during his studies. He was a psychiatrist in Berlin from 1911 to 1933. Publishing novellas and novels such as *Die Ermordung einer Butterblume* and *Die drei Sprünge des Wang-Lun* (1915), Döblin quickly established himself as a leading expressionist writer of his time. In 1929, the publication of *Berlin Alexanderplatz* completed his ascent. This, his major novel on life in WEIMAR REPUBLIC Berlin, was quickly made into a movie in 1931. In 1933, he emigrated via Zurich, Paris, Spain and Portugal to New York. He continued to write prodigiously, returning in 1946 to Germany as a member of the French army (he had taken up French citizenship early on during his emigration). He moved to Baden-Baden, then Mainz, then Paris, thoroughly disillusioned with post-war Germany. (**Holger Briel**)

Further reading

Schröter (1978). A classic with comprehensive information on Döblin.

Dörrie, Doris   Born 1955 Hannover. Director and writer. Dörrie shot to fame with the 1985 film *Männer* (*Men*), which was viewed by more than 6 million people in Germany. It was deemed the first post-war German comedy, and was successful also in the international markets. Dörrie studied in the USA and was relatively unencumbered by the German *Autorenfilm*, which dealt with serious subjects in very cerebral ways, mostly uninterested in reaching wider audiences. Her comedy style would have several successors, and she would also largely remain in this genre, with films such as *Paradies* (1986), *Happy Birthday, Türke* (1991, a detective story) *Keiner liebt mich* (1994), and *Erleuchtung garantiert* (2001). Dörrie is also a prolific writer, having worked as film critic for the *Süddeutsche Zeitung* in the 1970s, and then publishing short stories and novels such as *Liebe, Schmerz und das ganze verdammte Zeug* (*Love, Pain and the Whole Damn Thing*) (1987), *Der Mann meiner Träume* (*1991*), *Samsara* (1996) and *Was machen wir jetzt?* (2000). (**Holger Briel**)

Dürrenmatt, Friedrich   1921 Konolfingen, Switzerland–1990 Neuchâtel, Switzerland. Playwright, novelist, radio-play author, essayist and painter. Being rather in opposition to BRECHT, Dürrenmatt favoured the paradox and the grotesque as means of presenting a labyrinthine world. While tragedy overcomes distance because of its address of a commonly known myth, comedy, according to Dürrenmatt, creates critical distance and therefore becomes the only adequate form of drama of our time. Key texts: *Der Besuch der alten Dame*, *The Visit* (1956), *Die Physiker*, *The Physicists* (1962), and *Der Richter und sein Henker*, *The Judge and his Hangman* (1952). His output in later years clearly proves wrong accusations of his skill having run dry. (**Markus Oliver Spitz**)

Further reading

Whitton (1990). This is a compact introduction to the various aspects of his work.

East German identity Collective IDENTITY can be explained by the experiences of a nation. More than ten years after German reunification in 1990, East German identity and WEST GERMAN IDENTITY are frequently discussed issues because opinion polls are noting more and more clear differences between the two. The East Germans experienced dictatorship in the GDR. The official stance of GDR propaganda proclaimed the GDR as the better of the two German states. During the 40 years of separation, the East Germans always compared themselves with their compatriots in the Federal Republic of Germany. The poorer economic conditions meant that East Germans often felt that they were 'second-class Germans'. This feeling remains even after reunification, and has even intensified in some areas because there are still great differences in the economic capabilities of the 'old' (Western) and 'new' (Eastern) federal states. Today, one of the key determining factors of the East German identity is the disassociation of East Germans from West Germans. For example, in opinion polls East Germans may no longer consider themselves to be 'GDR citizens' but much more as 'East Germans' and less as 'Germans'. In many areas, this feeling of disassociation is based on being better than the western part of the Republic. Opinion polls clearly show that old German virtues such as morals and decency meet with greater approval in eastern Germany. At the same time, there is greater emphasis on values such as antifascism and anti-militarism which were officially imparted in the GDR. Equality among people is more important to them than freedom which tends to be a higher priority for West Germans. The experiences of many East Germans after reunification during which time previous lives and experiences were no longer acknowledged and had no bearing on their lives in the new Republic meant that these important identity-forming experiences were transfigured and contributed to a form of nostalgia for the GDR. The East Germans not only disassociate themselves from West Germans but also other foreigners. A greater prejudice towards foreigners can therefore be seen in the 'new' federal states and is also expressed in xenophobic attacks. This East German identity can be distinguished in all age groups, even among younger people who only experienced the GDR in their childhood. We can therefore assume that the emergence of a united German identity will take several years. (**Hendrik Berth**)

Further reading

Berth and Brähler (1999). The book contains various articles about East and West German identity and the inner unity of the Germans. Kahn (2000). Some aspects of the East and West German identity ten years after unification. Staab (1998). Thomas and Weidenfeld (1999).

Economic and monetary union   The accelerating economic and political collapse of the GDR state following the opening of the Berlin Wall on 9 November 1989 led to the key decision by the West German cabinet on 6 and 7 February 1990 to offer an economic, monetary and social union between the two states. The State Treaty to this effect was agreed immediately after a Christian Democrat (CDU)-led government was elected in the east on 18 May and came into effect on 1 July 1990. The Treaty exposed the rigid structures of the command economy overnight to competition: the largely prevailing state ownership of productive capacity, the central planning and direction, the administered prices and barter systems of trade with Comecon were all replaced by the West German economic constitutional order. The Deutschmark applied immediately, as did DM prices, the monetary and BANKING order, competition policy, pensions, SOCIAL SECURITY and employment legislation. The economy was exposed to EU and world competition immediately. The State Treaty specified the terms upon which the DM was to be applied in the monetary union, but to assist the transformation to a market economy, six main funds were established or extended to the East. These included the Federal Labour Office's budget to underpin the fundamental changes to the labour market, the German Unity Fund for pump-priming social insurance and paying for infrastructure developments, the *Kreditabwicklungsfonds* for the assumption of GDR state debt and the *Treuhandanstalt* budget for the restructuring and PRIVATIZATION of the state-owned productive sector. The currency exchange brought a fourfold over-valuation of the currency and so had a mortal effect on the East's competitiveness, but other factors contributed to the collapse – the end of Comecon, the very poor productivity, the rapid wage increases and the obsolescent, polluting plant and equipment. (**Chris Flockton**)

Further reading

Sinn and Sinn (1992).

Economic liberalization   German trade in manufactures and capital flows were liberalized in the early post-war period. Together with a non-interventionist policy in most of MANUFACTURING, the *soziale Marktwirtschaft* of the post-war decades demonstrated many liberal traits compared with European experience elsewhere. However, in key services, AGRICULTURE, shipbuilding and coal mining, water supply, TELECOMMUNICATIONS and energy supply, there were distinctive systems of regulation or subsidization, restricting the level of competition, in many cases inherited from the WEIMAR REPUBLIC. It was in the 1990s, often spurred by EU Single Market directives, that Germany opened previously heavily regulated sectors. The Deutsche Bahn AG was created and split into free-standing subsidiaries, and the Deutsche Post is in the process of a liberalization due to be completed in 2003. The Witte Commission report of 1987 into telecommunications regulation, reinforced by several EU directives over the 1990s, led to the splitting of the ministry into the incorporated subsidiaries of

Deutsche Post, Postbank and Deutsche Telekom and the progressive opening of all segments of the telecoms market to competition. Similarly, in the energy sector, the EU electricity directive of 1996 and the natural gas directive of 1998 provided for the opening of energy supply to competition. This built on the principle of third party access to the transmission networks and on the ability of customers to change supplier. The *Energiewirtschaftsgesetz* was revised in early 1998 to incorporate these principles and the *Kartellgesetz* renewed so as to expose electricity and gas to competition. While, in telecoms, electricity and gas, there have been substantial gains for customers in the form of significantly lower prices, nevertheless, evidence abounds of anti-competitive practices by the ex-monopolist and incumbent suppliers, which in the post and telecoms industries exercises the regulator (RegTP) and, in energy supply, has led to a series of court cases and formal complaints to the *Kartellamt*. Highly concentrated and vertically integrated, the power industries will be difficult to open fully. Separately, in retailing, the restrictions on shop-opening hours are being slowly relaxed, while the time-honoured *Rabattgesetz* was finally revoked in July 2001. (**Chris Flockton**)

Further reading

Wirtschaftsdienst. DIW-Wochenbericht. OECD, *Germany*, annual. Regular reviews.

Elections   Since the first belated onset of democracy, Germany has had at various times and in various regions a bewildering variety of election procedures. Historically, these include the Prussian system of four electoral classes, by which landowners and high taxpayers had much more influence than lesser men, and the WEIMAR REPUBLIC's disastrous experiment with American-style direct election for the *Reichspräsident*. Geographically, each *Land* has its own rhythm of elections to a *Landtag* (Assembly) or similar body, and since these send delegates to the Bundesrat, the composition of the German legislature is constantly changing. In many places direct elections to posts of *Bürgermeister* (mayor) and so forth foster interest in local democracy. The most important elections, however, are for the Bundestag, fought every four years and only brought forward if no party in the existing Bundestag is able to sustain a government. All citizens of over one year's standing and aged 18 or over have two votes. Participation is high (commonly 80 per cent). Half the seats in the Bundestag are available on the first vote, by constituency (*Wahlkreis*) first-past-the-post voting. The other half are allocated by a complex mathematical formula (since 1984 *Niemeyer-Verfahren*) to ensure that, *Land* by *Land*, the second votes (*Zweitstimmen*) cast for the different party lists are exactly reflected in the make-up of the Bundestag. Many voters vote for a constituency candidate of one party but a different party list (*Splitting*). Parties failing to gain 5 per cent of the popular vote are excluded from this allocation (*Fünf-Prozent-Hürde*, 5 per cent hurdle) unless they win one or more constituencies outright (thus in 1994 the PDS won four constituencies and was allowed the 30 seats corresponding to its 4.4 per cent share of the vote). Vacancies arising are filled by the next names on the party lists from the preceding election (*Nachrücken*). (**Alfred D. White**)

Further reading

Conradt *et al.* (2000). Close psephological study. Woyke (1992). Practical manual.

Emma   The magazine *Emma* was founded by Alice Schwarzer in 1977. *Emma* defines itself as a magazine by women made for people. Questioning women's traditional roles and positions in society it reports about and comments on a variety of women's issues. Subsequently the magazine has often provoked heated debates, be they on violence against women, pornography, unequal payment for women and men or women and religious fundamentalism. *Emma* appears twice a month and can financially sustain itself. (**Barbara Rassi**)

Further reading

Emma (Jan./Feb. 1997). Special edition ('20 Jahre *Emma*') on the twentieth anniversary of *Emma* which covers the decisive moments in the history of this magazine.

Employment structure   Including a statistical revision accounting for an extra 2 million people, total employment rose from 34.4 million in 1996 to 38.5 million in 2000. The great majority of employment contracts in Germany are full-time, open-duration contracts. Only 16.3 per cent of the total labour force was employed part-time (compared with 29.7 per cent in the Netherlands) and only around 600 000 employees were contract workers, employed on fixed-term contracts in 1999. The sectoral breakdown of employment in 1999 was of 1.3 per cent of employment in AGRI-CULTURE, forestry and fishing, 28 per cent in MANUFACTURING and 71 per cent in services. The services sector has continuously grown at the expense of manufacturing, with only 66 per cent employed in services as recently as 1996. Within production industries, of total employment of 6.335 million in 1999, 130 000 were employed in mining and quarrying, 981 000 in mechanical engineering, 767 000 in vehicles production and 542 000 in the food industry. The capital-intensive chemical industry employed 470 000 workers. Structural change has brought clear shifts over time, as expected, with the decline of first industrial revolution industries and the transfer of labour-intensive manufacturing operations to low-wage economies. With productivity gains overall of 3 per cent annually on average, there have been continuing reductions in the workforce in the staples of German export branches, namely mechanical and electrical engineering, vehicles and chemicals. The shift to the services sector is explained partly by shifts in demand as the population becomes wealthier, but business-related services have been growing strongly as a result of the continuing move to a knowledge-based economy and as companies out-source activities. Owing to their labour-intensity, personal services productivity rises slowly: there is a continuing shift away from public services to personal services, partly as a result of budgetary constraint, but also as personal services to the elderly, for example, rise. (**Chris Flockton**)

Further reading

Statistisches Bundesamt, *Wirtschaft und Statistik*, monthly. Statistisches Bundesamt, *Statistisches Jahrbuch*, annual.

Engagierte Literatur   Engaged literature includes writings that depict a commitment to religious, social, ideological, or political perspectives. The term *littérature engage* was popularized by Jean-Paul Sartre, in *Qu'est-ce que la littérature?* (1948), to distinguish *l'art pour l'art* (art for art's sake) from engaged art. Authors of *Engagierte Literatur* aim to confront present-day realities, to engage the reader in taking part in the creation of that reality. Thus they attempt to offer the reader an active part in solving day-to-day problems and raising the reader's consciousness. *Engagierte Literatur* does not necessarily offer resolutions to issues. Readers are encouraged to act (as opposed to react) and find solutions that respond to the demands of their environments. In Theodor W. Adorno's essay 'Engagement oder künstlerische Autonomie' ('Commitment or artistic autonomy', 1962 – see Adorno, 1974), he criticizes Sartre's existentialist definition of *engaged literature*. According to Adorno, Sartre understands the human individual as removed from its reality, neither part of it nor created by it. He conceptualized the individual as a form of absolute being that does not have space for any self-implemented changes. Therefore, Sartre does not grant the individual an interaction with his or her surrounding reality that could be represented in art, as Adorno understands it. Adorno's concept of *Engagierte Literatur* aims to help readers identify the difference between their reality and the representation of that reality so that they can interact with their reality. Yet, feminist critics maintain that Adorno's concept of *Engagierte Literatur* is also limited and uses normative ideas because he leaves out aspects of social changes that have taken place in Western societies such as the redefinition of women's space, agency, and labour. (**Britta Kallin**)

Further reading

Sartre (1948). Adorno (1974). See chapter 'Engagement oder künstlerische Autonomie'.

Environment   The maintenance of environmental quality and pollution control are highly effective in Germany, reflecting a strong environmental awareness among the population. Germany spends well over DM40 bn (or 1.7 per cent of GDP) annually on pollution control and clean-up, which puts the country in second place among developed nations. In recycling of paper and packaging, it achieves rates of over 80 per cent and over 1 million jobs are involved in environmental services and production of pollution control equipment. Anti-pollution controls were in place for water and air in the early decades of the twentieth century, but only from the early 1970s did the major clean-up of the Rhine take place. Opposition to nuclear power rose rapidly in the second half of the 1970s, buttressed by the Chernobyl disaster of 1986. Citizens' initiatives against nuclear power among other issues burgeoned and the BBU (*Bundesverband Bürgerinitiativen Umweltschutz*) grew rapidly such that ecological politics provided the base for the Green Party advances in the 1980s (see GRÜNEN). After many court cases, no further nuclear power project was approved after the early 1980s when approval was directly linked to a resolution of the problem of nuclear waste storage. Under the Red–Green coalition government in mid-2001, the details of a long-term exit from nuclear power to 2020 were agreed.

During the early 1990s, moves towards a more thoroughgoing recycling policy were in progress. The 1991 Packaging Recycling Law made wholesalers responsible for taking back product packaging, and at the retail level, the 'green dot' was introduced, signifying that the product would be collected and recycled by the DSD (Duales System Deutschland) organization. The DSD has, however, attracted widespread criticism for its quasi-monopoly status and its high cost. An ecology tax was finally introduced in 2000. It takes the form of an energy tax on petrol, power and gas, with the revenue largely recycled to cut SOCIAL SECURITY charges. (**Chris Flockton**)

Further reading

Bundesministerium für Umwelt, *Umweltbericht*, annual.

Ernst, Max 1891 Brühl–1976 Paris. Painter, sculptor and printmaker. A leading member of the Dada and Surrealist movements, Ernst brought Dada to Cologne after the First World War, pioneering collage, frottage and other innovative techniques. Closely associated with the surrealists around André Breton, he published the influential collage novel *Une semaine de bonté* in 1934. He experimented with automatic (drip) painting after emigration to the USA and inspired the young Jackson Pollock. He experimented with novel techniques of printmaking and painting after returning to France in 1953 with his fourth wife, the artist Dorothea Tanning. (**Martin Brady**)

Euro After three years operating as a shadow currency, the Euro finally took the shape of notes and coins on 1 January 2002, with DM1.95583: 1 Euro. The German population had to exchange their DM holdings of currency in circulation for Euros. They had prepared for this progressively over the last months of 2001 with the deposit of surplus notes into their bank accounts and then in the New Year, they received Euro notes from ATM machines at the bank and retailers exchanged DM currency for Euro notes and coins. The BANKING and retailing systems were the prime transmission mechanism for the physical issue of the new currency. DM280 bn in circulation (of which DM100 bn abroad) was withdrawn in an almost frictionless manner. Trial 'starter kits' in Euros of DM20 in value were available for the population from the middle of

December. On 1 January 2002, the DM ceased to be legal tender, although as a result of a 'friendly' agreement between the business associations for finance and trade, the DM can continue to be accepted for electronic payment because of the large foreign DM holdings. Banks accepted DM notes and coins until the end of February 2002. While there was very evident nostalgia for the Deutschmark, with consistently 55–66 per cent of the population opposed to the loss of the DM, nevertheless 70 per cent of those surveyed at the turn of 2002 professed a faith that the Euro would prove a stable currency. The greatest scepticism was among the old and East Germans. Whether the currency exchange provided the opportunity for price rises by rounding up was much debated. The population believes that it had: however, studies by the VZBV consumer organization concluded that price rises may have been made earlier in 2001 to avoid accusations of profiteering. (**Chris Flockton**)

F

Fashion Fashion is an identifying cultural marker, often used to delineate differences between oneself or one's group and others. In Germany, most areas retain their own fashion traditions with differing *Trachten* (regional costumes), such as the *Dirndl* in Bavaria, worn in different parts of the country. However, after the end of the Nazi-era, in which the ideology of specific German clothing styles was very much alive, these *Trachten* tend to be worn for official or cultural events only. In everyday life, German fashion is virtually indistinguishable from clothes worn by its neighbours in other Western countries. Beginning in the 1950s, clothing became a status symbol, closely related to the WIRTSCHAFTSWUNDER. Düsseldorf and Munich quickly established themselves as fashion capitals of Germany. The upper-middle and upper classes looked to Paris for inspiration, whereas the younger generation preferred the 'cool' and more 'legère' American look. Much of the clothing in Germany was sold through mail order companies, with Quelle (cf. SCHICKEDANZ), founded in 1927, Neckermann, (re-established in 1948) and Otto Versand (1949) leading the way. The most-read fashion magazines were *Constanze* and *Brigitte*. By the end of the 1950s, large department stores such as Kaufhof, Hertie and C&A were also doing a brisk trade in clothing. In the 1960s, boutiques began to spring up and attracted mostly younger shoppers. Internationally, German fashion houses did not play any important role until the 1980s, when designer clothing came into its own for the middle class, in particular the younger generation. Designers and designer labels such as Escada, Hugo Boss, Jil Sander, Wolfgang Joop, Helmut Lang (Austrian) and Karl Lagerfeld (in France) became household names and exports flourished. More recently, fashion has gone even more global and tribal at the same time. If in the 1960s, blue jeans were THE marker for all hip youths, nowadays it is almost only those youths of yonder who are still wearing them. Today, all over the globe, 'Goths' wear tight black, Skins Doc Martens, Technokids sports utility clothing, and other groups specific designer clothing. Germany is no exception. (**Holger Briel**)

Further reading

Loschek (1995); Strate (1994); Weber and Möller (1999).

Fassbinder, Rainer Werner 1945 Bad Wörishofen–1982 Munich. Film-maker, dramatist and actor. The most famous post-war German film-maker, he shot 42 films for cinema and television before an early death from a drug overdose. His work embraces gangster movies, thrillers, literary adaptations, melodramas, international co-productions (*Despair*, 1977 with Dirk Bogarde), political allegories (*The Marriage* *of Maria Braun, Die Ehe der Maria Braun* 1978) and historical costume dramas. Also a brilliant dramatist, he was as renowned for his wild private life as for his outspoken social criticism. (**Martin Brady**)

Further reading

Elsaesser (1996).

Fastnacht   *Fastnacht* (literally, the night before lent) describes the time period and its rituals immediately preceding the beginning of lent on Ash Wednesday. Other names given to this time period are *Fasching* (in the Hesse and Rhineland-Palatine area), *Karneval* (from the Latin for 'goodbye meat' (dishes)), mainly used in the Cologne and Düsseldorf areas, and *Fasnet* in South Western Germany, also known as *Alemannische Fasnett*. Traditionally, the *Fastnacht* period or *Narrenzeit* (crazy season) begins on the 11th day of the 11th month (November) at 11.11 o'clock, but things do not really get going before the weekend preceding Ash Wednesday. There are parades through cities, with sweets and other goodies thrown from the passing floats. People wear costumes and masks; in the *Fasnet* those are traditional masks whose symbolism (and sometimes the masks themselves) goes back hundreds of years. Many *Karnevals-Vereine* have a long tradition, and their official *Prunksitzungen* (Grand Annual Meetings) are broadcast on many TV stations. Famous *Büttenreden* (speeches given while standing in a large keg whose top has been sawn off) are given, traditionally poking fun of GENDER RELATIONS, current events and politics. A special day is also the *Weiberfastnacht*, when women symbolically take over the town halls of many cities. On *Rosenmontag* (Rose Monday) and *Faschingsdienstag* (Shrove Tuesday), many shops and businesses remain closed. (**Holger Briel**)

Further reading

Fuchs (1997). History of the Cologne Carnival.

FDP (Free Democratic Party)   The liberal party of Germany has played a very prominent role in post-war Germany. It was founded in December 1948 in an effort to unite all German liberals in one party and thus ending the pre-1933 tradition of splitting the liberal movement into several political parties. Liberals were among the most active members of the drafting committee for the German Constitution in 1948–49. Consequently liberal ideas still shape the foundations of present-day Germany to a large extent. Furthermore, the party managed to be part of the federal government for all but 11 years since 1949. It did so by entering into coalition governments in the past with both Christian Democrats (CDU) and Social Democrats. Changes in coalition partners frequently coincided with power struggles within the FDP. Since 1998 the FDP has been in the opposition at federal level.

The FDP's self-declared main aim lies in the strengthening of the rights and freedoms of the individual against state intrusion – a goal central to 200 years of liberalism in Germany. It believes that citizens know best what is good for them. Since differences in wealth might lead to gross and unfair inequalities between people, the present FDP identifies one of the main tasks for government as providing equal 'kick-off' opportunities for everyone rather than levelling out inequalities generally. The FDP also sees itself as the 'constitution party'. Consequently, liberals in Germany are struggling first and foremost for a market-oriented economy that leaves sufficient room for private initiative, an excellent education system available to everyone, a criminal justice system that takes into account the interests of victim and offender alike, effective data protection, a reduction of state influence in general and comprehensive protection of human rights. (**Hermann Christoph Kühn**)

Further reading

Watson (1992).

Feminism   Feminism is generally considered to be synonymous with the goals of the *Frauenbewegung* (women's movement), which aims to abolish discrimination against women in economic, social, political, and cultural areas. In West Germany, the middle-class feminist movement was marked by political struggles in the 1960s and 1970s. One aspect was the fight against abortion-paragraph 218, when women fought for a common cause to abolish the paragraph that restricted abortions. Between 1975 and 1979 women turned to more theoretical debates and focused on gaining a new self-awareness, a struggle that was strongly influenced by American feminist literature circulating in West Germany. Women set up libraries, coffee houses, workshops, founded day care centres, houses for battered women and rape victims, publishing houses such as the *Frauenoffensive* in Munich in 1976. Magazines such as *Courage* and *Emma* that were run entirely by a female staff and were independent of ads were created. Important publications include: Erika Runge's *Frauen: Versuche zur Emanzipation* (*Women: Attempts of Emancipation*, 1968), Verena Stefan's *Häutungen* (*Shedding Skin*, 1975), and Alice Schwarzer's *Der kleine Unterschied* (*The Little Difference*, 1975). The 1980s and 1990s saw similar developments in Germany as in other Western countries. The 1980s witnessed a backlash on women's rights and a reaffirmation of patriarchal hierarchies within society as a result of the post-feminist era. Simultaneously, however, women's groups continued their struggle for equal rights and a number of German universities implemented women's studies programmes during the 1990s. The influence of US scholarship on these programmes is obvious in the English term for these programmes: *Genderforschung* (gender research). In East Germany, women's issues were subsumed under the goals of the socialist government and the state provided support for women in the workforce and for their children. A feminist movement was not established in the East and even after unification of the two German states, interaction between feminists in the former East and West is marked by their different pasts and different understandings of feminism(s). (**Britta Kallin**)

Further reading

Abrams and Harvey (1996); Beinssen-Hesse and Rigby (1996).

Feuchtwanger, Lion   1884 Munich–1958 Los Angeles. Author. Feuchtwanger began his literary career in 1908 as the publisher of the short-lived journal *Der Spiegel* and as a writer for the theatre journal *Die Schaubühne*. From 1933 to 1940, he lived in southern France as an émigré, and then moved to Los Angeles, where he would remain until his death. Feuchtwanger became a literary star with his second book, the historic novel *Jud Süß* (1925), which sketched the rise and fall of the Jewish financial genius Joseph Süß. Feuchtwanger's historic understanding was firmly rooted in his belief of the necessary rewriting of history as literature from the vantage point of the here and now. *Jud Süß* would go on to become a *cause célèbre* with the 1940 cinematic adaptation by Veit Harlan, who illegally transformed Feuchtwanger's novel on the abuses of power into an anti-Semitic diatribe. In his successive novels *Die Geschwister Oppenheim* (1933) and *Exil* (1940), Feuchtwanger continues his themes of Jewish persecution and its psychological effects. His home in California would become one of the main centres of exile activities, attracting most of the German exiles, including Thomas MANN and Heinrich MANN and many others. After the Second World War, Feuchtwanger elected to remain in the USA and continue his writing on historical subjects. (**Holger Briel**)

Further reading

Arnold (1983).

Film   Partly due to the critical acclaim of the German expressionist films such as *Das Kabinett des Dr. Caligari*, the 1920s saw a veritable boom in cinema in Germany, culminating in 1926 in Fritz LANG's *Metropolis*, at the time the most expensive German film ever made. Another runaway success was *Der Blaue Engel*, launching the career of Marlene DIETRICH. INTELLECTUALS flocked to this new mode of expression, inquiring about its theory and cinematic manifestations. However, this boom came to a quick end in 1933; with HITLER's ascent to power, many of the most important film-makers fled German soil and made the USA's Hollywood their exile place of residence. In Germany, GOEBBELS brought the film industry under his control, resulting in Nazi film praising the new system, later on glorifying the German war effort, and still later, trying to detract from its imminent collapse by producing superficial comedy after comedy. After the division of Germany in 1949, the western and the eastern film industries developed very differently. The British and American military government of West Germany decided to split up ᴜꜰᴀ in order to counteract the perceived threat of centralization of the German film industry which had before served the Nazi regime's propagandistic power so well. In East Germany, UFA was replaced by its successor ᴅᴇꜰᴀ, and the Ministry of Culture established a Film Department which was 'responsible for all aspects of the film industry' (Pflaum and Prinzler, 1993).

In West Germany, the film market was overwhelmed by the American productions. The few successful German films were mostly of the genre *Heimatfilm* (folkloric films), but they never managed to challenge the cache of the much more professional American films. It was not until 1962, when young directors pronounced the death of the old cinema in the *Oberhausener Manifest* (Oberhausen Manifesto, named after the city in which the film festival where the manifesto was read to an amazed public was held) that German cinema began to be recognized as aiming for artistic objectives. However, largely due to arrival of ᴛᴇʟᴇᴠɪꜱɪᴏɴꜱ in most households, the 1960s saw a rapid decline in cinema audiences in West Germany, and German film, with its ᴀᴠᴀɴᴛ-ɢᴀʀᴅᴇ leanings was not suited to halt this decline. It took until the early 1970s for young directors such as Rainer Werner Fᴀꜱꜱʙɪɴᴅᴇʀ, Wim Wᴇɴᴅᴇʀꜱ or Werner Hᴇʀᴢᴏɢ to gain international recognition for feature-length films, prompting *Newsweek* in 1976 to publish 'The German Film Boom' as a title story. Meanwhile, the GDR maintained a film industry financed by the state. This method could have made directors more independent than seemed possible in a capitalist system; instead, GDR directors were forced strictly to follow the directives of the Ministry for Culture and the ꜱᴇᴅ party's Central Committee. So, in 1965 the Central Committee decided to ban films that allegedly fostered destructive ideologies and scepticism, such as *Karla* (Herrmann Zschoche), *Das Kaninchen bin ich* (Kurt Mᴀᴇᴛᴢɪɢ), *Jahrgang 45* (Jürgen Bᴏ̈ᴛᴛᴄʜᴇʀ) and others. West Germany had also recognized early on that public funding was essential for the survival of the German film industry. In 1951, a law on state subsidies for filmmaking was introduced. It guaranteed that the state would reimburse German film producers for up to 35 per cent of their production costs if a film was not successful enough to pay for itself through till receipts. This law has since been reformulated, but it still provides the basis for substantial funding for local film production. Furthermore, most *Länder* have additional venues for film subsidies. Germany has a large number of film festivals, the most important one being the *Berlinale*, which was established in West Berlin in 1951. The most famous GDR film festival was the Leipzig International Festival of Documentary and Animated Films. While American productions continue to take the lion's share of film revenues, a few noteworthy German films have been able to hold their own. For instance, the critically acclaimed as well as commercially successful *Männer* (Doris Dᴏ̈ʀʀɪᴇ, 1985), and the so far most successful German film, the comedy *Der Schuh des Manitu* (Michael Herbig, 2001). (**Corinna J. Heipcke**)

Further reading

Pflaum and Prinzler (1993). Includes a very accessible account of the history of West German film after 1945. Jacobsen *et al.* (1993). A collection of articles on German film covering a wide range of topics, from its beginnings to a feminist perspective. The chronology in this book gives a useful overview of events.

Folk culture   Folk or popular culture is a term introduced around 1900 and as opposed to 'high culture' implies the oral traditions of the lower social strata. It is a culture that arises from the poorest in society largely as a result of illiteracy. The distinction of high versus low culture corresponds to Herder's 'popular culture' (*Kultur des Volkes*) versus 'learned culture' (*Kultur der Gelehrten*). Folk culture manifests itself through a variety of cultural activities, such as folklore, folk music, folk dance. The carnival in particular is a folk cultural event that interrupts the seriousness of quotidian life. Its original function was to allow the powerless lower classes to be temporarily liberated from the authorities of church and state, although it has been argued that rather than having a subversive effect carnival actually reinforces official power structures. Folk culture is also present in literature, first and foremost the folktales. Certain manifestations of folk culture transcend genre boundaries: the carnival's harlequin and fool is, for example, a close relative of the mythological trickster, the Erlking and, in the novel, the picaro. The boundaries between these figures are indistinct and they all stem from what Bakhtin called the 'carnival sense of the world' that pervades popular culture. The distinction between popular oral culture and learned written culture is at times also blurred. While the folk tale derives from the oral tradition it enters written culture when the Brothers Grimm recorded them, and while the literary fairy tale (*Kunstmärchen*) is the result of written learned culture, it often reflects elements that are also found in folk tales.

   While the carnival is an event that used to fill the streets of Renaissance Europe, there is also carnivalesque literature, which according to Bakhtin replaced the celebration of the carnival after the Renaissance. The picaro tradition in particular poses a problem. The picaro, that 'shabby man without honor' as Spanish dictionaries of the sixteenth century define the hero of the picaresque novel, typically comes from the lower social strata and yet he is a part of written culture. Yet unlike the *Bildungsroman* the traditional picaro novel represents first and foremost the concerns of the lower class and not the bourgeois class. Bakhtin contrasted popular culture with official culture. Yet if one argues that since the Enlightenment official culture has largely corresponded to Herder's learned culture, then it seems peculiar that in the THIRD REICH and Stalinist Russia we witness a strange decline of learned written culture on the one hand, and an officialization of popular culture on the other hand. The fairy tale exemplifies this development: while the written literary fairy tale became unpopular in the Third Reich, the oral folk tale experienced its revival in support of party ideology. Yet this development has its paradoxes. The Nazis exploited certain themes of folk culture for their blood and soil ideology, such as the Germanic myths behind the folktales, while suppressing those which did not fit into their politics, such as the grotesque. In their persecution of *Untermenschen*, subhumans, they targeted primarily the *Unterschicht*, the lowest social classes because it was here that they saw emerge the greatest danger to the health of the collective body of the people, the *Volkskörper*. Thus popular culture became official but at the same time the class from which this culture originally stemmed became highly unpopular. Popular culture thus became detached from the people who had originally produced it and became entirely serviceable to party politics. Due to its increasing appropriation for nationalistic purposes from the beginning of the nineteenth century to its abuse as a tool for Nazi policies, folk culture fell into disrepute in Germany after 1945, where now it is more than ever reduced to its regional character, to such events as the celebration of local attires (*Trachten*), rustic furniture (*Bauernmöbel*), or different kinds of folk music. Since 1945 the patriarchal messages of the fairy tales have often been destabilized through parody and the picaro novel resurfaces in opposition to the conservative politics and the rationalist climate of the post-war years, primarily the ADENAUER era (eg. Heinrich BÖLL, *Ansichten eines Clowns* or Günter GRASS, *Die Blechtrommel*). (**Peter Arnds**)

Further reading

Bakhtin (1984); Berrong (1986); Burke (1978); Hamelmann (1989).

Food and drink   Staple foods throughout Germany include pork dishes, sausages, *Sauerkraut* (pickled cabbage), and potatoes. However, Germany has also a large number of varying regional cuisines. In the north, fish dishes are omnipresent, *Husumer Krabben* (prawns) are a famous delicacy, as is *Labskaus*, another fish dish. White asparagus, considered a delicacy all over Germany, comes mostly from the Altmark and south Hesse *Sauerbraten* (marinated braised beef) is a typical dish from the Rhineland. *Haxe* (pork knuckle) hails from Hesse and Bavaria. Especially in the more mountainous areas, game such as wild boar, rabbit and deer are considered delicacies. Bavaria is also famous for its *Weißwurst* (white sausage). *Spätzle* (homemade pasta) and *Flädlesuppe* (soup with egg) are specialities of Schwaben. Despite Germany's reputation as a meat-eater's paradise and a vegetarian's hell, there exists in Germany a long tradition of healthy, vegetarian eating. Starting around 1900 with the naturalists' movement, *Reformhäuser* (health food stores) became a common sight in many cities. Today, many of their functions have been taken over by the more upmarket *Bioläden*. Germans tend to be very conscious of food additives and colourings, and the market share for organic food and drink products is ever increasing. Furthermore, over the last 50 years or so, foreign influences have begun to influence available ingredients as well as dishes. Turkish *Döner Kebab* has become the most consumed food in Germany. American fast food outlets, Italian pizzerias and Spanish, Greek and Chinese restaurants have become ubiquitous. In eastern

Germany, much Vietnamese fast food can be had. German cuisine is also famous for its breads; there exist over 3000 different varieties within its borders. *Brötchen* (rolls) are the standard breakfast bread and grey and dark bread (*Pumpernickel*) are used for in-between snacks and supper. Its pastries and cakes are also renowned, with *Schwarzwälder Kirschtorte* from the Black Forest and *Stollen* from Dresden being the most famous. Special dishes are prepared for special occasions. The traditional Christmas roast is goose; New Year's Eve has carp, and Easter, lamb; *Kreppel*, or *Berliner* (deep-fried sweet buns) are for FASTNACHT (Mardi Gras). While German wines tend to have poor press outside of Germany, many vineyards from Baden, Rhine-Hesse, and those along the Moselle River have been producing excellent vintages; however, since the vintages are rather small, few of them make it to the international marketplaces. Another regional wine is *Apfelwein*, consumed mainly in the Frankfurt (Hesse) area. Germany is much more famous for its beer and its beer drinking, celebrated at such events as the Munich *Oktoberfest*. Statistically, every German consumes about 140 litres of beer per annum. There are over 1400 breweries in Germany, guaranteeing a large variety of different beers. Locals tend to be loyal to their local brewery. Famous for its adherence to the 1516 *Reinheitsgebot* (law on beer purity), most beers brewed in Germany will only contain malt, hops, yeast and water. Different beer varieties include *Export* and *Pilsner*, *Kölsch* (a light beer from Cologne), *Alt* (mainly from the Düsseldorf area), *Weizen* and *Hefeweizen* (wheat beer), *Bock* (dark and strong), and *Weißbier* (light, from Berlin). (**Holger Briel**)

Further reading

Heine (1998). A comprehensive overview of German wines. Horbelt and Spindler (2000). Good overview of German cuisine, with much social thought and many historic documents in between recipes. Olszewska Heberle (1996).

Football   Football is still the most popular SPORT in Germany, although tennis gained in importance with stars like Boris Becker and Steffi Graf, who dominated world tennis during the 1980s, and Formula One became trendy in the 1990s. The German Football Association (*Deutscher Fussballbund* – DFB) was founded in 1900 and is one of the biggest sports organizations in the world with over six million members. Highlights of the German football year are the DFB cup final held annually in Berlin and the premiership.

Professional football in Germany is organized in two divisions, the first Bundesliga and the second Bundesliga with 18 teams in each division. Regional and amateur leagues also play an important role, and the huge number of local teams prove the popularity of the sport today. Germany has some of the finest football arenas in the world and attendance is high with approximately 25 000 attending each premiership match.

The German international football team is one of the most successful sides in the world. The team won three World Cups (in 1954, 1974 and 1990 – see BECKENBAUER) and three European Cups although recently they have been less triumphant. The current team manager is Rudi Völler.

The best national clubs of recent years have been Borussia Dortmund, Bayer Leverkusen, Bayern München, and Schalke 04 (Gelsenkirchen) with Bayern having won the record number of 17 German championships. Internationally, Schalke and Dortmund were successful in the mid-1990s, but recently only Bayern were able to prove international top quality. They won the 2001 European Champions League Cup.

Despite football's popularity, however, the astronomical salaries being paid together with the rising budgets of the clubs cause increasing criticism in Germany. Bayern Munich, for example, is one of the wealthiest clubs in the world, and Borussia Dortmund for the season 2001–2 settled the biggest transfer deal in Bundesliga history by buying the Brazilian striker Amoroso for DM50 m. (**Anselm Heinrich**)

Further reading

www.dfb.t-online.de (website of German Football Association)
www.bundesliga.de (website of first and second football divisions)
www.kicker.de (most important German football journal)
www.borussia-dortmund.de (website of Borussia Dortmund)
www.schalke04.de (website of Schalke 04)
www.fcbayern.de (website of Bayern Munich)

Foundation of the FRG   The new (West) German state which arose out of the ashes of the THIRD REICH in 1949, was to a large extent the result of a realization by the Western allies that a new start had to be made in only part of the former Germany and the recognition of the undoubted desire among leading German politicians and statesmen, to regain independence and sovereignty along lines which would preserve what was best in German political life and democratic achievement.

Naturally, this state was also born out of the increasingly tense relationship between the USSR and the USA and its west European allies, Great Britain and France, known as the Cold War. This conflict was only in part about the future shape and size of Germany. It was more a conflict of ideologies and perceptions – perhaps even misperceptions – about one another's intentions for Europe and the world after 1947–48.

At any rate, in January 1947, the American and British zones of occupation were fused into a 'bizone' for both economic and political reconstruction. An early beginning to this was the fact that German representation was included in a *Wirtschaftsrat* (economic council) to begin the process of reviving employment and industrial reconstruction under western supervision. By late 1947, with the declaration of the Truman Doctrine of containing Soviet Communism, it had become obvious that further collaboration between the USSR and its former allies on the future of Germany was unworkable and the decision was made to go ahead and empower German politicians to set up a new German state. The documents of empowerment are known as the Frankfurt Declaration of American and British military governors, on the basis of which the *Wirtschaftsrat* was given enhanced powers and was to become the embryo of political reconstruction. Both the economic and political new beginning, however, could not have succeeded without a sound monetary base for the economy and the polity. The old Reichsmark was in any case worthless for all purposes of commerce and daily life and had been replaced by a black market and barter economy in which American cigarettes and luxury items such as chocolates and silk stockings were the main mediums of exchange. Thus in June 1948 a new currency, the DEUTSCHE MARK was introduced which almost overnight helped to kick-start the economy and increase confidence in the new administrative and political structures which had been put in place in the *Länder*. By refusing to allow this currency into the Soviet zone, the USSR ensured that the division of Germany would be long lasting and problematic for East–West relations for over 40 years.

Political reconstruction could only proceed on the basis of a new constitution. But this was not something that the western allies wished to impose. Instead, a Parliamentary Council was convened in Bonn, charged with drawing up a document that would form the legal basis of the new democratic order of the FRG. After lengthy discussion and compromise under the chairmanship of Konrad ADENAUER, the Basic Law (see LEGAL SYSTEM) was ratified as the new provisional constitution, although the German parliamentarians studiously avoided the word constitution. This document, with minor modifications – even after the reunification of the two German states in 1990 – remains the effective constitution to the present. The German Parliament (Bundestag) met for the first time on 7 September 1949, followed by the Federal Assembly (Bundesrat) five days later.

The years thereafter were characterized in many people's minds by the WIRTSCHAFTSWUNDER (economic miracle) and the period of reconstruction, which, together with the new currency, laid a solid foundation for political rehabilitation and the integration of the FRG into the western camp as an indispensable and valued member. They also saw the new FRG playing an important if necessarily subsidiary role in the creation of new European structures which eventually led to the setting up of NATO in its present form, the Common Market, the European Union and the introduction of the EURO. (**John Taylor**)

Foundation of the GDR   The German Democratic Republic of Germany (GDR) was founded in October 1949. It was premised on the theories of Marxism, and represented, according to Marxist-Leninist doctrine, an anti-fascist and socialist alternative to the capitalist FRG, founded just one month previously. Both German states emerged from the power vacuum after the defeat of HITLER's THIRD REICH. At the

Potsdam Conference in 1945, Germany had been divided into four zones of military occupation, administered respectively by the American, British, French and Soviet forces. With the onset of the Cold War from 1946, it became obvious that deep-seated ideological differences between the Soviet Union and the three Western powers of occupation ruled out international agreement on the political and economic framework for a united Germany. While the Western zones were rebuilt into a western-style democracy based on a free-market economy, the Soviet Union sought to transform its zone of occupation into a soviet-type society. Communists were installed into key positions and radical socio-economic changes, such as a land reform and the nationalization of industries, were implemented to establish a centrally planned economy.

The Soviet zone underwent a more thorough denazification in all areas of society than the Western zones as professional groups in education, the civil service, local administration and industry were purged of former Nazis. This provided a basis for the central 'foundation myth' of the GDR as the 'better', 'anti-fascist' Germany, together with a Marxist-Leninist historiography which allowed GDR citizens to see themselves as 'victors of history' by interpreting National Socialism as a product of capitalism. Unlike the Federal Republic which, in this view, continued the German history's chain of misery, the foundation of the socialist GDR marked a step forward in the historical struggle of working people against oppression by capitalist barons and fascist thugs.

When the GDR was formally founded in 1949, its first constitution still contained a catalogue of liberal democratic basic rights, but it was in effect already a one-party dictatorship. All political power lay in the hands of the SED (Socialist Unity Party) which had been founded in April 1946 from an amalgamation of the communist KPD and the social democrat SPD. A 'Party of the New Type' from 1949, it was organized along strictly hierarchical structures which prevented any internal opposition to the decisions of its executive committee. Other parties continued to exist nominally, but were subordinated to the SED. It occupied all leading positions in the government, with one chairman, Wilhelm Pieck, as President and the other, Otto GROTEWOHL as Prime Minister. The replacement of the position of Prime Minister by that of General Secretary of the SED, filled by its most influential figure, Walter ULBRICHT, in 1950, established the SED's authority even more firmly. With the exception of the JUNE 1953 UPRISING, and the emergence of small sub-cultural movements in the 1970s, these political and socio-economic structures remained largely unchallenged until the end of the GDR in 1989–90. (**Sabine Eggers**)

Further reading

Dennis (2000). Chapter 1 provides a concise overview of key events and cultural trends during the foundation years of the GDR. Fulbrook (1999). Analyses political and private ways of understanding the past in East and West Germany after 1945. Chapters 1–3 refer in detail to the foundation myth of the GDR and its continuing significance for EAST GERMAN IDENTITY today.

Frankfurter Allgemeine Zeitung (FAZ)   Daily newspaper published in Frankfurt, building on the tradition of the liberal _Frankfurter Zeitung_ closed under Hitler; one of the few serious German newspapers with a truly nationwide circulation (_Überregionale Zeitungen_). Strictly conservative in politics, and independent under the ownership of a trust, the _FAZ_ has avoided the controversies which the right-wing Springer press invited. Full and careful coverage of political, economic and high-cultural issues goes with a marked reluctance to increase sports, crime and popular culture reporting, to engage in investigative journalism, or to update the make-up of the paper by use of colour or more than a few photographs. (**Stuart Parkes**)

Further reading

www.faz.de (website with current edition, selected articles in English, and archive.)

Frisch, Max   1911 Zurich–1991 Zurich. Swiss author. One of the major German-language playwrights after 1945; important diarist and novelist. He developed an experimental yet approachable MODERNIST style in published diaries (1946–49 and 1966–71), major works which defy literary pigeon-holing. _Biedermann und die Brandstifter (Biedermann and the Fireraisers_, 1958) and _Andorra_ (1961) are plays epitomizing a left-liberal humanist viewpoint. The novels _Stiller_ (1954), _Homo faber_ (1957) and _Mein Name sei Gantenbein_ (translated as _A Wilderness of Mirrors_, 1964) ask radical questions about the nature of IDENTITY – civil identity, self-image, fantasy-lives, continuity and character development. Many interventions in public discussions showed strident radicalism, which alienated the Swiss establishment. His later literary works tend to be esoteric (_Neue Innerlichkeit_). (**Alfred D. White**)

Further reading

Koepke (1988). Well-balanced introduction. White (1996). A slanted interpretation of Frisch's development, but with a good select bibliography. Knowledge of German needed.

Fromm, Erich   1900 Frankfurt–1980 Muralto, Italy. Philosopher, sociologist and psychoanalyst. He studied law, sociology and psychology in Frankfurt and Heidelberg. After brief spells in Munich and Berlin, he became a member of the Institute for Social Research in Frankfurt. In 1934, he emigrated to New York and practised psychoanalysis while teaching at Columbia University. In 1941, he published _Die Furcht vor der Freiheit (Fear of Freedom)_ which established him as an important new psychoanalytical theorist, whose re-interpretation of Freud focused on societal drives rather than on individual ones. From 1941 to 1949 he lived and worked in Vermont, New Mexico and from 1953 near Mexico City. 1956 saw the publication of _Die Kunst des Liebens (The Art of Loving)_ which introduced his thought to a much wider audience. At this time, he also associated himself with the pacifist movement. In 1974, after severe health problems, he moved to Muralto (Italy). In 1976, *Haben oder Sein* (*To Have or to Be*) was published, once again propagating an existence without possessiveness and a move towards a more spiritual and inter-personal life. (**Holger Briel**)

G

Gastarbeiter (migrant labourers or workers) In the 1950s, the West German *WIRTSCHAFTSWUNDER* (economic miracle) required more workers than the population was able to supply. Furthermore, in 1955 the *BUNDESWEHR* was instituted, in effect taking a whole year's supply of 18-year-old men out of the economic cycle. In the same year a treaty was signed with Italy, allowing cheap labour to be imported from the south; similar treaties with Spain, Greece, Portugal, Yugoslavia, Turkey and others followed. (In East Germany, a much smaller number of foreigners was allowed to enter, hailing from the socialist countries of Cuba, North Vietnam and Angola; except for the Vietnamese, they did not remain in the country for long.) The idea was to have these workers stay and work in Germany for a few years only. However, many elected to stay and have their families follow them. When recession set in in 1967–68, tensions began to grow, built on the ubiquitous but fallacious argument that guest workers were taking away jobs from Germans. These tensions continued throughout the 1970s and 1980s, and were then highlighted again with German unification in the 1990s, once again exposing Germany to the charge of violent xenophobia, as foreigners were attacked in the street, and asylum seekers' housing firebombed. Successive governments grappled with this problem in different ways: the conservative side claimed the necessity of a German *Leitkultur* (leading or dominant culture), while the progressive side was much more willing to concede the necessity of MULTICULTURAL-ISM, allowing for Germany to be an 'immigration country' and providing legislation for double citizenship and other liberated measures. Today, there are about 5 million foreigners living and working in Germany, largely concentrated in urban areas such as Berlin and Frankfurt. (**Holger Briel**)

Further reading

Cohn-Bendit and Schmid (1992). Well-argued thesis on a liberal approach to multiculturalism.

Gastarbeiterliteratur Aka *Ausländerliteratur* ('foreigner literature') or *Migrantenliteratur* ('migrant literature'), this is the term used since the 1980s to describe the collection of literary creations in the German language by authors that were/are not born in Germany but were/are in the process of becoming a part of the German language or the German society. This collection of innovative and unusual perspectives has its own history and topics. Each author's unique experiences, images, and linguistic traditions are reflected in his/her poems, stories, and/or essays. Furthermore, each author possesses a deep knowledge of Germany as a country and a society. Very often authors use the German language as a vehicle to come to terms with conflicts or other puzzling phenomena in their process of obtaining a second home. Some creations reflect voices of authors that live in two worlds but are able to bridge all types of gaps between source and target cultures. A separate annual German literary award, the Adelbert-Chamisso-Preis was created in 1985 in order to honour excellence in the field of *Ausländerliteratur*. The first awardee was Aras Oeren from Turkey, the second one was Ota Filip from the former Czechoslovakia, and the third one was Franco Biondi from Italy. Authors' source cultures are: Iran, Italy, Japan, Spain, Syria, Turkey, Hungary, the former Czechoslovakia, Mongolia, Croatia, etc. *Ausländerliteratur* has been used by educators in classroom situations where students from various backgrounds faced communicative and cross-cultural challenges. Therefore, it can be hypothesized that some of the stories and poems perform a healing function in the new MULTICULTURAL contexts in Germany. (**Claudia A. Becker**)

Further reading

Ackermann (1996); Borries (1995); Raddatz (1994); Weinrich (1982).

GDR literature   For the East German authorities, literature was seen as a central weapon in the state's propaganda arsenal. Echoing the view of Stalin, writers were to be the 'engineers of the human soul', whose role it was to educate the masses in the ways of socialism. This made the GDR a very attractive place for many left-wing German writers who had spent the war in exile. However, early optimism was soon undermined due to the stifling limitations placed on writers by the official cultural policy of 'socialist realism'. This was a highly prescriptive mode of writing dedicated to providing its reader with an easily comprehensible model for socialist behaviour, in which a 'positive', 'historically aware' hero would point the way forward to the coming communist Utopia.

Although 'socialist realism' remained the official policy until well into the 1980s, as time went on, a more diverse range of books began to be published. The first major turning point came in 1959 with the *Bitterfelder Weg*, a movement designed to create stronger links between INTELLECTUALS and workers by encouraging both writers to spend time in factories and farms and workers to write about their daily experiences. Behind this movement was the wish to confirm the population's commitment to socialism, something the state never ultimately achieved. Gradually, more and more non-realist, experimental writing began to appear, and by the late 1960s the state was producing authors of international renown (e.g. Christa WOLF). Also, a small, but highly influential literary counter culture was beginning to develop, most famously in the Prenzlauer Berg area of Berlin. These artists completely rejected official aesthetics and embraced instead AVANT-GARDE modes of writing as a statement of their resistance to the authorities. Since the *Wende* many of these writers have had problems finding a market for their work, due in part to the dismissal of much East German culture in the new FRG. (**Paul Cooke**)

Further reading

Emmerich (1996). The standard work on the subject. Reid (1990). A good introduction to the literature of the final decades of the GDR.

Gender relations   In 1949, right at their founding, the Federal Republic and the German Democratic Republic both established gender equality legally, but did so in different ways and with varying outcomes. In West Germany, Elisabeth Selbert (SPD) insisted on not simply repeating the old WEIMAR REPUBLIC's Constitution's formula that men and women had the same rights and duties as citizens. This legislation had granted women suffrage but had not provided equal treatment legislation. Selbert achieved the inclusion of a paragraph in the Basic Law which guarantees women equal rights in all areas of society (§ 3 (2)). Nevertheless, it was for instance not until 1976 that revised family legislation described MARRIAGE as something in which not only the wife, but both partners should be responsible for the housework (§ 1356 German Civil Code). In East Germany, gender equality was allegedly established by the socialist constitution. The GDR version of socialism considered labour as the key to citizenship. § 18 of the Constitution explained that the government was responsible for establishing facilities which rendered it possible for women to reconcile their tasks as citizens and workers with their duties as housewives and mothers. When one compares the West German and the East German versions of gender equality, it becomes obvious that even though the GDR had no concept of a *Hausfrauenehe* (housewife marriage) in which the wife only seeks employment when necessary, housework was supposed to be exclusively women's work, as it had been in West Germany until 1976. With unification, the former East German federal states became part of the Federal Republic of Germany, thus adopting its LEGAL SYSTEM. Despite constitutional gender equality, Germany is far from having established it in reality. While § 611a German Civil Code requires equal pay for women and men, women's wages are still *ca.* 30 per cent lower than men's in some areas of the economy and the 'glass ceiling' remains hard to penetrate, e.g., in 1992, more than 40 per cent of German university students were women, but of their professors, only 4 per cent were (Kolinsky, 1995, p. 36). Nevertheless, the strong impact of European Community equal treatment law and its transformation into German law gives rise to hopes for future equality. One of the first immediate results of this looming legislation allowed for same sex marriages, the first of which were held in 2001. (**Corinna J. Heipcke**)

Further reading

Kolinsky (1995). Contains an overview of the history of gender relations from the nineteenth to the late twentieth century. The explanatory sections are completed by extracts from German legislation and statistics. However, in the meantime, some sections of the German Civil Code have undergone different paragraph codings.

Generation of 1968 (68ers)   Sociological discourse in Germany often concentrates on generational divides. This is not surprising in a society where, as a glance at German history shows, change has often been more abrupt than developmental. Within the Federal Republic most attention has undoubtedly focused on the 1968 generation that made its mark in the student movement of that year. At the least, this generation can be associated with cultural change, the move from a hierarchical, somewhat rigid society to a world of greater informality and wider choice of personal lifestyle.

The student movement's prime aim was of course to overthrow the existing political order. Although opinions vary over which, if any, of its radical demands have been realized, the 68 generation is responsible for many significant political developments since the 1970s: the growth of urban TERRORISM, the Green movement (see GRÜNEN) and the women's movement (see FEMINISM), for example. Since 1998, two of its members, both politically active in their youth, Gerhard SCHRÖDER and Joschka Fischer, as Chancellor and Foreign Minister, hold two of the highest offices of state.

Over recent years, there has been intense debate over the role of the 68 generation. Whereas apologists welcome the social changes it helped bring about, critics see the revolt against 'Nazi fathers' as self-indulgent, while its radicalism is said to have threatened social cohesion. The debate became particularly heated in early 2001 when Fischer's revolutionary past and his alleged links with terrorism came under the spotlight. In reality, it is possible to discern one major paradox in the political behaviour of the 68 generation. Although its revolt was directed against German nationalism, in power it has greater freedom to pursue certain policies than previous governments, for example, increased military intervention in the Balkans, because its members were either not born or just infants when the war ended. (**Stuart Parkes**)

Further reading

DeGroot (1998); Dirke (1997); Kraushaar (2000).

Germany   The Bundesrepublik Deutschland (Federal Republic of Germany) of today is situated in the centre of Europe. It comprises *ca.* 375 000 sq km, being only slightly smaller than France or Spain. It borders nine other countries: Austria, Switzerland, the Czech Republic, Poland, Denmark, the Netherlands, Belgium, France and Luxembourg. Germany's topography includes the islands in the North Sea and Baltic Sea, the northern lowlands, the *Mittelgebirge* (central mountainous area), the Rhine valley in the west, the *Alpenvorland* (alpine foothills) and the Alps in the south. Germany's highest mountain is the Zugspitze (2962 m) in the Alps, its longest river within its borders the Rhein (Rhine) (865 km), and its largest lake the German part of the Bodensee (Lake Constance) (305 sq km).

Its climate is changeable, Germany being situated in the moderate Atlantic as well as the Continental climate zone. In winter (roughly November to March), temperatures can drop to −15°C, and lower in the mountains. In summer (roughly June to September), temperatures can climb as high as 34 to 36°C, with much cooler temperatures during night-time.

Politically, Germany is divided into 16 *Länder* (states): Hamburg, Bremen, Schleswig-Holstein, Niedersachsen (Lower Saxony), Nord-Rhein Westfalen (North Rhine Westphalia), Mecklenburg-Vorpommern (Mecklenburg Western Pomerania), Sachsen (Saxony), Sachsen-Anhalt (Saxony-Anhalt), Thüringen (Thuringia), Brandenburg, Bayern (Bavaria), Hessen (Hesse), Rheinland-Pfalz (Rhineland-Palatine), Saarland, Baden-Württemberg, Berlin. Its capital is Berlin (since 1990, before then, it was Bonn for the Federal Republic and East Berlin for the German Democratic Republic).

There are about 82 million people living in Germany. Of those, almost 8 million are foreigners, with the largest contingent hailing from Turkey. Germany is very densely populated (229 people per sq km), but unevenly so. The highest population concentration can be found in Berlin, in the Ruhr area, in the Rhein-Main area and other expansive urbanized zones around cities such as Munich, Stuttgart, Dresden, Hamburg, and others. (**Holger Briel**)

Further reading

Kappler and Reichart (1996). Regularly updated extensive coverage of all aspects of modern Germany. www.government.de (government website.)

Globalization and multinational corporations Multinational corporations (MNCs) have long been a major factor in the globalization current, with more open economies, dense trade flows and capital movements, being closely linked with the increasingly global operation of companies. Global capital flows fund trade, mergers and acquisitions, new 'greenfield' subsidiaries of MNCs as well as government debt. Among the 25 largest world MNCs are the DaimlerChrysler, Volkswagen, Siemens and BMW AGs. The German economy is very open and dependent on trade and capital movements. Germans are very engaged in the globalization debate, concerned particularly about debt relief for the world's poorest countries. Many also believe that the very large net outflow of foreign direct investment (FDI) involves an export of jobs, reflecting the *Standort* debate over the FRG's international competitiveness. Originally slow, but from the 1970s onwards German multinational investment doubled every five years and it took off very rapidly at the end of the 1980s in advance of the creation of the Single Market. It expanded rapidly again in the second half of the 1990s. The total stock of German FDI at the end of 1999 amounted to Euro 405 bn and involved almost 30 000 companies. These employed 4 million people abroad. Geographically, EU countries accounted for 45 per cent of the total, although the USA had accumulated the largest German investment with Euro 129 bn. Total investments in developing countries reached only Euro 39 bn and a further Euro 25 bn in transition economies. By sector, German foreign holdings, at the end of 1999, amounted to Euro 152 bn in MANUFACTURING and Euro 136 bn in financial services. Within manufacturing, the branch breakdown reveals the export strengths of the German economy and this supports the view that FDI accompanies goods and services trade, penetrating markets: largely, it does not reflect a flight of production from Germany. (**Chris Flockton**)

Further reading

Deutsche Bundesbank, *Monatsbericht*, monthly. Includes biennial reports on German FDI and foreign FDI in FRG.

Goebbels, Joseph   1897 Rheydt–1945 Berlin. One of the most important Nazi leaders and chief propagandist of the THIRD REICH. Educated at a Jesuit grammar school, he studied at five different universities and finished his PhD in 1922. After that he struggled to make a living as a writer and journalist. From an early age Goebbels felt that he had a mission, he was ruthless and tried hard to overcome his inferiority complex caused by his clubfoot. In 1924 Goebbels attended a conference of the National Socialists (NSDAP), which proved to be a turning point in his life. He became a party member and found a job as a journalist for a Nazi newspaper. During the following years Goebbels developed into a brilliant orator, a fanatic anti-Semite and an ardent admirer of HITLER. In 1926 Goebbels became *Gauleiter* (regional party leader) in Berlin, founded his own newspaper, and started an aggressive agitation against Jews and communists. From 1929 he was the party's propaganda director who led the Nazis to their success in the 1930 general election when they became the second largest party. After the Nazi seizure of power in January 1933 Hitler made Goebbels 'Minister of Public Enlightenment and Propaganda'. In this function Goebbels tried to secure total control over the media and cultural life. The foundation of the 'Reich Culture Chamber' in autumn 1933 gave Goebbels the means to determine who was allowed to work in the arts. Entry into the different sub-chambers for music, theatre, broadcasting, etc. became limited to Aryans; Jews were excluded.

After the beginning of the Second World War, Goebbels' influence decreased. After the surrender at Stalingrad in February 1943, however, Goebbels held his infamous 'Sportpalast' speech in which he called for 'total war'. Hitler thereupon awarded him the title 'Reich Plenipotentiary for Total War'. A few days before the German capitulation in May 1945, Goebbels poisoned his children and killed his wife and himself in Berlin. (**Anselm Heinrich**)

Further reading

Fröhlich (1987 and 1993–96). The diaries are one of the most important sources for anyone interested in Goebbels. Trevor-Roper (1978).

Goethe-Institut   The Goethe-Institut is the organization for the teaching of German language and culture world-wide. The fusion of the Goethe-Institut with InterNationes in 2001 created Germany's biggest mediator of foreign cultural policy.

The Goethe-Institut was founded in 1951 as successor to the German Academy and has its headquarters in Munich and Bonn. The organization has 128 cultural centres in 76 countries today. The centres abroad implement arts programmes, run language courses, offer support to teachers, universities and local authorities as well as establishing co-operations with organizations, clubs and individual persons in the respective local communities. They promote the German language and provide up-to-date information on Germany. Apart from the activities abroad there are 15 centres in Germany which mainly offer language courses. The Goethe-Institut also runs a visitors' service in Germany and organizes language courses for children from all over the world.

Despite the Goethe-Institut's successful work, however, many cultural centres are under threat of closure, especially in Western Europe and Northern America, because of cuts in the budget carried out by the German government. Apart from that, the Goethe-Institut itself intends to shift the emphasis increasingly towards Eastern Europe, developing countries and crisis areas such as Palestine and South Africa. In countries like Britain, France or Italy this development has led to a substantial loss and has met with much disapproval.

The overall budget of the Goethe-Institut is DM487 m, of which DM130 m are generated by the Goethe-Institut itself. The remaining sum of DM340 m is a grant from the German Foreign Office. Legally, Goethe-Institut InterNationes e.V. is a registered association, its president is Prof Hilmar Hoffmann. (**Anselm Heinrich**)

Further reading

www.goethe.de (official website of the Goethe-Institut.)
www.inter-nationes.de (website of InterNationes.)
Grünbein *et al.* (2001). The most recent and comprehensive history of the Goethe-Institut.

Grass, Günter   Born 1927 Danzig. Novelist who transformed the West German literary scene with his Danzig trilogy: first *Die Blechtrommel* (*The Tin Drum*) 1959, fulfilling the perceived need for a treatment of the HOLOCAUST. By tricks of style and narration, and obsessive grotesque imagination, Grass sidestepped the difficulties of the huge tragic theme. A short sequel, *Katz und Maus* (*Cat and Mouse*), portrayed life during the war. *Hundejahre* (*Dog Years*) 1963, another complex narrative with grandiose themes (myth, creativity), included more satire on the post-1945 world. His prolific work since has not repeated the influence (acknowledged by Salman Rushdie among others) of these books. Grass is an active publicist – prominent SPD speaker in ELECTION campaigns in the 1960s, critic of reunification in 1989–90. (**Alfred D. White**)

Further reading

Preece (2001). Full and authoritative study. Pelster (1999). Most recent German-language survey.

Gropius, Walter   1883 Berlin–1969 Boston. Architect. Germany's most important architect of the inter-war years, he achieved early fame with the revolutionary design in glass and concrete for the *Fagus Factory* (1912) which heralded the modern movement in ARCHITECTURE. Founded the BAUHAUS design school in 1919 and built its headquarters in Dessau in 1926; director there until 1928. Emigrated to England (Impington Village College, 1936) before settling in the USA and founding the Architects Collaborative. Post-war buildings include an elegant apartment block for the Berlin Interbau exhibition of 1957 and the Berlin Bauhaus Archive (completed 1978). (**Martin Brady**)

Grotewohl, Otto   1894 Braunschweig–1964 East Berlin. GDR functionary. Grotewohl was a figurehead of the SPD in the 1920s. During the THIRD REICH, he became a member of an illegal Social Democrat group in Hamburg and later worked together with a Social Democrat resistance group in Berlin. In 1945, he was made chair of the SPD's Central Committee in Berlin and helped guide the SPD in the Soviet zone into a fusion with the KPD (*Kommunistische Partei Deutschlands*), from which sprang the SED (*Sozialistische Einheitspartei Deutschlands*). From 1946 to 1954, he and Wilhelm Pieck held the two chairmenships of the SED. In 1949 Grotewohl became the first GDR Prime Minister. (**Corinna J. Heipcke**)

Gründgens, Gustav   1899 Düsseldorf–1963 Manila. Actor and director. Active on stage from 1920 and in films from 1929. Legendary performances as Mephistopheles in his productions of Goethe's *Faust*. (**Martin Brady**)

Further reading

Blubacher (1999).

Grünen, die   Political party whose defining policies are ecological: anti-nuclear, anti-pollution, pro-organic and communitarian. (See ENVIRONMENT.) Local pressure groups for particular causes (Bürgerinitiativen), common in the 1960s, included many ecological groups, anxious about the ecological price of the economic miracle; a national umbrella organization was constituted in 1972, the party 1979–80. Commitment to a high level of internal democracy (*Basisdemokratie*) at local, *Land* and national level rendered the party chaotic, one meeting often reversing the previous one's decisions, or a meeting of members imposing policies which the political office-holders found unfeasible. Other disruptive elements were the division between those willing to make compromises, form coalitions and exercise power even if diluted (realists, *Realos*), and those who wanted to keep pure doctrine at any price (fundamentalists, *Fundis*); and discussions about making common cause with alternative radical movements less committed to ecological issues. Policies on economic affairs, foreign relations and so forth slowly developed. Helped by the second votes of other parties' supporters, the party built power bases at all levels, entering the Bundestag in 1983 (failure at the 5 per cent hurdle in 1990 was redressed in 1994 by operating a common list of candidates with Bündnis 90, successor to the East German civil rights movement) and participation in federal government in 1998 with Joschka Fischer, veteran of 1968 and leading exponent of the move of old radicals to respectability, as Foreign Minister. Whether this is sufficient to keep the party's support buoyant in the absence of membership policies to recruit and retain young activists remains to be seen in the light of recent electoral setbacks. (**Alfred D. White**)

Further reading

Lees (2000). Most up-to-date view of the political situation. Scharf (1994). Authoritative view of the party's history and policies.
www.gruene.de (the party's website, German-language only.)

Gruppe 47   This literary group was founded in 1947 by Hans Werner Richter, who convened the group twice before 1955 and from then on it gathered annually. Given this informal system, despite widespread perceptions, it is hard to speak of a clear membership. The aim of the Group was to provide a forum where writers could read from their works and hear the reactions of colleagues. From modest beginnings it had established itself by the late 1950s as a leading literary force in the Federal Republic. Meetings increasingly took on fixed forms. Those reading from what became known as the 'electric chair' were subject to the comments of 'star critics', the most controversial of whom was the trenchant Marcel Reich-Ranicki. There was much media, including television, interest, while the winners of the Group's prize (they included Heinrich BöLL, Martin WALSER and Günter GRASS) attracted widespread attention.

   The Group also increasingly involved itself in politics, generally taking stances opposed to the ADENAUER government, which led one CDU politician, Josef Hermann Dufhues, to compare it to the Nazi Writers Union (*Reichsschrifttums-kammer*). The *de facto* end of the Group came in 1967 when protesting students disrupted the annual gathering, exposing the increasing strains within its ranks. For many years the *Gruppe 47* was linked with the social and cultural changes that gathered strength throughout the 1960s. More recently, its role has been questioned. Critics have pointed to collective misjudgements of certain writers, not least the poet Paul CELAN, whose work received a frosty reception in 1952, the patronizing treatment accorded to women authors and the limits of the Group's supposed radicalism. Many participants, including Richter, had fought in the *Wehrmacht* and seemed reluctant to question the Nazi past very deeply. Nevertheless, its significance within the development of West German literature remains undeniable. (**Stuart Parkes**)

Further reading

Cofalla (1997); Lettau (1967); Parkes and White (1999).

Handke, Peter   Born 1942 Griffen, Carinthia, Austria. Dramatist, novelist and film-maker. Prolific writer of the 'new subjectivity' tendency (e.g. *Der kurze Brief zum langen Abschied*, 1972) with a predilection for philosophical and linguistic discourse (e.g. the play *Kaspar*, 1967). (**Martin Brady**)

Further reading

Arnold (1999).

Haneke, Michael   Born 1942 Munich. Film-maker and journalist. Haneke is regarded as Austria's most important international film director. Recently, two of his feature films received major critical attention across Europe. *Code Inconnu* (*Code Unknown*, 2000) was filmed in French and starred Juliette Binoche. *Die Klavierspielerin* (*The Piano Teacher*, 2001) also stars a leading French actress, Isabelle Huppert. It is an adaptation of the Jᴇʟɪɴᴇᴋ novel of the same title. Haneke's earlier films include corrosive critiques of contemporary Austrian society. His first major feature *Der siebente Kontinent* (*The Seventh Continent*, 1989) tells the story of an average Austrian household. It is a portrait of daily routines and there have been few better cinematic depictions of middle-class drudgery. However, Haneke does not lack a wry sense of humour or a dramatic use of film-making techniques. Citing Jacques Bresson as an influence, Haneke is a welcome addition to the ranks of international cinema that seeks to go beyond the Hollywood formula. (**Hugo Frey**)

Further reading

Steiner (1995).

Health services   The German model of health provision is based on solidaristic, compulsory social insurance coverage and a self-governing system of health provision, where doctors and dentists practise independently: the individual patient can also choose freely among general practitioners and specialist doctors. The federal government and the *Länder* have important regulatory activities and the *Länder* themselves are responsible for hospital planning and investment. While the system is of high quality, it is also expensive: in the 1990s on average 10 per cent of GDP was devoted annually to health care (8 per cent in the old states and 13 per cent in the new) and this proportion had risen by approximately 1.5 percentage points since the early 1970s. There are obviously considerable cost pressures and questions of efficiency, resulting in a succession of partial reforms from 1989 and continuing to the present.

If only for the reason that the costs of health insurance are borne equally by employers and employees, with a present contribution rate of on average 12.5 per cent of gross earnings, cost containment is important, since it is a tax on employment. Some 90 per cent of the population is covered by the compulsory non-profit-making public health insurance system (with the remainder, largely higher earners opting for private insurance), comprising the public funds (GKV - *Gesetzliche Krankenkassen*). The statutory insurance funds account for one-half of all health care spending. While patients generally do not see the charges for health services, they often have to make co-payments as a contribution to pharmaceuticals costs. The doctors and dentists, while operating as independent professionals, must form regional associations (KV *Kassenärztliche Vereinigungen*) which are public corporations. They are under contract to the insurance funds, which act as a single purchaser of services. A further distinction concerns that of ambulatory care (outpatients and surgery consultations) and hospital care. The latter is supplied by a split provision whereby fixed investments are funded by the *Land* and the services are provided by the hospital organization. (**Chris Flockton**)

Further reading

OECD, *Germany*. See especially 1997 edition, but also other editions, of this annual publication.

Heidegger, Martin   1889 Meßkirch, Baden–1976 Freiburg, Breisgau. Philosopher. Heidegger is one of the most important philosophers of the twentieth century. He began his career with studies on Aristotle and Heraclitus, but then turned to ontological questions concerning the problem of 'being' as well as concerning the status of art and language. Heidegger's most important work is *Sein und Zeit* (1927). It develops an 'existential hermeneutics', i.e. a form of hermeneutic reasoning which does not refer to the interpretation of texts but to the interpretation of the finitude and temporality of human existence as 'being-in-the-world'. Other works include *Der Ursprung des Kunstwerkes* (ed. 1960) and *Unterwegs zur Sprache* (1959). (**Christian J. Emden**)

Further reading

Figal (1999). A very short, but very readable overview of Heidegger's work and career. Guignon (1993). Collection of essays by prominent scholars on most aspects of Heideggers's work. An ideal starting point for further study. Heidegger (1962). Standard translation of *Sein und Zeit* (1927). Heidegger (1993). Very accessible collection of other important essays and central passages of Heidegger's work. Sluga (1993). Examines Heidegger's involvement with the Nazi Party during the 1930s and the philosophical implications of his political beliefs.

Herzog, Werner (Werner Stipetic)   Born 1942 Sachrang. Film director. Herzog is one of Germany's most powerful directors and was central to the 'New German Cinema' revival of the 1970s. To date, he has made over thirty films, including *Aguirre, Der Zorn Gottes* (1972) and *Fitzcarraldo* (1982). His screen alter ego is the actor Klaus

Kinski (1926–91) who has starred in five of his works. Herzog is frequently described as an 'idiosyncratic' or 'eccentric' director and his major features do often seem to pose impossible challenges for his cast and crew. However, notwithstanding the dramas of filming *Fitzcarraldo*, Herzog has also offered mystical, poetic work like his meditation on the desert, *Fata Morgana* (1971). More recently, Herzog has returned to documentary. *Little Dieter Needs to Fly* (1997) is an account of a German émigré to the United States whose passion for flying leads him to serve in the US Air Force and to subsequently be held as a prisoner of war in Vietnam. This remarkable story represents a continuation of the director's fascination with historical and social extremes. (**Hugo Frey**)

Further reading

Brady and Hughes (1998); Cronin (2002).

Hesse, Hermann   1877 Calw–1962 Montagnola, Switzerland. Writer. Hesse, the son of a pietistic preacher, in many ways revived German romanticism and updated its search for a spiritual life through art. In 1919, deeply troubled by German patriotism on display before and during the First World War, he moved to Switzerland, where he would take up Swiss nationality and remain for the rest of his life. In 1946, he was awarded the Nobel Prize for Literature. Already in his early texts, such as *Peter Camenzind* (1904), *Unterm Rad* (1906) and *Roßhalde* (1914), he described the tensions between the artist and reality, a subject he would take up time and again. His writing reached a new quality with *Siddartha* (1922), retelling the spiritual journey of Gautama Buddha. In this text, many of the descriptions are due to Hesse's own journey to India in 1911. In 1927, *Steppenwolf* was published, cementing his reputation as a spiritual author, who nevertheless remains firmly grounded in reality. *Steppenwolf* tells the story of Harry Haller and his search for spirituality in the animalistic world of the 1920s. Hesse's last novel, *Das Glasperlenspiel* (*The Glass Bead Game*), is also his most esoteric. It describes the quasi-hermetic world of an order led by Josef Knecht. Within this society, the game of the glass beads represents the search for spirituality of the highest rank, and, if played correctly, leads to serenity and truth. While Hesse's novels were often criticized for their apparent non-political messages, he nevertheless gained many readers, especially during the 1960s and 1970s, when the search for a new spirituality, informed by a *mélange* of Eastern religions, was in its heyday. (**Holger Briel**)

Further reading

Mileck (2002); Unseld (1973).

Heym, Stefan   1913 Chemnitz–2001 Jerusalem. Author. Born Helmut Flieg. Son of a Jewish merchant, Heym had to emigrate in 1933 to the USA in order to escape the

Nazi terror. In Chicago, he was made editor-in-chief of the German language weekly *Deutsches Volksecho*. In 1943 he joined the US Army and fought in France and Germany. He had his problems in the new Germany, and returned to the USA until 1953, when he moved to the GDR. His work was recognized, but after his protest against the BIERMANN expatriation in 1976, he was thrown out of the GDR Writers' Association. He was only reinstated after German unification in 1989. Already his first poem, written in 1931, led to his exclusion from school, as it attacked a political figure of the Right. In 1948 he published *The Crusaders*, an account of the Second World War from the perspective of American soldiers. While in America, his texts were considered rather highbrow European, but back in Germany he was often chided and criticized for writing in an American, too easy-to-read style. This would only change in 1979 with his novel *Colin*, which attempts to work through the effects of Stalinism in GDR society. His 1981 *Ahasver*, written in a mix of styles and staged during three different epochs, tells the story of the eternal Jew at the time of Luther, in the GDR and in Israel. *Schwarzenberg* (1989) tells the short story of a post-war unified German state, a fact which would finally come about in the year of its publication. Finally, his 1995 novel *Radek* tells the story of a troublesome German Communist Party functionary, who is illegally imprisoned in the USSR. (**Holger Briel**)

Hindemith, Paul   1895 Hanau–1963 Frankfurt am Main. Composer. Pre-eminent composer of the inter-war years who developed a soberly modern style spanning Expressionism and *Gebrauchsmusik* (functional music). (**Martin Brady**)

Further reading

Briner *et al.* (1988).

Hitler, Adolf   1889 Braunau, Austria–1945 Berlin. Became *Führer* of the Nazi Party and was appointed Chancellor in 1933. Hitler built up a total dictatorship and started the Second World War, in which Nazi Germany planned and organized the HOLOCAUST, the systematic extermination of the European Jews.

Hitler was born into a petty bourgeois family. His parents died early but left him an allowance on which he could live. Hitler left school without graduating at the age of 16. His ambition was to become an artist, but he failed to secure entry to the Vienna Academy of Fine Arts. Between 1907 and 1913 Hitler lived an unsettled life, during which he developed his political consciousness, and became an anti-Semitic pan-German nationalist. At the outbreak of the First World War he volunteered for service in a Bavarian regiment and was twice awarded the Iron Cross. After the war Hitler moved to Munich and joined the German Workers' Party, which changed its name to National Socialist German Workers' Party (NSDAP) in 1920, and became its leader in 1921. He soon developed into a brilliant orator with a unique talent for mass leadership. After the abortive Munich ('Beer Hall') Putsch of 1923 Hitler was arrested. During his imprisonment he wrote *Mein Kampf* (*My Struggle*), in which he summed up his central political aims and beliefs. On his release in 1924 he reorganized the Nazi Party, which profited from the economic problems after 1929. Hitler found the support of influential conservative circles, was appointed Chancellor in January 1933, and after the death of Hindenburg also became head of state. His two central political aims were the acquisition of new territory (*Lebensraum*) to create a Germanic superpower and the extermination of the Jews. After the first *Blitzkrieg* victories of the war the 'new order' began to take shape, and in 1940 Hitler stood at the height of his power. In 1941 he began the war against his great ideological enemy: the Soviet Union. At the end of the same year the Holocaust started, and extermination camps, in which approximately six million Jews died, were built. With the first military defeats, Hitler increasingly avoided public appearances. Although it had become obvious that the war was lost, Hitler demanded the fight to go on. He retreated to the chancellery in Berlin and killed himself on 30 April 1945. (**Anselm Heinrich**)

Further reading

Kershaw (1999). The most detailed and most recent highly acclaimed study by one of the experts in the field. Kershaw (2000a). Fest (1974). Still one of the most important studies. Geary (1993). Gives a short, concise overview. Domarus (1990).

Hochhuth, Rolf Born 1931 Eschwege. Author. A member of the Bavarian Academy of Fine Arts, Hochhuth practised the writing of documentary drama and became famous in the 1960s with his bold attack on institutions such as the CATHOLIC Church. In 1963, his play *Der Stellvertreter* (*The Representative*) was published, a scathing attack on Pope Pius XII and his active support for HITLER and his politics. Another play of his, *Soldaten: Nekrolog auf Genf* (*Soldiers: Necrologue on Geneva,* 1967) also caused an uproar during its premiere because it charged Churchill with crimes against humanity, committed by ordering the death of hundreds of thousands of civilians during the Second World War. Among other reactions, the play caused theatre censorship in England to be abolished. Hochhuth continues to attack social and political wrongdoings with his plays; *Guerrillas* (1970) predicts a military coup in the USA; *Judith* (1984) chronicles the attempt to kill the American president because of his decision to allow for chemical weapons once again; and *Sommer 14: Ein Totentanz* (*Summer 14: A Dance of Death,* 1989) decries the patriotism leading to the beginning of the First World War. More recently, he has taken up the German–German relationship after unification (*Wessis in Weimar,* 1994), and a novel about Alan Turing and artificial intelligence (*Alan Turing,* 1998). (**Holger Briel**)

Further reading

Puknus (2002).

Holidays   Germans have been dubbed the 'world champions of holidays'. Statistically, Germans take more holidays than any other nation in the world. Depending on which state they live in, public/religious holidays can add up to 18 working days' worth of holidays to begin with. Due to a generous welfare system, individual holiday allocations might be as high as 30 to 40 days per annum. Furthermore, many Germans are entitled to *Kuren* (spa visits), which are co-sponsored by the national HEALTH SERVICE. While these *Kuren* were very much *de rigueur* with the upper class in the early 1900s, they have since become a common occurrence. Starting in the 1920s, beach holidays in summer and mountain holidays in winter were (and still are) viewed as important status symbols. During the Nazi era, the *Sommerfrische* (refreshing summer holidays) was viewed as an integral part of staying fit for the service of the Fatherland. In the 1950s, going on holiday to the Mediterranean countries became an important part of the WIRTSCHAFTSWUNDER. Favourite holiday locations continue to include Austria, Italy, Spain, Greece and increasingly Turkey, the Dominican Republic and Thailand. (**Holger Briel**)

Holocaust   In its most commonly used form, the term 'Holocaust' refers to the murder of about 6 million Jewish victims by Nazi Germany during the Second World War. Most scholars regard the Holocaust as a unique event in history, mainly because of the sheer scale of the killings but also because of their bureaucratically planned and technically advanced execution.

After years of social discrimination in the aftermath of Adolf HITLER's accession to power in 1933, the persecution of Jews entered a new phase with the so-called Wannsee Conference on the outskirts of Berlin in January of 1942. At that conference steps to implement the decision to annihilate European Jews were co-ordinated. Concentration and extermination camps (such as Auschwitz, Bergen-Belsen and Treblinka) played a major role in this process.

ANTI-SEMITISM was central to Nazi ideology but a number of other social groups also fell victim to the extreme racism and social Darwinism of the National Socialist regime. Several hundreds of thousands of Sinti and Roma, tens of thousands of homosexual men and a similar number of physically and mentally handicapped people were also killed. Very often these killings are also subsumed under the heading of 'Holocaust'.

Since the end of the Second World War, the term 'Holocaust' has also been used to describe other mass killings and genocides. The usage of the term for such modern killings is contested since some scholars argue that the uniqueness of the Jewish Holocaust is thus questioned. As the term invokes such strong reactions in most people, it is not surprising that it is instrumentalized for political purposes. Anti-abortionists have laid claim to the 'Holocaust' to refer to abortion, as have animal rights activists to refer to vivisection or slaughter houses. (**Manuel Gull**)

Further reading

Hilberg (1985); Novick (2000).

Horkheimer, Max   1895 Stuttgart–1973 Nuremberg. Philosopher and sociologist. Horkheimer studied psychology and philosophy in Munich, Freiburg and Frankfurt. In 1930 he was made Professor of Social Philosophy at Frankfurt and co-founded the Institute of Social Research, together with Fromm and Adorno.

In 1933 Horkheimer emigrated to Switzerland and in 1934 moved to New York, where he re-opened the Institute at Columbia University. In 1940, he moved to California, where he co-wrote the *Dialektik der Aufklärung* (*Dialectic of Enlightenment*) with Adorno. He became Editor of *Studies in Philosophy and Social Science*. From 1943 to 1949 he headed the scientific department of the American Jewish Committee and worked on anti-Semitism research. In 1944 *Dialektik der Aufklärung* was published, one of the most influential philosophical texts of the twentieth century. In this text, Horkheimer and Adorno attempted to prove why the Enlightenment as a closed system was doomed to failure and how Enlightenment thought has to undergo continuous criticism in order to fulfil its goals, thereby establishing a practical philosophy unable to come to rest in any identity. In 1949 Horkheimer returned to the University of Frankfurt, re-opening the Institute in 1950. In 1970 he published *Traditionelle und kritische Theorie*, in which he once again extolled the virtue of continuous critical theory (see Kritische Theorie). (**Holger Briel**)

Huillet, Danièle and Straub, Jean-Marie   Huillet born 1936, Straub born 1933 Metz. Political film-makers whose literary adaptations (of Heinrich Böll, Brecht, Kafka, Hölderlin, Pavese and others) and music films (*Chronicle of Anna Magdalena Bach, Chronik der Anna Magdalena Bach*, 1967; *Moses und Aron,* 1974) are uncompromisingly rigorous and inhabit a zone between documentary and fiction. Brechtian film-makers inspired by Robert Bresson and Jean-Luc Godard, they left for Italy in 1968, but have repeatedly returned in their films to German history, culture and politics from a radical, Marxist perspective. (**Martin Brady**)

Further reading

Byg (1995).

Identity   Terms like 'national identity' and 'gender identity' have become much used concepts in social science research, especially in cultural studies. For a number of scholars the notion of 'identity' has replaced traditional categories like class or hegemony. Identities are considered to be fluid and bound to change. What one identifies with at any given moment may depend upon the situation and the threat or challenge one is facing. Cultural theorists argue strongly for the existence of multiple identities in human beings. A German woman, for instance, is German and a woman, she may also be white and of a particular sexual identity, not to mention her religion. All these social categories have meaning to the individual and form someone's personal identity.

The notion of identity is closely linked to concepts of 'difference' and of 'the other'. What one identifies with depends as much on what one is (e.g. a woman) as on what one is not (in this case: a man). It is in those polarities that difference is expressed and lived.

History is an important marker of identity, especially with respect to national identity. A common history may result in a shared feeling of belonging to a nation or a political state. Germany's past is dominated by the memory of the Second World War and the HOLOCAUST, two decidedly negative events in history. For this reason Germans have been struggling to come to terms with their national identity. To identify as a German means for many Germans to accept the legacy of the NAZI regime, a usually painful and difficult process. (**Manuel Gull**)

Further reading

Hall and du Gay (1996); Fulbrook (1999).

Inflation   Germany has been known through the second half of the last century as a relatively price stable country, after two searing episodes earlier of the rapid erosion of monetary value. The post-First World War inflation jumped from an annual 2420 per cent in 1922 to an annual 1 869 999 900 per cent in 1923, when the US dollar became worth 4.2 thousand billion Reichsmarks. Here escalating public debt following the Versailles Treaty was met by printing money. After the Second World War, by contrast, there was repressed inflation in the form of rationing and a black market based on barter. The 1948 currency reform deliberately cut the volume of Reichmarks in circulation, which had become almost valueless. The currency reform cut nominal prices at a stroke. From a high point of 7.7 per cent consumer price inflation in 1950, this fell to the Bundesbank's price stability target of 2–2.5 per cent, but rose again with the oil crises to 7 per cent in 1974 and 6.3 per cent in 1980. With the oil price fall in dollars in 1985, consumer price inflation fell to −0.1 per cent. While inflation has averaged 2 per cent over the 1990s in a unified Germany, unification brought price alignment in the east, and so a large rise in administered prices such as for heating, transport and rents. Both the level and growth in the consumer price index in the east now mirror the west. Historically, much inflation in Germany has been imported, through higher world inflation, oil crises, etc., but there have been phases of wage push and of VAT-induced price rises. Generally, the monetary targeting of the Bundesbank had an announcement effect which induced a relative discipline on wage bargainers. Centralized, sectoral collective bargaining of the German type tends to produce wage moderation and avoids wage-price spirals after oil crises. Wage bargainers tend to keep unit costs stable, which sustains price stability. (**Chris Flockton**)

Further reading

Deutsche Bundesbank, *Monatsbericht*, monthly.

Intellectuals   According to *Brockhaus*, 'Intellektuelle' (Intellectuals) are 'Menschen, die in der Regel wissenschaftlich gebildet sind, eine geistige, künstlerische, akademische oder journalistische Tätigkeit ausüben' ('people who are generally scientifically trained and pursue an intellectual (as opposed to physical), artistic, academic or journalistic career'). This definition, however, represents only the denotative aspects of the term. Ardagh (1991) discusses in his chapter 'Arts and Intellectuals: Lively Activity, but Low Creativity' the connotative aspects of the term 'Intellectuals'. Ardagh claims that solid knowledge seems to be a definite asset of the German intellectuals, but a certain lack of creativity seems to be present at the same time. The causes, according to him, are deeply rooted in the German past as opposed to France, for instance, too rigid study habits, too formalized discussion patterns, and intense peer pressure. This might also have contributed to the fact that 'the vast majority of worthwhile intellectuals and creative people ... moved either into exile or into prison' (ibid., p. 298), especially during the Nazi period. (**Claudia A. Becker**)

Further reading

Ardagh (1991, pp. 298–314). For a detailed discussion.

Islam   Islam is the third largest religion in Germany, after CATHOLICISM and PROTESTANTISM, numbering about 2.7 million believers. The overwhelming majority are Sunnite Moslems, with only about 6 per cent being Shiites. In Germany, Islam is still a very young religion; beginning with the mid-1960s, most of its practitioners came as GASTARBEITER (migrant workers) or as their family members to Germany; more recently, many asylum seekers are also practising Moslems. Due to the large number of Moslems, mosques are beginning to spring up in many German cities; Halal meat is now widely available, at least in major industrial centres and large cities. Islam is taught in schools and Koran schools have also begun to appear; however, the latter still have difficulties with accreditation within the German education system (see SCHOOLS AND EDUCATION). (**Holger Briel**)

Further reading

Kolinsky (1996); Tibi (2000).

J

Jahnn, Hans Henny   1894 Hamburg–1959 Hamburg. Author and organ builder. In 1915, during the First World War, Jahnn emigrated to Norway as a pacifist and returned to Hamburg only in 1918. In 1920 he received the Kleist prize for his play *Pastor Ephraim Magnus* (1919). His topics describe the beauty of humanity, which is tragically lost through acts of violence and hatred; this beauty can only be recreated by individuals and only for individuals, such as lovers and artists. In 1933 he emigrated to Switzerland and then settled in Denmark until 1945, when he once again returned to Hamburg. His magnum opus, the novel *Fluß ohne Ufer*, only posthumously published in its entirety in 1961, deals with the ultimately doomed search of its main character, the musician Gustav Anias Horn, for positive absolutes and justice in a cold and ever-changing world, a world in which even the artist is helpless. (**Holger Briel**)

Further reading

Niehoff (2001); Wolffheim (1989).

Jaspers, Karl   1883 Oldenburg–1969 Basel. Philosopher and medical doctor. Jaspers studied first law, then medicine, receiving his degree in medicine from Göttingen. From 1908 to 1915, he worked in a psychiatric ward in Heidelberg, moving steadily from psychiatry to philosophy. At the time, his influences were Weber, Husserl and Dilthey, later also Heidegger. In 1922, he was made Professor of Philosophy at Heidelberg. In 1931 he published *Die geistige Situation unserer Zeit* (*The Spiritual Situation of Our Time*), questioning the scientist view of truth and moving towards existentialism. He was a great influence on Hannah Arendt. In 1933, Jaspers was forced to leave university; later on during the Nazi regime, he was prohibited from publishing. In 1948 he was made Professor of Philosophy at the University of Basle, and in 1957 he published what he believed to be the first of three volumes of *Die großen Philosophen* (*The Great Philosophers*), but which would remain the only one. In 1958 he was awarded the *Friedenspreis des Deutschen Buchhandels*. (**Holger Briel**)

Jelinek, Elfriede   Born 1946 Mürzzuschlag, Steiermark, Austria. Writer. Prose: *wir sind lockvögel, baby* (1970), *Die Liebhaberinnen* (1975), *Die Klavierspielerin* (1983), *Lust* (1989), *Gier* (2000). Plays: *Was geschah, nachdem Nora ihren Mann verlassen hatte* (1977–78), *Krankheit oder Moderne Frauen* (1984), *Ein Sportstück* (1998).

Jelinek is one of the most prolific and successful contemporary authors in German. In addition to her plays and prose narratives, she has written poetry, film scripts, radio plays, essays on poetics, literary politics, as well as contemporary political issues. (**Corinna J. Heipcke**)

Further reading

Fiddler (1994). Janz (1995). Investigates how Jelinek deconstructs modern myths. The book thus may serve in-depth studies of Jelinek.
ourworld.compuserve.com/homepage/elfriede (Elfried Jelinek's homepage, giving a survey of her works, prizes she has won, and also recent texts by her.)

Johnson, Uwe   1934 Kammin–1984 Sheerness-on-Sea. Author. Johnson studied with Hans Meyer and Ernst Bloch and in 1959 moved to the FRG, as the GDR cultural and ideological establishment refused to print his texts. He finally achieved recognition with *Mutmaßungen über Jakob* (1959), in which he tries to reconstruct the death of Jakob, an East German railroad technician, applying elements of the crime story and the psychological novel in the process. As in his other texts, the tableau of a torn-apart Germany and its societies is ever-present. Johnson's main work, which goes beyond the scope of a single novel, is *Jahrestage*, its four volumes having been published in 1970, 1971, 1973 and 1983. In this voluminous text, he comes back to one of the characters already present in *Mutmaßungen*, Gesine Cresspahl, and follows her to New York, where her 365 days of reminiscing will inform the division of the novel into 365 chapters. The memories of her East German youth, reports from newspapers, political changes and the clash of ideologies/cultures all have a role to play, thereby creating a vivid tapestry of Western life in the second half of the twentieth century, albeit from a decidedly German perspective. (**Holger Briel**)

Further reading

Grambow (1997).

June 1953 uprising   The suppressed uprising of 17 June 1953 was the most traumatic event in the history of the East German GDR. In the preceding years, popular dissatisfaction with travel restrictions and socio-economic restructuring on communist terms had been building up. When the regime decided to increase work-norms for industrial workers by 10 per cent, unrest broke out. It started as a spontaneous protest by workers engaged in the construction of the East Berlin *Stalinallee*, but soon spread to over 350 places in East Germany. Spearheaded by industrial workers, more than 500 000 people participated in mass demonstrations. The uprising was crushed by the *Volkspolizei* (peoples' police) and Russian tanks. At least 50 demonstrators were killed in clashes, 21 were summarily executed, along with over 20 policemen and 40 Russian soldiers who refused to raise their arms against the demonstrators. The regime interpreted the event as a western, fascist attempt to overthrow the GDR government. The uprising served as a pretext to arrest and purge disloyal SED party members. Party leader Walther Ulbricht was able to stabilize his position by reinforcing the peoples' police, reorganizing the Ministry for State Security (*Stasi*) and receiving further backing from the USSR. Up until 1989, no similar widespread protest against the SED regime was made. In West Germany, 17 June became a national public holiday (Day of German Unity) until replaced by 3 October in 1990. (**Stefan Manz**)

Further reading

Baring (1972). Classic study by one of the leading German political scientists. Detailed account in a readable style. Mitter and Wolle (1993). Read Chapter 1. Good analysis of the wider historical context; based on new sources after the opening of archives.

Jünger, Ernst   1895 Heidelberg–1998 Wilflingen. Author and entomologist. Made his name in the 1920s with a theory of the new synthesis of worker and soldier, amounting to a right-wing ideology which was congenial to the Nazis, though when they came to power he soon became disillusioned and wrote veiled oppositional works. In the occupying forces in France, he became a francophile. After 1945 he reconquered a literary position now with less overt political stance, but towards the end of his life was fêted by leaders of the right in Germany and France. Discoverer of several species of ephemera. (**Alfred D. White**)

Further reading

Seferens (1998). Specialized study of Jünger's political work and influence. Plard (1992). Authoritative survey of his literary and publicistic work.

Kandinsky, Wassily   1866 Moscow–1944 Neuilly-sur-Seine. A leading painter and theoretician of German Expressionism, Kandinsky only took up painting in 1896 after quitting the legal profession. A brilliant colourist, pioneer of abstraction and founder in 1911 of the *Blaue Reiter* circle (which also included Franz Marc and August MACKE – see ART), he was an influential theorist, whose tract *On the Spiritual in Art* was translated into English as early as 1914. After the First World War he taught at the BAUHAUS and settled in France in 1933. His later canvases are meticulously planned constellations of calligraphic and biomorphic shapes. (**Martin Brady**)

Kiefer, Anselm   Born 1945 Donaueschingen. Painter and sculptor. A pupil of Joseph BEUYS who works on a monumental scale in painting and sculpture (including a library of giant lead books). Frequently controversial, his paintings (often incorporating straw, glass, charred wood and plants embedded in thick paint) tackle taboos from German history, philosophy, mythology and culture. Perennially maligned as politically conservative, he moved to France in the early 1990s. From there he has engaged with themes as diverse as cosmology and the Chinese Cultural Revolution in colossal paintings that are lighter in tone if not in weight. (**Martin Brady**)

Klemperer, Otto   1885 Breslau–1973 Zurich. Conductor and composer. Outstanding conductor from the 1920s with a broad repertoire of classics (especially Beethoven and Mahler), opera and contemporary music. (**Martin Brady**)

Kluge, Alexander   Born 1932 Halberstadt. Trained lawyer, philosopher, teacher, political activist, cultural and media critic and, of late, a television producer for German cable television on the RTL and SAT.1 channels. Kluge is regarded both as a major film-maker and as a major social theorist in the tradition of the Frankfurt School. He began his career as a lawyer in 1958 and soon became a writer and a film-maker after a brief internship with the legendary film director Fritz LANG, to whom he was introduced by the philosopher ADORNO. Kluge is also a well-known author, recipient of numerous literary awards, including the prestigious Fontane Prize in 1979 and the Kleist Award in 1985. His theoretical books, *Öffentlichkeit und Erfahrung* (*Public Sphere and Experience*) and *Geschichte und Eigensinn* (*History and Stubbornness*), co-authored with Oskar Negt, are written in opposition to Jürgen Habermas's theory of the bourgeois 'public sphere'.

Kluge's career as a lobbyist for the New German Cinema began at the Oberhausen Festival of short films, on 28 February 1962, when 26 film-makers, writers, and artists, headed by Kluge, protested against government economic and cultural policies that ignored the problems encountered by the West German film-makers. The manifesto this coalition produced marks the inception of *Das Neue Kino* (New German Cinema). 'The old cinema is dead', proclaimed the Oberhausen Manifesto: 'We believe in the new.' The principle behind the manifesto was that the film-maker should have autonomy in giving shape to his or her idea without having to take legal or financial risks.

Kluge made his first short film with Peter Schamoni, *Brutalität in Stein* (*Brutality in Stone,* 1960), an experimental documentary on the ruins of the Nuremberg monuments. In 1966, his first feature film, *Abschied von gestern*, based upon one of his short stories, 'Anita G.', received numerous international awards, including the Special Jury Prize (Silver Lion) at Venice Film Festival. Two years later, he won the Golden Lion at Venice for his *Die Artisten in der Zirkuskuppel: ratlos*. Kluge's reputation as one of the finest German film-makers was once again established when he won the International Critics Prize at Cannes in 1976 for *Strongman Ferdinand* and an award at Venice in 1983 for *The Power of Emotion*. His other significant films are *Deutschland im Herbst* (1978), a 'collective film', and *Die Patriotin* (1979), probably his most accomplished but also his most inaccessible film. Despite this artistic success, Kluge remains the least known film-maker in and outside Germany among his contemporaries, such as Fassbinder, Herzog, Wenders and Schlöndorff. His films are considered too cerebral and eclectic for the box office.

Kluge's films are an ongoing dialogue with the identity of German history, located between the reality of everyday experience and its ever-present antagonism with German history. His historiography rejects the narrative thread of the conventional cinema of Hollywood, which follows the official project of logical continuity; he reveals the inadequacy of such projects to confront the 'peculiarities' of a history, especially of German history. In what could be a statement of Kluge's own project, Gabi Teichert remarks in *Die Patriotin*, 'What else is the history of a country but the vastest narrative surface of all? Not one story but many stories.' The stories in his films are not consistent or continuous; they are a vertiginous collage of many fragmented and disrupted stories which are linked together in free association. (**Amresh Sinha**)

Kohl, Helmut   Born 1930 Ludwigshafen. Statesman, father of German reunification. (See *Wiedervereinigung*.) Rose in the cdu machine and *Land* politics in Rheinland-Pfalz from 1959. CDU president 1973–99, *Bundeskanzler* 1982–98 in succession to Helmut Schmidt. A pragmatic politician but noted for autocratic style, Kohl saw his generation as the first after 1945 not to bear responsibility for Nazism. Upon the gradual collapse of the GDR, he quickly saw a political chance, promulgated a ten-point programme for Germany's reunification, settled matters with the USSR as early as July 1990, and enforced his line on the economic and political implications. Later scandals (*Kohlgate*) concerning illegal CDU funding and possible corruption in disposal of East German state assets have dented his reputation. (**Alfred D. White**)

Further reading

Clemens and Paterson (1998). Wide-ranging collection of academic papers.

Konkrete Poesie   Concrete Poetry can be defined in three ways: (1) poetry as craft; (2) as concretism; and (3) as sound poetry or visual art, which uses letters as material. A poem by the Austrian writer Jandl, written in English, demonstrates all three criteria:

> i love concrete
> i love pottery
> but i'm not
> a concrete pot

There are three translations or interpretations for Jandl's text: (1) 'ich liebe konkrete / ich liebe töpferware / aber ich bin k / ein konkreter topf' (2) 'ich liebe beton / ich liebe töpferei / aber ich bin k / ein betonkübel' (3) 'i love concrete / i love poetry / but i'm not / a concrete poet' (translation Reinhard Döhl). *Concrete / pottery / po(e)t* here can be read as building material, craft art, as well as a word game. The Swiss writer Eugen Gomringer, whose first poems were published under the title 'konstellationen constellations constelaciones' in 1953, however, favoured the visual as the most common part of Concrete Poetry, referring back to an exhibition on 'concrete art' in Basel in 1944. Therefore the history of Concrete Poetry is bound to the history of ART after 1945. Important German artist schools with international connections to Brazil, Japan, USA, Sweden, France, and Czech Republic, were: Vienna Group (Achleitner, Mon, Rühm), Stuttgart School (Döhl, Heißenbüttel, Bense), Darmstadt Circle (Bremer, Williams, Spoerri), International Forum for Form Ulm (Gomringer, Schäuffelen), studio UND Munich (Gappmeyer, Wezel). Concrete Poetry was influenced by the AVANT-GARDE movement Dada, especially by the poet Hugo Ball and the artist Hans (Jean) ARP. Baroque emblems, Apollinaire's 'Calligrammes', Italian Futurism, Russian Formalism, BAUHAUS typography, Gertrude Stein's language games, as well as Concrete Music have contributed their aesthetics. As diverse, highly experimental and philosophically reflected as concrete poems are, they all focus on the communicative function and materialism of language. (**Markus Hallensleben**)

Further reading

Solt (1968). Includes an introductory chapter on German movements, which can also be found on-line, with further materials and translations, at www.ubu.com Gomringer (1972). Anthology in German with short introduction and biographical/bibliographical information on main authors. Some poems can be understood without translation. Jandl (1998). Bilingual edition with an introduction to Jandl's work in the context of contemporary literature.

Kraus, Karl   1874 Gitschin–1936 Vienna. Poet and literary critic. In 1897, Kraus began his literary career as a correspondent for the *Breslauer Zeitung*. But his claim to fame remains the publication and editorship of the irreverent and critical journal *Die Fackel*, which ran from 1899 until 1936. During the First World War, copies of the *Fackel* were confiscated because of its pacifist leanings. In 1918–19, Kraus's influential anti-war play, *Die letzten Tage der Menschheit* was published. In the 1920s, Kraus began to write against the Nazi's apparently unstoppable rise to power, but ceased to publish the *Fackel* only in the year of his death. (**Holger Briel**)

Further reading

Timms (1999).

Krautrock   German Rock Music (from 1968). A collective term for diverse rock and electronic MUSIC groups with influences ranging from The Velvet Underground to New Music (most famously Karlheinz STOCKHAUSEN's *Hymnen*, 'Anthems for Electronic and Concrete Sounds'). Prefiguring Punk, New Wave, ambient and electronica, groups including Kraftwerk, Can, Faust, Neu and Tangerine Dream gave Germany a unique claim to international fame in popular music during the 1970s – 'not remotely "hippy" … soaringly idealistic and hard as nails' (Julian Cope). (**Martin Brady**)

Further reading

Cope (1996).

Kritische Theorie   A term coined by German philosopher Max HORKHEIMER in 1937. It is a concept most closely associated with the German Frankfurt School (officially known as the Institute for Social Research at the University of Frankfurt). The School was set up in 1923 by Felix Weil as an interdisciplinary institutional centre for research into political economy and cultural production. From 1931, under the direction of Horkheimer, it moved its focus to philosophy, culture and the media. The institution closed in 1934, when Horkheimer and other leading members (such as ADORNO and MARCUSE) emigrated to New York because of the pressures of the German political regime. The School returned to Frankfurt in the early 1950s. Critical theory is inherently suspicious of the ideology of modern, capitalist-orientated society, and its hegemonic tendency to exploit and subjugate both individuals and culture in the effort to capitalize on profits. The School's most famous member was Adorno, a philosopher, sociologist and musicologist whose thought was permanently marked by the rise of fascism in Germany. He diagnosed the ills of modernity in *Dialektik der Aufklärung* (*Dialectic of Enlightenment*) (1944), where he launched an attack on an Enlightenment thought which had moved from critical philosophy to an affirmation of the status quo by default. It is, however, in *Negative Dialektik* (*Negative Dialectics*)

(1966) that a more general account of his thought can be found: in contrast to Hegel, Adorno did not believe that a system, or a philosophy of 'identity', could be extrapolated from the criticism of other philosophers or institutions. Negative dialectics rejects any methodology applicable to all conditions of modern society.

Critical theory has since become an umbrella concept which covers such areas as anthropology, sociology, hermeneutics, feminist theory, film studies, POSTMODERNISM, etc.; it is therefore of crucial importance to anyone interested in understanding German culture and society of the past six or seven decades. (**Katya Bargna**)

Further reading

Adorno and Horkheimer (1972). This is without doubt one of the most celebrated works of modern social philosophy, and it represents the keystone of the Frankfurt School. Jay (1996). Provides a history of the Frankfurt School, and includes a new Preface which focuses on the relevance of critical theory in today's society.

Kroetz, Franz Xaver   Born 1946 Munich. Dramatist and actor. Author (and director) of muscular socially critical realist dramas, frequently in Bavarian DIALECT (including the famous *Wildwechsel, Jailbait*, 1971). During the 1980s and 1990s, he successfully intensified his television work. (**Martin Brady**)

Further reading

Mattson (1996).

Kultur/Zivilisation   According to *Meyers Encyclopaedia, Kultur* is defined as 'Gesamtheit der geistigen, künstlerischen und praktischen Lebensäußerungen einer Menschengruppe, zeitlich und örtlich begrenzt' ('the summation of the intellectual, artistic, and practical expressions of a group of humans that is limited by time and space'). Depending on the specific research focus, various definitions of 'culture' co-exist. One could attempt a general definition of 'culture' as follows: 'culture' could be defined as 'the shared patterns of behaviours and interactions, cognitive constructs, and affective understanding that are learned through a process of socialization. These shared patterns identify the members of a culture group while also distinguishing those of another' (cf. Carla.acad.umn.edu/culture.html). Especially in the German context, the old formula 'Kultur für Alle von Allen' ('Culture for everyone by everyone') has been replaced by the leitmotif of 'Urbanität' ('urbanity) according to Frömming, Schwark, and Stiller in their preface to *Hauptsache Kultur*. In this context, *Kulturpolitik* (cultural politics) deals with the issues of providing '*Orientierungsmarken*' (orientation guidelines) and *Orientierungshilfen* (orientation assistance) in order to prevent randomness. Committees formed by citizens and representatives of the *Kulturbehörden* ensure that operas, THEATRES, libraries, MUSEUMS, musical events, films, monuments, general art and cultural assistance programmes, cultural administrations, and neighbourhood culture (= '*Stadtteilkultur*') are engaged in planned '*Kunst- und Kulturarbeit*' ('artistic and cultural activities') from the largest city to the smallest village. (**Claudia A. Becker**)

Further reading

Ardagh, (1991, pp. 479–96, 563–80). Kulturbehörde Hamburg, Referat für Stadtteilkultur (1991). Moos *et al.* (1997). Trompenaars and Hampden-Turner (1998). Banks and McGee (1989); Damen (1987, p. 367); Hofstede (1984, p. 51); Kluckhohn and Kelly (1945, pp. 78–105); Kroeber and Kluckhohn (1952); Lederach (1995, p. 9); Linton (1945, p. 45); Parson (1949, p. 8); and Useem and Useem (1963, p. 169). Carla.acad.umn.edu/culture.html ('What is Culture?')

***Kultusministerkonferenz* (KMK)** The permanent Conference of the *Länder* Ministers for Culture and Arts in Germany consists of all the ministers or senators for education, universities and research as well as cultural affairs of each federal country (16). It was founded in 1948 by the ministers for education in the three parts of Germany administered by the French, English and American forces. The German Constitution of 23 May 1949 gives the federal states the sole responsibility for education and cultural affairs (*Kulturhoheit der Länder*). Therefore it is the federal ministers' task to deal with their local issues concerning education and cultural affairs. Together they provide some consensus on issues which concern the whole of Germany in the KMK. Some of these general tasks are to ensure that exams and certificates issued by schools are comparable within Germany, to safeguard care of similar quality standards in schools, vocational education and university. One of the main tasks of the KMK is the representation of the individual states and the German education system as a whole vis-à-vis the public and international bodies. The conference is also an instrument for co-operation between the federal countries and the central government in issues which fall into the responsibility of both parties involved, such as vocational training. Vocational training within companies is regulated by the central government whereas the vocational education in schools is the responsibility of the governments of local states. There are three central services offered by the KMK: the pedagogical exchange service for teachers and those studying to become teachers, the central office for education in other countries and the central office for norms and effectiveness in the educational system. Current high priority discussions include the Bachelor and Master degrees in Germany in order to make German degrees comparable to those of other countries around the world. (**Inge Strüder**)

Further reading

Lau (1996).   www.kmk.org (website of the KMK, in German only.)

Kunze, Reiner   Born 1933 Oelsnitz. Author. In the 1950s and 1960s, Kunze had relative success with his poems on the stagnation of social(ist) progress in the GDR. While in those early poems, the belief in communist principles is still unbroken, his collection of poems entitled *zimmerlautstärke* (1972) clearly highlights that poetic admonitions were not enough to change the reality of GDR socialism for the better. He rose to fame with his poetic novel *Die wunderbaren Jahre* (1976) in which he describes the life of a young generation, who, having grown up in the GDR, are subsequently faced with the fallout of the invasion of Czechoslovakia and begin to reflect upon their own lack of freedom, a lack of freedom which apparently can no longer be relieved by any internal changes made to the political system. Because of this novel, Kunze was forced to leave the GDR and settled in Bavaria in West Germany. Together with Volker BRAUN and Wolf BIERMANN (who was forced out of the GDR only five months before Kunze had to leave himself), Kunze formulated the protest of the younger GDR citizens against a corrupt and dictatorial system. The seeds sown by his texts played an important part in creating a culture of dissent that would ultimately lead to the demise of the GDR. He continues to live in Germany and publish poems and young adults' stories. (**Holger Briel**)

L

Lang, Fritz 1890 Vienna–1976 Beverly Hills. Film director. Lang was one of the world's greatest film directors and his name is mentioned in the same breath as those of Hitchcock and Renoir. Lang is best known as an exponent of German Expressionism. Among a deeply impressive canon of work dating from the Weimar period, one must highlight his innovative science fiction piece, *Metropolis* (1926) as well as adaptations of Wagner's *Die Nibelungen* (1924). Equally famous is the disturbing portrayal of a child-murderer in *M* (1931). Images from these films have literally entered into the public imagination. They are frequently borrowed and copied by others and were also even much admired in their day by the Nazi propagandist, Joseph GOEBBELS. Lang's post-war reputation was built in Hollywood and Paris. Lang left Germany in 1934, after refusing an invitation to work for the Nazi film industry. In Hollywood he made further films such as *Rancho Notorious* (1952) and the sophisticated *film noir*, *The Blue Gardenia* (1953). These and other Lang films were then picked up and promoted by the influential French film critics associated with the journal *Cahiers du cinéma*. Lang was now identified as a master film-maker: an 'auteur' or 'author'. Parisian intellectual support for Lang reached its height in 1962 when he was asked to play himself in Jean-Luc Godard's *Le Mépris* (*Contempt*). (**Hugo Frey**)

Further reading

Eisner (2002). Classic study of Lang. Gunning (2000). Recent, impressive survey of the director's films. Cook and Bernink (1999). Provides a very good introduction to the cinema of Fritz Lang.

Legal system In German Law, the *Grundgesetz* (Basic Law) as Constitution takes precedent over all other laws. The *Grundgesetz* was drafted after the Second World War as a deliberate reaction to the Nazi regime.

It is called *Grundgesetz* rather than *Verfassung* (Constitution) as it was initially thought to be merely an intermediate solution for the old Federal Republic of Germany (i.e. without the territory of the former German Democratic Republic). Since the reunification in 1990 it is indisputably the Constitution for all of Germany.

Article 1 of the *Grundgesetz* states that Human Dignity (*Menschenwürde*) is inviolable. Articles 1–19 of the *Grundgesetz* constitute Basic Rights (*Grundrechte*) for the individual citizen. Hereby the *Grundgesetz* makes a clear statement that it is the state's duty to serve its citizens (and not, as in socialist regimes, vice versa). Furthermore, after the abuse of civil liberties during the THIRD REICH the *Grundgesetz* makes these

Basic Rights binding for all branches of state power (Art. 1 subsection 3 of the *Grundgesetz*). Should the state violate a Basic Right of any one of its subjects, the citizen has a right to file a complaint to the Federal Constitutional Court (*Bundesverfassungsgericht*).

The central provision defining Germany's structure as a democratic and social federal state is Article 20 of the *Grundgesetz*. Democracy, as a subsection of the same article states, means all state authority is derived from the people. 'It shall be exercised by the people through elections and other votes and through specific legislative, executive, and judicial bodies.' The requirement for a social state is to strive for social justice and security in its society. This objective is to be achieved by various further laws, foremost by the *Bundessozialgesetz* (Federal Social Law). German Federalism, the final requirement of Article 20 is based on two pillars: there was no unified German state until 1871. Before this date the German Empire consisted of very many independent German states. Thus decentralism was not a new concept to Germany and the Germans. The second reason for Germany being a Federal State lies in a requirement of the Allied powers in post-war Germany: a strong central power had to be prevented; in today's Germany the executive is dominated by the *Länder* (for example, the police are the responsibility of the *Länder*).

In fact, the provisions of Article 1 and Article 20 are deemed to be of such importance that they are placed under the special guarantee of Article 79, subsection 3 of the *Grundgesetz*: 'Amendments to this Basic Law affecting the division of the Federation into *Länder*, their participation on principle in the legislative process, or the principles laid down in Articles 1 and 20 shall be inadmissible.'

There are various further Federal and *Länder* laws relating to every aspect of life. Obviously, they cannot be described in detail in this publication.

The German Legal System is a codified system. As stated above, Germany was not a unified state until 1871. Indeed, it took until this time for Germany to have a single legislator. Many of today's codifications date back to the end of the nineteenth and beginning of the twentieth century. These codifications have undergone a multitude of amendments and reforms; nonetheless the core can easily be traced back to that period. (**Andrew Otto**)

Further reading

www.iuscomp.org/gla (website of the German Law Archive, with a comprehensive account of all publications on German Law in English.)

Lenz, Siegfried   Born 1926 Lyck. Author. Together with Günter GRASS and Walter Kempowski, Lenz is one of the foremost German authors to thematize life in Eastern Prussia. His collection of stories, *So zärtlich war Suleyken* (1955), would firmly establish him on the literary map of Germany. In his *Deutschstunde* (1970), Siggi Jepsen, a prisoner, is forced to write about his memories of his father, a policeman and his quarrels with a 'degenerate' painter during the THIRD REICH. This intricate story recreates the lives of people during the Third Reich and exemplifies the problems the German post-war generation had with the guilt of their parent generation and their involvement in the Nazi regime. Lenz would continue his analysis of what *Heimat* (home/land) means for Germans with the novels *Heimatmuseum* (1978) and *Exerzierplatz* (1985). In those and also in subsequent short stories, Lenz weaves a tapestry of snippets from the lives of the people in what used to be Prussian territory, all the time reflecting on notions of home and local culture. He does so with empathy, yet also with the distancing view of somebody who knows what brutal and negative effects some of the protagonists' actions would have. While his more recent texts do not create the publicity of his earlier work, he continues writing on his traditional subjects (*Ludmilla*, 1996; *Arnes Nachlass*, 2001). (**Holger Briel**)

Further reading

Wagener (1985).

Library system   As in most other European countries, libraries in Germany date back to the Middle Ages when monasteries held Latin manuscripts that were manually copied and exchanged.

Owing to industrialization and science in the nineteenth century which led to a vast increase in the publication of scientific literature, academic libraries became more important than ever before. Public libraries on the other hand were then founded to meet the demands of the rising number of educated people. This distinction between 'public' and 'academic' libraries has been prevalent in Germany ever since. During the 1990s hypertext, multimedia and the Internet added to the traditional linear approach to information, and as a result libraries in Germany developed to become more of general information centres with access to books, journals, multimedia products, software, and Internet information.

Today German libraries co-operate on a local, regional and national basis. Most of them offer free access to their own collections, and they participate in the countrywide interlibrary loan system. Over recent years the SUBITO (www.subito-doc.de) project emerged which enables library users to electronically order and receive within 48 hours digitized or hardcopy versions of academic articles from home. The final step of this project will provide the quick ordering and delivery of complete books for academic purposes on a loan basis. In 1998 there were 400 million media in over 14 000 German libraries available which is equivalent to one library per 5800 inhabitants and to 4.8 media per person. Germany's national library is *Die Deutsche Bibliothek* (www.ddb.de) which since the reunification of 1990 comprises the former West 'Deutsche Bibliothek' in Frankfurt, the 'Deutsches Musikarchiv' in Berlin and the former East 'Deutsche Bücherei' in Leipzig with the original locations having been retained. (**Dieter Aichele**)

LIVERPOOL JOHN MOORES UNIVERSITY
LEARNING & INFORMATION SERVICES

Further reading

Thun (1998). Excellent and concise overview of the contemporary German library system.

Literary canon A privileged group of literary works deemed suitable for study in (state) universities and schools, production in (court, later state-subsidized) literary THEATRES and so forth. The German canon originates in the formation of a German consciousness in the early nineteenth century, as the cultural achievement of a 'Volk der Dichter und Denker' previously overshadowed by French culture. The lyric and dramatic works of the Weimar classics Goethe and Schiller, with the proudly national works of the Romantics, are central. Politically unacceptable, internationalist or radical writers, Jews, women and popular writers are disregarded. The canon is extended during the nineteenth century: in academia with Middle High German poetry, in the theatre with Shakespeare (an honorary German) and later serious national dramatists (Kleist, Hebbel), for the general reader with more narrative literature (Goethe, Keller, Storm), much of it found in the ever-growing series of super-cheap classics published by Reclam from 1837 on. Foreign writers appear only if long dead (Dante, Calderon) or seen as embodying a common Nordic heritage (Strindberg). The twentieth century sees, especially with the political pluralism of the 1920s, acceptance of political radicals, past (Heine, Büchner) or present (Hauptmann). National Socialism narrows the canon again to authors who are interpretable nationalistically. In the GDR further radical authors come in; it privileges Russian socialist classics (Gorki). The Federal Republic favours older Jewish writers (Schnitzler), movements banned by Nazism (Expressionism), and more modern writers regardless of political attitude. Subsidized theatres attempt greater range, with rediscoveries (Grabbe) and new playwrights (FRISCH, DÜRRENMATT, and despite political doubts BRECHT).

The structuralist slogan of the death of the author casts doubt on the idea of a canon. Today texts are viewed more as expression of a context, less as lonely pinnacles of individual achievement. Women's writings, workers' literature (*ARBEITERLITERATUR*), travel writing, popular fiction and other groupings come into their own. At school level the canon survives in the lists of authors issued by *Land* authorities. (**Alfred D. White**)

Further reading

Kammler (1997). Sketch of implications for schools. Heydebrand (1998). Magisterial collection of studies.

Low German (See also DIALECTS.) This is a collective term for a number of linguistic varieties in northern Germany that are very distinct from standard German, although related to it. There is much debate over whether Low German is a dialect (i.e. subvariety) of German or a separate language, but it is described in the European Charter for Regional and Minority Languages, parts of which Germany has ratified, as a regional language. Today there is no accepted standard variety, although a relatively standardized written variety, based on Lübeck usage, was used widely along the coasts of the Baltic and North Sea up to about the sixteenth century. With the emergence of standard German, Low German became associated with low-status social groups and was ousted by the former, first in writing, then in formal speech. In recent years it has regained prestige, and nearly all school curricula produced by states with Low-German-speaking communities refer to it. In practice it is still used more in private situations than in public, formal ones, which makes it difficult to judge how wide-spread competence in it really is. Efforts to teach it are hampered by the lack of a standard variety, but a recently published grammar based mainly on North Low Saxon (one variety of Low German) (Lindow *et al.*, 1998) may encourage standardization tendencies and play a symbolic role in bolstering the status of Low German. Whether the European Charter for Regional and Minority Languages can do anything to help it remains to be seen: not all states have ratified every part of the Charter, so they are under no obligation to protect it and promote it actively. (**Winifred Davies**)

Further reading

Lindow *et al.* (1998). A comprehensive description of one variety of Low German. Wildgen (n.d.). A brief but informative account of the history and current situation of Low German.

LIVERPOOL JOHN MOORES UNIVERSITY
Aldham Robarts L.R.C.
TEL. 051 231 3701/3634

Macke, August 1887 Meschede–1914 Champagne. Painter. Expressionist painter of the *Blaue Reiter* (Blue Rider) group (see ART). Painted colourful street and park scenes in Germany and Tunisia. (**Martin Brady**)

Maetzig, Kurt Born 1911 Berlin. Film-maker. Founder in 1946 of the newsreel *The Eyewitness* (*Der Augenzeuge*) and co-founder of DEFA, the state-run East German film industry. His first feature, *Marriage in the Shadows* (*Ehe im Schatten*, 1947) tells the tragic story of actor Joachim Gottschalk and his Jewish wife during the THIRD REICH. Maetzig's feature films frequently used historical and documentary material (the armaments industry, the life of Ernst Thälmann, the JUNE 1953 UPRISING, everyday life in East Germany) but he also made comedies and a sci-fi film. A critical realist, he exerted a considerable influence on younger GDR directors. (**Martin Brady**)

Mann, Heinrich 1871 Lübeck–1950 in exile. He was one of five children of a very upper-class, traditional Senator. Although most dictionaries will carry a much longer entry on his younger brother Thomas MANN, someone looking for social and political engagement in a work of fiction may prefer to turn to the writings of Heinrich Mann. In his early writings a protagonist of the neo-romantic and the Expressionist movements, later, he displayed liberal and anti-nationalist ideas and in later life a humanitarian socialism. His novels caricature the staid narrow-mindedness of the 'Bourgeoisie' who set great store by outward appearances and the so-called '*Sekundartugenden*' ('secondary moral qualities') of the era of Emperor William I and the ensuing WEIMAR REPUBLIC.

'*Die kleine Stadt* (*The Little Town*, 1909) is considered a masterpiece of his early writings, but Heinrich Mann soon turned from the praise of the carefree adventurer to scathing criticism of bourgeois life. His pathos changed into satire and finally turned into grotesque, sketchy caricature: *Im Schlaraffenland* (*In Paradise*, 1900), *Professor Unrat* (about a tyrannical professor who gets caught in his own web laid to catch out 'amorality') was turned into the famous Marlene DIETRICH film *The Blue Angel*). His novel *Der Untertan* (*The Underling*, 1918) caricatures the subservient, power-hungry personality he saw as the typical representative of the era of Wilhelm I.

Heinrich Mann left Germany in 1933 and completed his two-volume novel *König Heinrich IV* (*King Henry IV*) in exile. His autobiography, *Ein Zeitalter wird besichtigt* (*An Era is Visited*, 1943–44), combines accounts of his personal existence with the historical epoch. (**Astrid Küllmann-Lee**)

Further reading

Haupt (1980).

Mann, Klaus   1906 Munich–1949 Cannes. Writer. The son of Thomas MANN, he began writing for theatre early, with limited success. He emigrated from Germany in 1933 to flee the HITLER regime, and lived in Amsterdam, Prague, Paris and Zurich, where he continued writing and also edited the Amsterdam emigrant newspaper *Die Sammlung*. In 1936 he emigrated to the USA and returned to Germany as an American soldier, writing for *The Stars and Stripes*. Mann wrote his most famous novels while living as an émigré. *Mephisto* (1936) sketches the ruthless career of one Hendrik Höfgen, an actor whose character had a lot in common with Gustav GRÜNDGENS, who at one time had been married to Klaus Mann's sister Erika, and who fought the publication of the book for a long time. In 1981 Istvan Szabo turned the novel into a film. *Der Vulkan. Roman unter Emigranten* (1939, *The Volcano: A Novel among Emigrants*) is highly autobiographical and tells the story of emigrants in Paris, of their resignation and desires. It also problematizes homosexuality and suicide, topics which would also act as defining markers for Klaus Mann's own life. (**Holger Briel**)

Further reading

Naumann (2001).

Mann, Thomas   1875 Lübeck–1955 Kilchberg, near Zurich. Author, known internationally for *Der Tod in Venedig* (*Death in Venice*), the tragic story of a platonic paedophile, inspiration of a Visconti film and a Britten opera. Mann commented on German society in his great novels: *Buddenbrooks* 1901, story of the decline of a patrician family; *Der Zauberberg* (*The Magic Mountain*) 1924, exploration of spiritual and intellectual tensions before 1914; the tetralogy *Joseph und seine Brüder* (*Joseph and his Brothers*), whose biblical setting encodes topical references; *Doktor Faustus*, 1946, symbolic of the Nazi catastrophe. Conservative in politics until after 1919, Mann became a prominent defender of the WEIMAR REPUBLIC, going into American exile after 1933. (**Alfred D. White**)

Further reading

Koopmann (1990). All the facts one needs. Reed (1996). Most perceptive analysis.

Manufacturing and energy   The share of manufacturing in national output is significantly higher in Germany than in other European countries and generally 50 per cent of production is exported, with between 60 per cent and 75 per cent of exports shipped to the EU area. The German business cycle is therefore more directly influenced by world demand. Productive industry comprises manufacturing and mining: at the end of the 1990s manufacturing accounted for DM605 bn in output, while mining and quarrying output reached DM12.7 bn. In all, there are 6.24 million employees in manufacturing and 129 000 in mining and quarrying. The productivity, quality and innovation of German manufacturing have carried much of Germany's post-war growth, with an important export share, although total output growth has been less than the EU average since the early 1970s. Key sectors of manufacturing are mechanical engineering, AUTOMOBILE manufacture, chemicals and electronics and electrical engineering. The largest employer is mechanical engineering with almost 900 000 employees in 2000: the sector covers the full range of capital equipment and much of output is produced by medium-sized enterprises with a high level of specialization. The opposite is found in automobile assembly and parts production, which is the second largest branch having DM84 bn of output at the end of the 1990s and 755 000 employees. Here five companies have the largest share, and 10 companies account for 79 per cent of output. In chemicals, feedstock output is the most important segment, while the allied branch of pharmaceuticals is well represented internationally. Though less-concentrated, the share of Bayer, BASF and Hoechst in output is very large. Manufacturing subsidies are the highest in the EU, principally because of aid to the east. Technologically, Germany surpasses in the medium rather than the high technology branches. In energy, hard coal production output has been reduced by two-thirds over the last decades and subsidies are falling from DM5 bn to DM3 bn annually. East German lignite production has halved since 1990. (**Chris Flockton**)

Further reading

Bund Deutscher Industrie publications. Deutscher Industrie- und Handelstag publications.

Marcuse, Herbert   1898 Berlin–1979 Starnberg. Philosopher. Studied philosophy at Berlin and Freiburg, where he wrote a PhD thesis on the *Künstlerroman*. He then continued his studies there with Husserl and HEIDEGGER. In 1932 Marcuse emigrated, via Geneva and Paris, to New York, where he became one of the founders of the Institute for Social Research. He became an American citizen and worked at the Office of Strategic Services in Washington. After the war, he worked at Columbia University, Harvard and Brandeis. In 1955 he published *Eros and Civilization*, in which he described present-day society as repressed due to its repression of sexual drives. In 1964 *One-Dimensional Man* was published which was to become one of the most influential texts of the student revolt. In this text, Marcuse sketches the crises of capitalism which can only survive by making humans one-dimensional money-seekers and by destroying their more liberating drives. In 1965 Marcuse moved to the University of California, San Diego. Unlike other exponents of *KRITISCHE THEORIE*, such as ADORNO and HORKHEIMER, Marcuse denied complete negativity of today's society and believed in the possibility of change for the better. (**Holger Briel**)

Further reading

Jansen (1999).

Marriage   Article 6 of the Federal Republic's Basic Law places marriage and the family under 'the special protection of the state order'. This is reflected at federal government level, with a cabinet minister having specific responsibility for the family, currently within the Ministry for the Family, Older People, Women and Youth.

Not surprisingly this state of affairs has not prevented similar developments to those in comparable countries, specifically the overall decline in the significance of the institution of marriage within society. In 1998 every fourth inhabitant of a large city lived alone, while 36.2 per cent of all households in the western part of Germany, the largest group, consisted of only one person. This compares with a figure of 19.4 per cent in 1950. Reasons for these changes include increasing secularization (particularly marked in the east) and individualization, not to mention the financial burdens of family life. These developments are reflected in: the decline in the number of marriages from 750 000 in 1950 to 423 000 in 1997, the more than doubling of divorce rates between 1965 and 1997 and the almost doubling of non-married partnerships in the decade up to 1998 in the western states.

One further consequence has been a decline in the birth rate from over a million in 1970 to 812 000 in 1997. Around a fifth of children are born outside marriage, which is, however, well below the EU average. Despite all these changes, the outlook for marriage is not entirely bleak. Married people generally profess more satisfaction with their lives than other groups. Moreover, in Spring 2001 the Federal Constitutional Court required changes in the welfare state to be made by 2004 so that parents of children should no longer be discriminated against, thus alleviating one reason for the decline of marriage and the family. (**Stuart Parkes**)

Further reading

Bundesministerium für Familie, Senioren, Frauen und Jugend (1998); Kolinsky (1998); Urmoneit (1991).

Marshall Plan   As a programme of economic help – food, raw materials, technical assistance – from the United States, the Marshall Plan permitted 16 European countries to restore industrial capacity after the Second World War. The programme was proposed by the American Secretary of State George C. Marshall in a speech at Harvard University on 5 June 1947. US motives were both economic and political: massive aid was necessary before the European states could provide for their own needs and become trading partners again. But the programme has also to be seen in the context of the Truman Doctrine, announced in March 1947, which called for the prevention of the further spread of communism. Social tensions resulting from poor economic conditions were seen as a major cause for the strength of Communist parties in France and Italy and for support of the communist guerrillas in Greece. Although Marshall had extended his offer to all European countries, the countries in the Soviet bloc and neutral Finland refused to participate. The Marshall Plan was therefore also part of the Cold War: the already growing antagonism between Moscow and Washington made economic co-operation between East and West impossible. Between 1948 and 1952 the 16 participating countries received $13.15 billion with outright grants accounting for seven-eighths of the aid. Economically, the plan contributed to a fast recovery of Western Europe: the recipient countries' gross national product rose by 25 per cent, industrial production increased by 35 per cent and agricultural production by 10 per cent. For West Germany the programme had an enormous psychological effect: confidence in economic reconstruction was rebuilt, and the West German zones became, for the first time, economically linked to Western Europe. Thus, the programme became a corner stone of pro-Americanism among the West German population. (**Jörn Leonhard**)

Further reading

Hardach (1987). Useful overview of Marshall Plan's impact on post-war Germany. Nicholls (1994). Readable and convincing analysis of the long-term development of SOZIALE MARKTWIRTSCHAFT in Germany.

Mies van der Rohe, Ludwig   1886 Aachen–1969 Chicago. Architect and designer. Hugely influential architect whose early (unexecuted) projects include majestic glass skyscrapers and a reinforced concrete office building (1919–22). The glass, steel and marble *Barcelona Pavilion* (1928–29) and International Style Tugendhat House in Brno remain icons of modern design. Director of the BAUHAUS (1930–33), he emigrated to America in 1937, where he built landmark domestic and commercial towers including the elegant and minimalist Lake Shore Drive Apartments (Chicago, 1950–51) and the Seagram Building (1954–58). (**Martin Brady**)

Further reading

Carter (1999).

Minorities   Already at the beginning of the twentieth century, there were many migrants living in Germany. Many of them came from Poland and worked in the mines of the Ruhrgebiet. During the THIRD REICH, millions of mostly East Europeans were forced to work as slave labourers in German factories and in the agricultural sector. Nowadays, there are ca. 9 million non-Germans residing in Germany, which is about 10 per cent of the whole population; this group is comprised of GASTARBEITER (migrant labourers or workers) and their families, who by far make up the largest segment, Sinti and Roma, refugees and asylum seekers. Partly due to the immediately preceding events, the West German GRUNDGESETZ (Basic Law) of 1949 stipulated that refugees and asylum seekers were welcome in Germany and that they had a legal right to apply for asylum. In the beginning, numbers were small, but by the mid to late 1980s, their numbers swelled to hundreds of thousands each year. The overwhelming majority had their applications rejected, being classified as *Wirtschaftsflüchtlinge* (economic refugees), rather than political refugees. Since then, an emotional political discussion has been going on regarding how to deal with this large number of foreigners, who, while awaiting the outcome of their application, were forbidden to work and therefore incurred a huge cost to the tax payer. Recently, partly due to changes in legislation (the Schengen Agreement), their numbers have dropped considerably. However, a convincing political solution, allowing for the quick settlement of genuine asylum seekers while at the same time stopping economic refugees, remains elusive. (**Holger Briel**)

Further reading

Herbert (2001). Comprehensive overview of the role of politics in migration. Münz *et al.* (1999). Overview of migration process and its social implications. Schmalz-Jacobsen and Hansen (1995). Spoerer (2001). Study of slave labour during the Third Reich. Tebbutt (2001). Comprehensive essays on the situation of Sinti and Roma in Germany.

Mittelstand   The *Mittelstand* or owner-led business has always been considered the backbone of the German economy and is defined as companies having 500 employees or less. They account for one-half of the country's businesses, employing two-thirds of the German private sector working population and training four-fifths of the young people there. Typically the *Mittelstand* enterprises are *Personengesellschaften* (non-incorporated companies), where the owner has unlimited liability but also maintains unlimited management control. In fact, the great majority of German firms are unincorporated. The owner-entrepreneur retains the *Personengesellschaft* status, rather than adopting the *Aktiengesellschaft* (AG) or *Gesellschaft mit beshränkter Haftung* (GmbH, Limited) incorporated forms because he does not want to relinquish control to new shareholders. Typically, important sectors of German MANUFACTURING, such as mechanical engineering and especially machine tools are dominated by *Mittelstand* firms. This is because they are flexible, innovative and yet can specialize in a narrow range of products or pursue series production, where size in itself is not a prime advantage. There is, however, a very wide range of firms within the category, whether grouped by turnover or profitability. For example, some 6700 *Personengesellschaften* generated sales of more than DM50 million, compared with 6300 corporations achieving the same. Because of the close personal identity between ownership and management in *Mittelstand* firms, considerable upheavals arise with the question of succession, as many sons and daughters are unable or unwilling to take over the family firm. While there may be around 3 million family-run businesses, over the period 1999–2004 one in nine owners of *Mittelstand* companies will step down. This raises the question of whether such companies will be bought out, merge or become incorporated. There are also important tax issues which differentiate between incorporated and unincorporated firms. One possibility would be to convert to the non-listed, so-called 'business AG' form, which has a sound equity basis but is simpler than the exchange-quoted AG. (**Chris Flockton**)

Further reading

Statistisches Bundesamt, *Statistisches Jahrbuch*, annual.

Modernism A term used within the sphere of culture to refer to experimental forms of art which began to appear around the beginning of the twentieth century throughout Europe and America. Although the actual work produced by modernist artists was highly varied, certain common strands can be identified. Be it the Expressionists in Germany, or the Surrealists in France and Spain, these artists were driven by the need radically to break with earlier traditions, particularly nineteenth-century realism, since these traditions were viewed as being unable to provide them with satisfactory models for the representation of a world in which the pace of industrial, philosophical and technical change was becoming ever faster. The art of the period tended to be highly self-reflective, with many writers and painters self-consciously exploring the process of artistic production. Consequently, particular emphasis was placed on the form of the work, a tendency which can be seen, for example, in narrative experimentation of Alfred DÖBLIN's *Berlin Alexanderplatz*.

Artists' attitudes to the pace of change in twentieth-century society varied greatly. However, many of these attitudes are permeated by a deep-seated sense of unease. In Germany this was encapsulated in the title of Kurt Pinthus's seminal anthology of Expressionist poetry *Menschheitsdämmerung* (*The Twilight of Humanity*) – a title which suggests that this age could signal either the end of humanity, or the beginning of a new era. In either case, writers of the period viewed their work as a vehicle to imbue the world with new meaning, providing their audiences with a powerful critique of the forces of modernity. This tradition remained strong in German art right though the twentieth century, as can be seen, for example, in the novels of Günter GRASS. However, since the late 1960s it has begun to be challenged ever more by POST-MODERN artistic production. (**Paul Cooke**)

Further reading

Sheppard (1993). A very good introductory overview of the socio-political and cultural developments connected with modernism.

Morgner, Irmtraud 1933 Chemnitz–1990 Berlin. Writer. Important texts by her include *Rumba auf einen Herbst* (published posthumously, 1992), *Hochzeit in Konstantinopel* (1968), *Leben und Abenteuer der Trobadora Beatriz nach Zeugnissen ihrer Spielfrau Laura* (1974), *Amanda* (1983), *Das heroische Testament* (published posthumously, 1998). Morgner was one of the most renowned GDR authors. In *Trobadora Beatriz*, the protagonist wakes up after 800 years of sleep to find out whether the situation of women has improved in the supposedly exemplary GDR. For this novel, Morgner developed a much acclaimed narrative technique which she herself called 'operativer Montageroman' (operative montage novel). Among other things, this allowed her to include clippings from texts that had not passed censorship before. (**Corinna J. Heipcke**)

Further reading

Gerhardt (1990). Serves well as an introduction to Morgner. Westgate (2002). Focuses on the system of state control and surveillance that accompanied cultural production in the GDR and draws on new biographical material.

Müller, Heiner 1929 Eppendorf–1995 Berlin. Playwright and theatre director. Arguably the most important figure in German theatre after Brecht, and his most significant spiritual heir, Müller lived through Germany's turbulent history: from the rise of Hitler to the Soviet occupation, to the building and eventual collapse of the Berlin Wall – all subjects which would form part of his dramatic œuvre. An awkward Marxist, Müller was heavily critical of the East German government, which in turn often censored his works. Famously claiming for himself the title of '*zweifellos größter lebender Dramatiker*' (without doubt the greatest living playwright), Müller was honoured with a remarkable number of awards and, in 1995, became the sole artistic director of the Berliner Ensemble. His plays include *Der Bau, Die Schlacht, Germania Tod in Berlin, Der Auftrag, Quartett*, and, perhaps most famously, *Hamletmaschine*. His last play, *Germania 3*, was premiered in Bochum in 1996. (**Katya Bargna**)

Further reading

Weber (2001). This anthology, translated by former Brecht-collaborator Carl Weber, is the only publication in English to offer a selection of Müller's works spanning various genres, and includes an introduction to each separate section. Kalb (1998). Kalb's critical investigation of Müller's work sheds light on the playwright's deliberate 'borrowings' from other greats of European theatre: Shakespeare, Büchner, Artaud, Beckett, and, of course, Brecht.

Multiculturalism Multiculturalism is deeply connected to the various complex relationships towards what one defines as 'one's own' and what one defines as belonging to 'the other'. These vital processes of cross-cultural encounters are not free of internal contradictions and external conflicts; such an unstable and conflict-prone state within an individual, a family, a company, a neighbourhood, a city, a region as well as a society should not be confused with beautiful folkloristic presentations, potlucks or international shows of merely decorative and/or entertaining functions. Multiculturalism will probably increase in the Federal Republic of Germany in the future due to general migration processes, the EC, and a new openness for external cultures; the idea of cultural homogeneity will ultimately be replaced by cultural plurality. This process will have an effect on set values and conventional ways of behaviour. In order to achieve a peaceful coexistence, an awareness of different conceptualizations in terms of living, working, the relationship between men and women, etc. needs to be raised as early as in kindergarten or even earlier in the earliest socialization phase at home. Furthermore, cultural differences should be explained in their contexts while trying to preserve one's existence as an individual as well as a group. In conclusion, a resolution in conflict management is successful when an individual as well as a group recognizes that any foreign culture does not have to pose a threat to one's own existence because self-confidence or a lack thereof are the real issues and affect each culture, foreign or home. (**Claudia A. Becker**)

Further reading

Ardagh (1991, pp. 479–96, 563–80); Enzensberger (1992); Kuhnhardt (1994); Kulturbehörde Hamburg, Referat für Stadtteilkultur (1991); Trompenaars and Hampden-Turner (1998); Zinn (2000).

Münchener Abkommen   After the annexation of Austria in March 1938, the German dictator Adolf Hɪᴛʟᴇʀ turned to new goals in his foreign policies. Since the foundation of Czechoslovakia after the First World War in 1919 this new state had encompassed a significant German minority of 3.2m (22.5 per cent of the overall population) who mainly lived on the border with Germany, in the so-called Sudetenland. After Hitler's seizure of power in 1933 the German minority started to demand greater autonomy. The 1935 general election, in which the German nationalist party *Sudetendeutsche Heimatfront* managed to secure the majority of the German vote, together with the intensified pressure from Nazi Germany, resulted in increased demands on the Czech government. Hitler deliberately encouraged Konrad Henlein, the leader of the *Heimatfront*, to come up with ever new demands, which he knew Prague could not accept. The situation gradually deteriorated and Hitler prepared for war. Much depended on the moves of the Western allies who had tried to meet Hitler's demands before in order to preserve peace. According to this 'appeasement' policy the British Prime Minister Neville Chamberlain flew to Munich in September 1938 and eventually managed to convince Hitler to refrain from military action. On 29 September Chamberlain, Hitler, the Italian leader Mussolini, and the French Prime Minister Daladier signed the Munich treaty without consulting the Czech government. It allowed the German army to occupy the Sudetenland but also guaranteed the continued existence of the rest of the Czech state. Although the annexations left Czechoslovakia nearly defenceless and subject to German influence, Chamberlain celebrated the treaty, which in his opinion had saved 'peace for our time'. For Hitler, however, it meant only another step on the way to war. Five months later he breached the Munich treaty and invaded Czechoslovakia turning it into a German protectorate. (**Anselm Heinrich**)

Further reading

Wendt (1995). Chapter V, 4 gives a concise overview of the most important developments.

Museums   Today's Germany is home to about 3000 museums, which enjoy much interest from the public and a relatively high level of public funding. As is the case with many other cultural institutions, these museums and galleries are not only concentrated in the large cities, but are distributed throughout the country. Museums in smaller towns such as Tübingen, with its world-renowned *Kunsthalle*, play as much an important part in the cultural life of Germany as do museums in the large cities. Many of the latter have a long history, such as the Deutsche Museum and the Alte and Neue Pinakothek in Munich or the Germanisches Nationalmuseum in Nuremberg. However, throughout the 1980s and 1990s, major architectural and cultural initiatives added new and exciting fora for artistic display. Such initiatives included the Neue Staatsgalerie in Stuttgart, the Museumsufer (containing several museums), the Schirn and the Museum für Moderne Kunst in Frankfurt, the Wallraf-Richartz-Museum/Museum Ludwig in Cologne, the Museum für Deutsche Gegenwartsgeschichte (Museum for Contemporary German History) in Bonn and the re-vamping of the Museumsinsel and the opening of the Jüdisches Museum (Liebeskind) in Berlin. Berlin also profited from the 'open-air' museum that was the Berlin Wall, of which a stretch continues to be an ART exhibit, and the many new galleries opening in the 1990s, especially in its erstwhile eastern parts of Prenzlauer Berg and Mitte. An even more recent development is the virtual history museum the Deutsches Historisches Museum Berlin (www.dhm.de) has mounted, which gives an interactive overview of German history. (**Holger Briel**)

Further reading

www.dhm.de (website of the Deutsches Historisches Museum, with an excellent tour of German History.)
www.museumsbund.de (website of the Association of German Museums.)

Music   Music plays an important part in German life. After the USA and Japan, Germany is the third-largest market for music in the world. German used to differentiate between *E(rnster)-Musik* (serious music), comprising classical and AVANT-GARDE music *U(nterhaltungs)-Musik*, pop, rock, dance, etc, and *Volksmusik* (literally people's music, folkloric music), but rapid changes in the global music industry and in tastes have increasingly led to a fusion-driven cross-over globalization of music, which also reverberates within the German music market. Recent mega-mergers within the music industry have left fewer than five companies dominating the global market. In Germany, only Bertelsmann has been able to remain an independent global player. Furthermore, starting in the WEIMAR REPUBLIC, technological advances began to have an impact on music. Arnold SCHOENBERG's twelve-tone music became an important innovation in AVANT-GARDE music and film music and popular music were played on the RADIO, which, along with the phonograph shaped musical history in the twentieth century. Hans Eisler and Kurt Weill (especially in his collaboration with Bert BRECHT) greatly influenced the music market of the time. During the Nazi era, the musical tastes and needs of the people in power shaped the programming available, with Wagner and military marches playing an important role. After the Second World War, classical music, film music and operettas would dominate the tastes of the middle-aged middle class. Important festivals such as the Bayreuth Wagner Festival, the Salzburger

Festspiele and the Oberammergauer Passionsspiele would captivate the slightly more upmarket audiences and create international interest. Only a small market segment would be taken up by avant-garde music from composers such as Karlheinz STOCKHAUSEN, Hans Werner Henze, Wolfgang Rihm and Bernd Alois Zimmermann. Overall, however, it was music in English that began to exert its ever-increasing influence on the emerging and financially all-important German youth market. Especially the American Forces Network (AFN) would re-introduce Germans to jazz and swing, both prohibited during the THIRD REICH, but also open the German market to rock 'n' roll. This predominance of English music is still the case today. With little or no market share outside of the German speaking countries, German rock 'n' roll never really managed to challenge English language dominance. However, exceptions did occur. One was the period of the *Liedermacher* (Song writers, mid-1960s to late 1970s), with singers such as Franz-Josef Degenhardt, Konstantin Wecker, Klaus Hoffmann and Hannes Wader, who, influenced by American folk music and French Chanson, specialized in political music. Another was the period of the early 1980s when the *NDW* (*NEUE DEUTSCHE WELLE*, New German Wave) insisted on German language music. The most famous exponents of this music were Ideal. (During this same time period, East German music, represented by such groups as Puhdys and Karat received some airtime in West Germany, but due to the tightly controlled East German musical production, they largely remained celebrated exceptions.) Other successful German music of the time included Udo Lindenberg, BAP and the *KRAUTROCK* phenomenon with bands such as the Scorpions, whose lyrics were in English, though. Another hugely influential band were Einstürzende Neubauten, whose industrial music shaped the taste of a whole generation and who have found valiant successors in bands such as And One. In the 1980s and 1990s, foreign influences were taken up and reshaped into German language music; punk music was also very successful, with bands such as Slime and the early Toten Hosen having much success. More recently, Techno music has exerted a very strong influence in Germany. DJs such as Sven Väth have received international attention. The most visible manifestation of this style is the Love Parade, held annually in Berlin, and with up to 1.5 million participants Europe's largest. Partly due to unification, a new phenomenon could be observed in the 1990s, namely that of right-wing music. A typical example was the band Böhse Onkelz, whose early music was prohibited as it was deemed to contain neo-Nazi propaganda. In the meantime, their political outlook has changed somewhat and they have been allowed to publish their music once again. Also due to unification, the focus of at least some *U-Musik* shifted east, with songs such as Stefan Raab's *Maschendrahtzaun*, Ö La Palöma Boys' *Ö La Palöma Blanca*, and Niemann's *Im Osten* highlighting eastern experiences. In the 1990s, German Hip Hop bands began to repopularize German language lyrics, with bands such as Die Fantastischen Vier, Fischmob and Fettes Brot picking up on critical lyrics once again, albeit in a more POSTMODERN stance than their songwriter predecessors in the 1960s and 1970s. (**Holger Briel**)

Further reading

Gilliam (1994). Dahlhaus and Eggebrecht (1995). Authoritative guide to German music. Hansen (1999); Krekow *et al.* (1999); Niketta and Volke (1993).

Musil, Robert   1880 Klagenfurt–1942 Geneva. Author. After attending a military academy, Musil received a diploma in engineering and later on studied psychology and philosophy. Before the outbreak of the First World War he was an editor at the *Neue Rundschau* in Berlin. In the First World War, Musil served as a soldier on the southern front. After the war, he initially worked as a civil servant and in 1922 became a freelance writer living in Vienna and in Berlin. In 1938 he emigrated to Switzerland. His main text is the unfinished novel *Der Mann ohne Eigenschaften* (*The Man without Qualities*) which depicts the collapse of the Hapsburg Empire, symbolizing the dissolution of the world order. In *Die Verwirrungen des Zöglings Törless* (*The Confusions of Young Törless*), Musil deals with the abuse of power, sexuality and bullying among pupils at a military academy. Robert Musil has been described as an Austrian Joyce or Proust. (**Barbara Rassi**)

Further reading

Musil (2001).

National Socialism   Political party formed in the confusion of 1919 by A. Drexler as the *Deutsche Arbeiterpartei*, soon changed to *Nationalsozialistische Deutsche Arbeiterpartei* (NSDAP; National Socialist German Workers' Party). The common abbreviation *Nazi* arises from analogies with *Sozi* (socialist) and *Bazi* (ruffian). Its policies were formulated in 1920 by Drexler and A. HITLER, who became chairman in 1921. Part of a Europe-wide nationalist trend, the party aimed to reconcile social differences without recourse to dogmatic socialism, but in the process adopted a divisive ideology of racism derived from vulgar Social Darwinist theories. Consequently it lacked a democratic commitment. Opposing the Versailles Treaty and needing an explanation for defeat, the NSDAP – like other groups – fixed on Jews as the scapegoat, adopting a friend-and-foe pattern of historical interpretation. Apart from appealing to lower middle-class resentments, the NSDAP early on developed a camaraderie of *Parteigenossen* (Pg.; party members), which included disillusioned soldiers who could not adapt to civilian life after 1918. It found support in Bavarian beerhalls thanks to the oratory of Hitler, who attempted a putsch in Munich in 1923 to remove the WEIMAR REPUBLIC. He was sentenced to five years' imprisonment when it failed and used the time (much reduced for good behaviour) to write the party's effective manifesto, *Mein Kampf* (*My Struggle*). He affirms his role as steersman; political aims are thoroughly personalized. Other ideological input came from writers such as A. Rosenberg, but their role remained subordinate.

Hitler's underlying belief was in the manipulability of people; he used emotional appeals to liberate their will-power and energy. Actual policies were opportunistic and flexible. Revolutionary and anti-democratic rhetoric put at the service of rabid ANTI-SEMITISM and expansive nationalism – the demand for *Lebensraum* (living space) in the east – concealed generally conservative attitudes.

The party organization was built up, including two groups of young men: the frightening paramilitary *Sturmabteilung* (SA) of E. Röhm which specialized in beating up political opponents and intimidating voters, and the impressive elite *Schutzstaffel* (SS) under H. Himmler, originally meant as Hitler's bodyguard. Financial support came from industrial and commercial backers, notably in the Düsseldorf *Herrenklub* of Ruhr coal and steel magnates. As long as Germany was relatively prosperous, this produced little success, but the beginnings of the Depression from 1928 favoured the party which offered opportunities of identification and release of aggression to various groups: a socialist party to the workers and unemployed; a nationalist party to those who hankered after the old larger Reich or the incorporation of Austria; a party of strong and stable government to the industrialists; a friendly support to the artisanate, the lower middle class fearing proletarization and the rural population. However, the socialist wing of the party led by O. Strasser seceded in 1930.

No area of possible recruitment and influence was overlooked. Seats were won in *Land* and Reich assemblies, eventually bringing the Nazis to power in the monster *Land* of Prussia and allowing the key post controlling the Prussian police to be occupied by H. Göring, while in the Reichstag GOEBBELS set the tone with ranting speeches. More established right-wing parties regarded the NSDAP with distaste for its populist approach and rough tactics, but could not disregard its popular appeal. When Reichspräsident Hindenburg was persuaded that the party could be tamed by allowing it to participate in national government, Hitler held out until political circumstances allowed him to demand the Chancellorship for himself, though the party's electoral support was already waning. Helped by the REICHSTAG fire of February 1933, and massive SA intimidation, Hitler and Göring were able to pass draconic laws and to gain a popular mandate in the elections of 1933, after which it was clear that the NSDAP was not going to relinquish power (see THIRD REICH).

The civil service and those who wanted something from the government rushed to join the party in large numbers (*Märzgefallene* – March victims). Any remaining political opponents and dubious INTELLECTUALS were brutalized in local party premises or the newly-founded concentration camps. The party was developed as an alternative government, with its *Gauleiters* all over the country and eventually in occupied areas, effective control of the secret police (*Gestapo*), and the heads of its divisions telling ministers in Berlin what to do. The fusion of party and government was completed when Hindenburg died and Hitler succeeded him, while the last internal challenge to Hitler was removed with the murder of Röhm. All organizations of public life were subordinated to the party (*Gleichschaltung*: parallelization) as affiliated bodies or branches: employers and trade unions yoked together in the *Arbeitsfront*, farmers in W. Darré's *Bauernschaft*, youth under the unlikely leadership of B. von Schirach enrolled in the *Hitlerjugend* and *Bund deutscher Mädel* (girls), women in the *NS-Frauenschaft*, students, doctors, lawyers, civil servants and so forth each in their own body. Party congresses became masterpieces of organization to demonstrate mass support for Hitler. The divisive party ideology showed itself in the systematic use of sanctions against identifiable real or potential opponents: Jews, the churches, communists and so forth. Indeed, continual campaigns against these groups covered the lack of positive policies, while the chance of personal preferment through the party gave an impression of classlessness and modernity.

During the Second World War, when the strategy adumbrated in *Mein Kampf* became bloody reality with the mass murder of Jews and others and the occupation of most of Europe, some parts of the party were diluted or confused with state organs, for instance by recruitment of non-Germans into the SS, but most organizations survived into 1945, when they suddenly disappeared.

Under the Allied Occupation, party membership became a rough-and-ready test of whether individuals were suspect (denazification), though many had joined only opportunistically, while some serious criminals were not party members. The party was outlawed and constitutional measures taken to prevent its return in another guise, though extreme right-wing parties loosely known as neo-Nazis have enjoyed some support in the Federal Republic. (**Alfred D. White**)

Further reading

Bracher (1970). Classical overview, comprehensive and still useful as a general introduction. Broszat (1981). Balanced and sophisticated analysis of the domestic structure of the Third Reich. Crew (1994). Specialist papers. Geary (2000). Small book by big expert. Survey aimed at A-level students, with further bibliography. Gregor (2000). This reader presents many useful articles by leading experts on a variety of subjects, including women, the Holocaust and Nazism's legacy. Kershaw (2000b). Important overview of controversies and interpretations of Nazism and the Third Reich. *Meyers Grosses Universal-Lexikon* (1981–86). Article 'Nationalsozialismus'. Full encyclopedia entry with history, analysis, and chart of party organization.

NATO   (See also *BUNDESWEHR*.) The North Atlantic Treaty Organization is an alliance developed to implement the North Atlantic Treaty, signed in April 1949, to establish a military counterweight to the Soviet military presence in Eastern Europe. The United States, Canada, and most European states were original signatories. Greece and Turkey joined in February 1952, West Germany in May 1955, and Spain in May 1982. France withdrew from the military command in 1966 but remained a member of the organization as such. West Germany's participation in the alliance, a key element of Chancellor Konrad ADENAUER's concept of full political, economic and military integration of West Germany in the West, provoked widespread unease in Germany herself and abroad. The prospect of a rearmed Germany just ten years after the end of the Second World War led to intense debates in the West German political public. However, West German economic strength had already been recognized by the other NATO-members as an important part of the response to the Soviet military threat, especially during the Korean War. The Paris Agreements of October 1954, which led to West Germany's accession to NATO in 1955, not only included provisions for the limitation of Germany's armaments, but also ended the military occupation of West Germany by the Allies. Adenauer's concept – West German sovereignty and military integration in the West – was successful. However, this policy directly led to the Soviet Union's formation of the Warsaw Pact in 1955, a military counter-alliance of Eastern European countries. The modernization and stationing of nuclear weapons in the 1980s (Pershing missiles) led to intense political conflicts in West Germany and contributed to the formation of a new peace movement. A fundamental part of the process of German unification in 1990 was the fact that the unified country would adhere to NATO. Full international responsibility of Germany within NATO has recently caused new domestic controversies, as the German military engagement in the Kosovo War demonstrated. (**Jörn Leonhard**)

Further reading

Kirchner and Sperling (1992). Useful overview of Germany's NATO-membership. Reed (1987). Concise analysis of the complex relationship between Germany and NATO.

Neue Deutsche Welle (NDW)   A term originally coined by the Hamburg music journalist and entrepreneur Alfred Hilsberg to denote the German variant of the 'New Wave' of rock music which emerged in the late 1970s. Hilsberg first used the NDW tag in October 1979 as the title of a series of articles in the German rock periodical *Sounds*. Hilsberg also founded his own record label ('Zick Zack') and shop ('Rip Off'). The first NDW records to appear were by the Düsseldorf bands Male and Mittagspause, and by the end of 1979 nearly 30 new German groups had committed their music to vinyl. The number of releases accelerated sharply in 1980 – supported by a burgeoning network of independent record labels and sales outlets – and show-cased a wide range of contemporary musical styles. The common denominator was the use of the German language for both lyrics and band names. Previously, German had been considered ill-suited to rock rhythms, but NDW bands like Geisterfahrer, Abwärts, Deutsch-Amerikanische-Freundschaft and Der Plan made an inventive and often ironic use of their native tongue.

   Language barriers notwithstanding, the NDW quickly gained an international audience through the BBC's John Peel and US college radio. Critical acclaim was showered on bands such as Einstürzende Neubauten, X-Mal Deutschland and Die Krupps by the influential British music weekly *New Musical Express*, which made no fewer than three German records 'Single of the Week' in the course of 1980. By the end of 1982 the NDW meant big business, and many bands were signed by major record labels. The new-look NDW took the European sales charts by storm, giving a host of minor talents a brief taste of stardom: Trio, Peter Schilling, Markus, Hubert Kah, and Nena ('99 Luftballons') among them. By the mid-1980s, however, the movement had lost most of its original vitality, and the NDW tag was henceforth only used pejoratively. (**Matthew Jefferies**)

Neue Innerlichkeit   After the events of around 1968 and the considerable pressure to abandon literature as we know it in favour of committed and operative texts, the reaction came in the form of *Neue Innerlichkeit*, a label for the more personal writing engaged in by HANDKE and others, particularly well epitomized in FRISCH's *Montauk*, a text on the boundary of autobiography and novel which self-referentially revisits parts of his life and tells the reader where he adapted them for previous novels. Paradoxically, renewed interest in the individual, meaning also in the family, was then to lead back to political commitment by way of meditations on the misdeeds of the fathers' generation. (**Alfred D. White**)

Schlösser (1992). Tangential to our approach, but with valuable analyses. Kämper-Van den Boogaart (1992). Specialized treatment.

Neuss, Wolfgang 1923 Breslau, now Wroctaw, Poland–1989 Berlin. Cabaret artist, playwright and actor. Important texts: *Das jüngste Gerücht, Neuss Testament, Asyl im Domizil.* Wolfgang Neuss was sent to the Eastern Front in 1941. After having been wounded several times he shot off his left index finger to be sent back to hospital, where he acted in sketches for his fellow patients. After the war he toured the country and became famous as a member of the *Bonbonniere Company* in Berlin. During the 1960s, he was renowned as West Germany's leading political satirical cabaret artist. He appeared on stage, in films and in print. When Neuss protested against West Berlin newspapers' fundraising for the Vietnam War, a press campaign against Neuss ensued, ending in his exclusion from the SPD. In the 1970s his fame decreased, but in the 1980s he had a comeback with weekly columns, written in his inimitable style, for *Stern* magazine. He was awarded the *Deutscher Kleinkunstpreis* in 1983. (**Corinna J. Heipcke**)

Nitsch, Hermann Born 1938 Vienna. Austrian painter and *Aktionskünstler* (actionist artist); one of the most prominent representatives of the *Wiener Aktionismus* (Viennese Actionism), the Austrian form of the 1960s' happening and fluxus movement. Since the late 1950s, Nitsch has been developing the idea of the *Orgien-Mysterien-Theater* (orgy mystery theatre), a six-day festival comprising music, dance and ritual killing of animals whose blood he uses for his monumental *Schüttbilder*, to paint on canvas, garments, robes. These, together with 'documentations' of the orgies are shown in his exhibitions. Nitsch intends to revive and re-interpret ancient and Christian rites, transcending the secondary nature of the fine arts and to release the repressed natural human instincts. This provocative form of art led to accusations of blasphemy, cruelty and pornography (trials and prison sentences) particularly in the conservative atmosphere of the 1960s. In 1995 he devised a stage set for the Vienna State Opera, and in 2001 for Philip Glass's opera *Satyagraha*, thereby demonstrating his acceptance by and his 'arrival' on the established art scene. (**Stefan Hauser**)

Nolde, Emil 1867 Nolde–1956 Seebüll. Painter and printmaker. Born Emil Hansen. A German Expressionist painter celebrated for his vibrant colour and energetic brushwork. Associated with the *Brücke* circle, he became fascinated by 'primitive' art following a trip to Russia, China and Polynesia in 1913–14 and is best known for dramatically distorted studies of figures in ecstatic movement and luminous flower and landscapes paintings. An early member of the Nazi Party, he was nevertheless branded degenerate by the Nazis and retreated to Seebüll, where he spent the war years painting a striking series of miniature 'unpainted pictures'. (**Martin Brady**)

PDS (Party of Democratic Socialism)   The PDS is a German left-wing, socialist party which is only of political significance in eastern Germany. It was founded on the former GDR governing party, the SED, during the course of the peaceful revolution in the GDR and German unification.

In autumn 1989, thousands of people demonstrated against the policies of the SED, which had governed the GDR for 40 years. Erich Honecker, Party Chairman since 1971 had to resign on 18 October 1989. Egon Krenz was the new Chairman for a short period. At a party conference held in December 1989, a lawyer from Berlin, Gregor Gysi, was elected new Chairman. The party immediately changed its name to 'SED-PDS' and as of January 1999 was known simply as the PDS. The former SED functionaries were stripped of their offices and were expelled from the PDS. Huge numbers of people left the party (more than 1 million resignations were received by February 1990). At the first PDS party conference (24–5 February 1990), the PDS voted in favour of gradual reunification. During the first all-German ELECTIONS in December 1990, the PDS gained 2.4 per cent of the total number of votes and entered the Bundestag (the lower house of German parliament) with 17 seats. In 1994, the party obtained 4.4 per cent (30 seats) and in 1998, 5.1 per cent (37 seats). In 1998, the party managed to enter the European Parliament (5.8 per cent, 6 seats). Gregor Gysi was replaced as Party Chairman in 1993 by Lothar Bisky who held this position for seven years. Gabi Zimmer was made PDS Chairman in October 2000. Although the PDS has had federal associations in western Germany since March 1990, many people tend to view the party as the successor to the SED and therefore reject it. It does not really enjoy any political significance. For example, in the 2000 elections to the *Landtag* (the state parliament) in Schleswig-Holstein, the party only obtained 1.4 per cent. In the East, the PDS has been able to win back a great amount of sympathy because it concentrates on East German issues. In the 1998–99 elections to the state parliaments in the East German states, it gained around 20 per cent. There has been a SPD/PDS coalition government in Mecklenburg-Vorpommern since 1998. The PDS's present party manifesto was adopted in January 1993 and characterizes the party as a left-wing socialist initiative. In 1999, the PDS had 88 594 members (of which 3773 were in western Germany); in 1998 this figure was 94 627. (**Hendrik Berth**)

Further reading

Moreau (1998). Sturm (2000). These two books very critically discuss the political aims of the PDS as successor of the SED.
www.sozialisten.de
www.pds-online.de (official website of the PDS, in German only, with information about the history of the party, election results and current political aims and activities.)

Piscator, Erwin   1893 Ulm–1966 Starnberg. Theatre director. Pioneer from the early 1920s of anti-illusionistic, multimedia proletarian theatre, often in the round and incorporating documentary techniques. (**Martin Brady**)

Plenzdorf, Ulrich   Born 1934 Berlin. Author. Plenzdorf, together with Wolf BIERMANN and Volker BRAUN, belongs to a group of GDR authors who in the 1970s began to challenge the system by airing the dissatisfaction and disillusionment of the young GDR generation. He shot to fame with the publication of *Die neuen Leiden des Jungen W.* (1973), in which he uses 'street language' to update Goethe's *Werther*, the story of a young man's unrequited love and its deadly effects. It had originally been a film script and was subsequently turned into a hugely successful play and finally also a film (1976). (**Holger Briel**)

Polke, Sigmar   Born 1941 Oels, Silesia. Painter, graphic artist and photographer. Early works, from the mid-1960s, belong to the so-called 'capitalist realism' movement (see Gerhard RICHTER) and show the influence of American Pop Art. Simultaneously comic and militant, they deconstruct and caricature consumer society and its off-spring the Art Market, often juxtaposing trite and hackneyed images (enlarged from newspapers for example) with icons of High Art (ancient and modern) to startling effect. A meticulous technician and fine colourist, Polke's deconstruction of the banal has been complemented since the 1980s by experiments with novel artistic materials, some of them unstable or toxic. (**Martin Brady**)

Postmodernism   A notoriously difficult term to pin down, referring to a range of philosophical and cultural phenomena, originating primarily in France, which have begun to appear since the late 1960s. A key aspect of postmodernism is a voracious eclecticism, manifesting itself in ARCHITECTURE, ART and literature constructed from a parodic collage of a range of traditions and styles. If MODERNISM saw itself as attempting to imbue the world with new meaning, the function of much postmodernist culture is to undermine all those meanings we have traditionally used in our quest to explain reality, what the postmodern theorist Jean-François Lyotard defines as society's *grand narratives* (e.g. Christianity, Marxism or the Enlightenment). Postmodernism entered the cultural vocabulary of Germany in 1968, heralded by Leslie Fiedler's lecture 'The case of post-modernism' to the University of Freiburg. Here Fiedler praised a new generation of writers who were rejecting the post-war consensus on the need for literature to be socially committed. However, what Fiedler read in the late 1960s as the radical liberation of the individual from the need for political responsibility was seen by many leading German INTELLECTUALS in the 1980s, particularly Jürgen Habermas, as the death of the Enlightenment and a resurgence of the political Right within German culture. Such critics argue that since the aim of much postmodern thought is simply to destroy all preconceived notions of 'truth', it appears to be reconnecting with the irrationalist, anti-Enlightenment philosophical tradition of the 1920s and 1930s, from which Germany had been purged – one hoped – after the demise of the THIRD REICH. (**Paul Cooke**)

Further reading

Wittstock (1994). A good survey, tracing the development of postmodernism within German literature. Jencks (1992). Especially Chapter 2, which contains key essays by Lyotard and Habermas. Briel (1991). An assessment of the differences between modernism and postmodernism.

Post-unification   In 2000, ten years of German unity was celebrated. Since the beginning of October 1990 the Federal Republic of Germany and the German Democratic Republic have been united in one state after having been separated for 40 years. In 1990 the central government developed a 'Recovery East' programme which is aimed at diminishing the differences in the standard of living between East and West Germany. This was necessary as the infrastructure and the GDR economy were only developed at a low level in comparison to the market economy of West Germany. So far billions of DM have been spent on the following areas:

- *Education*: The entire education system has been overhauled, in order to remove the communist content in the curricula. (See SCHOOLS AND EDUCATION.)

- *Housing*: By 2000, 50 per cent of the housing stock of 1990 was modernized and new houses built.

- *Transport*: 11 700 km of roads and 5400 of railroad lines were upgraded or newly built. (See TRANSPORT.)

- *Economy/Social welfare*: Over 500 000 companies were founded with more than 3.2 million employees. The UNEMPLOYMENT rate is still much higher in the Eastern federal states.

- *Communication*: About 5.7 million new telephones were newly installed by 2000.

In 1995 the federal government introduced the 'solidarity surcharge' in order to fund the investments in East Germany. In 2001, 5.5 per cent is deducted from each taxpayer's gross income and used to finance the 'Recovery East' programme.

Internal unity has not been fully accomplished so far. Germans in the Eastern and Western federal states still have problems in understanding each other as they have lived in different political states for 40 years. With the recent SED (former communist party of the GDR) Crime Adjustment Act, a political step has been made to assist the mental process of unification which improves the compensation and rehabilitation of victims of SED crimes. (**Inge Strüder**)

Further reading

Berdahl (1999); Müller (2000).

Post-unification literature   The agenda for POST-UNIFICATION literature was, in part at least, set by events in the immediate aftermath of the fall of the Berlin Wall, and in particular the infamous *Literaturstreit* (Literature Debate) sparked by the publication of the GDR writer Christa WOLF's *Was Bleibt* (*What Remains,* 1990). This story, which describes the experience of being put under surveillance by the *Stasi*, caused an uproar among critics in the West, who saw it as an attempt by a GDR state-endorsed writer to redefine herself as a dissident. The debate then snowballed into a general attack on the artistic merit of all East German literature (an attack which was subsequently fuelled by revelations about the connection of many GDR writers with the *Stasi*). Finally, it developed into an assault on politically and socially committed literature in general, a mode of writing which had been dominant not only in the GDR but also in the FRG since the state's founding.

The *Literaturstreit* can be seen as symptomatic of a number of important trends in post-unification literature. First, the dismissal of East German writing is read by many easterners as part of the West's dismissal of the whole of their pre-*Wende* experience. This has produced a backlash among some East German writers who have attempted to provocatively re-appropriate the East German past in their work. Second, it can be seen as heralding in a new generation of writers dedicated to a *neue Lesbarkeit* (new readability). These writers are ostensibly more preoccupied with telling 'good stories' rather than making political points. This move away from politics in literature has been seen by some commentators as a resurgence of a conservative tradition within German culture, a resurgence which has unfortunately coincided with a rise in right-wing extremism and racial violence in the 1990s. However, this would not seem to be able to undermine the increasing self-assuredness of Germany's more established ethnic MINORITIES, and the growing number of books written by, for example Turkish-German writers, a fact which has brought a strong MULTICULTURAL dimension to German literature. (**Paul Cooke**)

Further reading

Brockmann (1999). The best survey available of 1990s' German literature.

Poverty   In the early years of the Federal Republic inequality was not a major issue. The currency reform of June 1948, which gave everyone DM40 in cash, created an impression that all had begun from the same point so that the advantages of those who held capital in forms other than money were often overlooked. At the same time, the first Economics Minister Ludwig Erhard promised 'prosperity for all'. Indeed, with the rapid economic growth of the 1950s, the expansion of the welfare state and the achievement of almost full employment it did seem that everyone was enjoying the fruits of the *Wirtschaftswunder* (economic miracle). In reality there were always major differences in income and wealth with the self-employed and public servants (*Beamte*) over-represented among high earners.

In recent years more attention has been paid to the problem of poverty. Most figures identify households earning only up to 40 per cent of the average income as living in severe poverty and those earning only up to 50 per cent as living in poverty. In the pre-1990 Federal Republic, these were in 1997 3.7 and 9.1 per cent respectively of households in these categories. Lower average incomes in the East mean that the figures were lower if seen in a purely eastern context (2.0 and 6.2 per cent, respectively). Equally relevant are the kinds of people likely to be affected by poverty. In 2001 the Federal government published its first report on wealth and poverty. Whereas, according to the figures, there were 1.5 million millionaires, twice as many people lived on the basic form of SOCIAL SECURITY (*Sozialhilfe*). UNEMPLOYMENT and poor education were identified as major factors leading to poverty, while the most affected group was single mothers. (**Stuart Parkes**)

Further reading

Böhnke (1999); Bundesministerium für Arbeit und Sozialordnung (n.d.); Hanesch (2000).

Privatization   Privatization is primarily a phenomenon of the 1990s in Germany, both in the west and the east, since earlier in the old *Länder* it was taken forward only on a modest, hesitant scale. In the post-war period, there were no nationalizations in the FRG although, clearly, inherited public holdings were very considerable in TRANSPORT and the utilities, the savings banks and *Landesbanken* at *Land* and local levels. The Bundesbank (see BANKING AND THE DEUTSCHE BUNDESBANK) in 1988 valued all enterprises belonging to public authorities at DM370 bn. In the tradeable, competitive sector itself, the scale of public enterprise is relatively modest. In 1978, major public sector enterprises accounted for a total of only 14 per cent of the turnover of the 270 largest companies in the country and also their share of tradeables' turnover amounted only to 4 per cent. The limited privatization occurring in the period 1957–65 was pursued to generate people's shares (*Volksaktien*), sold at reduced prices to low income groups and employees. In the early 1980s, partly for ideological reasons, the incoming KOHL government sought a reduction in state holdings but the initial list of 100 companies with 900 subsidiaries was reduced to only 12 candidates, including VEBA, VIAG, Salzgitter steel and VW AG. In the early 1990s, under the influence of EU Single Market directives, network utilities were opened and the Lufthansa, Deutsche Telekom and the Deutsche Post were sold in stages. Public debt was thereby reduced. In the east, the *Treuhandanstalt*, responsible for privatizing the East German state assets, quickly got the blame for the collapse of eastern industry and its first President, Detlev Rohwedder, was assassinated at Easter 1991 by the Rote Armee Fraktion. It broke up the giant socialist combines into 12 000 enterprises and these, together with 26 000 small businesses, were sold by tender, auction or buy-out. Its assets, valued in late 1990 at DM600 bn, melted away to a cumulated debt of DM250 bn in late 1994. (**Chris Flockton**)

Further reading

Flug (1992); Wright (1994).

Protestantism   There are around 27.6 million Protestants in Germany since reunification in 1990, i.e. formal members of the *Evangelische Kirche Deutschlands* (EKD, Protestant Church of Germany). In addition, there exist a much smaller number of free and independent Christian churches (*ca.* 328 000 members) that do not belong to the EKD although some may join with the EDK and the Catholic Church within ecumenical organizations and worship services.

Despite its title, the EKD is more akin to a federation of independent churches of the reformed Lutheran, United Reformed or Calvinistic persuasion based on a *Landeskirche-Principle* which, however, is not so much based on the current *Länder* boundaries but on those of the Reich of 1871. The EKD represents its members *vis-à-vis* the state authorities but can exercise no doctrinal control over individual churches or pastors. Currently it is characterized by involvement in many national, international and ecumenical organizations and programmes, by a strong element of female involvement (women ordained to pastorates and bishoprics) and a broadly liberal theology. Outside the strictly religious domain, the EKD is highly influential in social, political and educational fields. Through its social policy organs and its role in education, the EKD has considerable influence on political party programmes and government policy making, where it has a constitutional right to be heard. Its traditional links with the SPD and the trade union movement make it an influential voice in the area of interest articulation and broader social consciousness-raising. Examples are the EKD's 1965 *Ostdenkschrift* (Memorandum on the East) that influenced public opinion in West Germany ahead of the *Ostpolitik* of chancellor Willy Brandt and its involvement with the peace movements in the old FGR and Europe in the 1970s and 1980s. Most Protestants live in northern and west/south western Germany although they are present in reasonable numbers in every *Land* (state) in Germany. (**John Taylor**)

Publishing industry   Beginning with the 1920s and the media empire built by Alfred Hugenberg, Germany has enjoyed an ever-increasing number of publications. Although the freedom of the press has been anchored legally since the late nineteenth century, during the Third Reich this freedom was rescinded. All publications had to go through the censorship of Goebbels' *Propagandaministerium*, and furthermore, in order to publish, one had to be a member of the *Reichsschrifttumskammer* (Reich Chamber of Written Texts). After the Second World War, at first it was the Allies who decided what publications were allowed, with some writers such as Ernst Jünger and Gottfried Benn, and the philosopher Martin Heidegger, whose political allegiance was considered somewhat questionable, prohibited from publishing. This changed rather quickly, and by 1949, the freedom of the press was once again legally guaranteed in West Germany by the GRUNDGESETZ. In the GDR, censorship continued, and continued mostly along ideological lines. Today, Germany has a large publishing sector, which in 2000 published about 400 daily newspapers, over 1700 magazines and journals, and more than 80 000 book titles (new and reprints) annually. The book trade is organized in the *Börsenverein des Deutschen Buchhandels* (Association of German Book Traders). The world's largest book fair is held annually in Frankfurt am Main. The most important publishing houses are Suhrkamp, Berliner Verlag, Rowohlt, Fischer, Luchterhand, Reclam, Insel, and Hanser. In regards to magazines, their numbers have skyrocketed during the 1980s and 1990s, with special interest publications leading the way. The German newspaper market is split into transregional and regional presses, with subscribers often subscribing to one of each. Large transregional daily German language newspapers are the *Süddeutsche Zeitung*, the FRANKFURTER ALLGEMEINE ZEITUNG, *Tageszeitung* (TAZ), *Bild*, *Die Welt* and the *Neue Zürcher Zeitung*, which although published in Zurich, does enjoy a considerable following in Germany as well. Other German-language Swiss newspapers include the *Tagesanzeiger* and *Blick*; large Austrian newspapers are the *Neue Kronen Zeitung* and *Der Standard*. Weekly newspapers in Germany include *Die ZEIT*. In Germany, the Sunday newspaper market is by far not as important as it is in the English-speaking world. The downmarket *Bild am Sonntag* has a virtual monopoly in this market segment. Only in 2001 did the *Frankfurter Allgemeine Zeitung* launch its own Sunday paper. Large German publishing houses for magazines and newspapers are Bertelsmann, Gruner und Jahr, Axel Springer and the Westdeutsche Verlagsgruppe. (**Holger Briel**)

Further reading

Briel (1998). Faulstich (1999). The standard text on media in Germany. Humphreys (1994). Still the standard text on German media in English. Wittmann (1991).

Qualtinger, Helmut 1928–86 Austrian political satirist, writer and actor. Most prominent representative of the post-war Viennese *Kabarett*. Shortly after the Second World War Qualtinger, then an actor, film critic and playwright, e.g. 'Reigen '51', a parody on A. Schnitzler's 'Reigen', together with G. Bronner, G. Kreisler and C. Merz, founded a satirical and political revue group which was highly successful especially in the 1950s. The cabaret songs (*Couplets*) and characters, e.g. Travnicek, are in the tradition of the *Wiener Volksstück* (Viennese folk drama/popular theatre) as defined by J. Nestroy and Ö. v. Horváth, with its ironic style and the imitation of spoken language. This is especially true for one of the most important and controversial texts of Austrian post-war literature, *Der Herr Karl* (Qualtinger and C. Merz, 1961), which started the public debate on contemporary Austrian history (the First Republic, Austrofascism, the repercussions of the Nazi period, etc.). In this satirical monologue the petty bourgeois Herr Karl tells the story of his life from the 1920s to the present showing the callousness and opportunism with which he survived and gained advantage throughout all of the political changes. Qualtinger went on tour with this portrayal of the Austrian 'type' of a suburban, opportunist fellow traveller who does not accept responsibility beyond his own petty interests, thereby also making HITLER possible. In the 1970s and 1980s, Qualtinger continued to act and write and also recorded famous readings of K. KRAUS's *Die letzten Tage der Menschheit*, and A. Hitler's *Mein Kampf*. His last role was that of a monk, Pater Remigius, in the 1986 film *The Name of the Rose* (loosely based on U. Eco's novel *Il nome della rosa*). (**Stefan Hauser**)

R

Radio   The 1920s marked the beginning of civic broadcasting in Germany, Switzerland and Austria. However, in the First World War information technology had already played a very important part and hence boosted the use of radio technology. These first years of broadcasting history in Germany are predominantly associated with one man, Hans Bredow. His activities ranged from experimenting with the medium radio, broadcasting radio programmes to becoming Broadcasting Commissioner in Weimar Germany. The seizure of power by the National Socialists tightened the already quite strict state control over radio broadcasting. Radio became a tool of National Socialist propaganda. In order to enable everyone to listen to it, cheap radio sets, *Volksempfänger* ('people's wireless'), were produced.

After the Second World War, the Allied forces played a crucial role in shaping the radioscape of Germany as well as Austria. As occupying forces, they issued radio licences, set up their own radio stations and regarded broadcasting as one means of building a democratic and/or antifascist German society. The Western powers created broadcasting organizations that reflected their own national broadcasting systems (e.g. the British had established a broadcasting corporation in Hamburg following the BBC model). Their common goal was to hand back to Germans broadcasting organizations that were 'public service bodies'. These *Anstalten des öffentlichen Rechts* ('corporations under public law') should be neither state nor privately owned, with listeners' fees as their prime source of income. In East Germany, the Soviet forces helped the SED to set up a centralized broadcasting system. This organization was eventually terminated after East Germany had been united with West Germany (1990). In the mid-1980s, broadcasting laws were deregulated in West Germany. These reforms enabled broadcasting by local and regional private radio stations. In Austria, this development came later and it was not before the mid-1990s that radio licences were granted to selected private radio stations. As well as the public broadcasting sector and commercial private radio stations, Germany, Austria and Switzerland also offer many independent local radio stations. These non-commercial stations want to guarantee open access to broadcasting. Examples: *Radio Dreyeckland* (based in Freiburg, Germany) or *orange 94.0* (Vienna, Austria). (**Barbara Rassi**)

Further reading

Briel (1998). A concise overview of the history and development of mass media in (West) Germany. Humphreys (1994). Very detailed and comprehensive description and analysis of the German media system.

Railways   The first railway in Germany opened in 1835 between Nuremberg and Fürth. Thereafter expansion was rapid, as industrialization advanced, particularly following unity in 1871. A feature of this early development was the part played by the state, with some lines built more for strategic than economic reasons. Full nationalization took place after the First World War when the Deutsche Reichsbahn was created. The Second World War not only led to much destruction, but also, when Germany was divided in the post-war period, to the creation of separate companies. Whereas in the East, the old name survived, the Deutsche Bundesbahn (Germany Federal Railways) was created in West Germany. Division also meant the loss of several lines that had crossed the new frontier, as links between the two Germanies were reduced.

While railways retained a key role in the East, the Bundesbahn had to compete increasingly with other means of TRANSPORT and began to incur substantial losses. However, unification in 1990 provided a boost with several cross-border lines reopening and fast connections to Berlin being added to the new western high-speed lines. It also provided the opportunity for restructuring the network. In 1994 Deutsche Bahn (German Rail) came into existence as a private company, but with the Federal government owning all the shares. Separate divisions e.g. for freight were also created, while *Land* (state) governments took over responsibility for financing loss-making regional services. While this semi-PRIVATIZATION initially led to a working profit, it has not been a panacea. Current debates centre around how far private companies should be allowed to use the network and whether a separate infrastructure company is required. The government target of rail traffic taking an increasing share of the market, not least in freight, seems remote, as mounting losses lead to line closures and a reduction in services. (**Stuart Parkes**)

Further reading

Gall and Pohl (1999).

Reichstagsbrand   The Reichstag had been home to the German parliament since 1894. On the night of 27 February 1933 it was set alight and was damaged considerably. The Nazis used the burning of the Reichstag to pursue brutal persecution of political opponents and to pass anti-democratic laws. This 'emergency decree' denotes one of the decisive steps on their way to establishing a total dictatorship in Germany.

Half an hour after the fire was detected, the Dutch anarchist Marinus van der Lubbe was arrested as the main suspect for the arson. The Nazis immediately claimed that Lubbe had acted on behalf of the Communist Party whom they accused of planning a *coup d'état*. They used this claim as a pretext to start a wave of arrests, which started the same night. Some 4000 communist functionaries were arrested, and communist and social democratic newspapers were forbidden with immediate effect. The following 'emergency decree' of 28 February 1933 practically annulled the basic political rights laid down in the Weimar Constitution. The government awarded itself far-reaching legal powers and extended the possibilities of imposing capital punishment. The result of the decree was a permanent state of emergency as the Weimar Constitution was never formally cancelled during the THIRD REICH. Thereby, the Nazis managed to lend a legal outlook to their open terror.

The burning of the Reichstag came at a most convenient time for the Nazis. Claims that they had set the fire themselves, therefore, started to being raised immediately, and the question is still not entirely settled. In any case, in September 1933 at Leipzig Marinus van der Lubbe was found guilty and was executed in January 1934. (**Anselm Heinrich**)

Further reading

Pritchard (1972); Raithel and Strenge (2000); Schmädecke and Bahar (1999).

Reitz, Edgar   Born 1932 Morbach. Film-maker, director, producer, author, lecturer, director of the Europäisches Filminstitut, Karlsruhe. Studied theatre, history, and art in Munich after graduating from Herzog-Johann-Gymnasium, Simmern (Hunsrück) in 1952; deeply involved with the 'Avangarde'; member of the *Oberhausener Gruppe* that declared during their short film festival 'Papas Kino' to be dead; consequently, cosigned the *Oberhausener Manifest* in 1962; co-founder (together with Alexander KLUGE) of the *Hochschule für Gestaltung* in Ulm; created his first experimental films, documentaries, short films, and commercial films in the mid-1950s; 1957–58: short film (together with Bernhard Dörries): *Schicksal einer Oper*; 1959–60: documentary *Baumwolle*; 1960: short film *Yucatan*; 1961: experimental film *Kommunikation – Technik der Verständigung*; 1962–63: experimental film *Geschwindigkeit. Kino Eins*; 1964–65: cinematic experiment *VariaVision*; 1966: short film: *Die Kinder*; 1965: cameraman in Kluge's *Abschied von gestern*; 1966: first feature film *Mahlzeiten*, the story of a tragic marriage; both films represent the beginning of the 'New German Cinema'; 1973: feature film: *Die Reise nach Wien*; 1974: feature film (together with Alexander Kluge) *In Gefahr und größter Not bringt der Mittelweg den Tod*; 1976: feature film *Stunde Null*; 1977–78: road film episode: 'Grenzstation' in *Deutschland im Herbst*; 1978: feature film: *Der Schneider von Ulm*; 1980–81 documentary: *Geschichten aus den Hunsrückdörfern*; 1981–84 film novel: *Heimat: Eine Chronik in elf Teilen*; 1985: four TV films (together with Alexander Kluge): *Die Stunde der Filmemacher*; 1985–92: film novel *Die Zweite Heimat: Chronik einer Jugend in 13 Filmen*; currently working on the continuation of *Die Zweite Heimat*; since 1971 owner of his own production company; for his cinematographic work on *Heimat*, Reitz was awarded the 'Fipresci Award' at the Venice Film Festival, the Berlin and London Film Critique Awards, the German Federal Film Award, the Golden Camera as well as the Adolf-Grimme Award in Gold; the British Film Academy voted *Heimat* best foreign film; for *Die Zweite Heimat*, Reitz received the Special Award of the Venice Biennale and the

Kulturellen Ehrenpreis by the City of Munich; his theoretical work is published in the volume *Liebe zum Kino* (1984); a series of interviews and essays with German directors and producers is published in *Bilder in Bewegung: Essays – Gespräche zum Kino (1995); Edgar Reitz im Verlag der Autoren: Drehort Heimat* (1993) is an account of the creation processes of *Heimat* and *Die Zweite Heimat* by Reitz himself. (**Claudia A. Becker**)

Further reading

Ardagh, J. (1991, pp. 331–54); Jacobsen *et al.* (1993); Radevagen (1993).

1918–19 Revolution (including *Räterepublik*)   At the end of the First World War, political unrest emerged in Germany, and in January 1918 many German cities saw demonstrations and strikes. In October sailors of the imperial navy started a mutiny, which spread quickly to other ports. Sailors', soldiers' and workers' soviets were formed, united and brought many coastal towns under their control. Soon the revolt also reached the inland. On 7 November the Bavarian Wittelsbach dynasty was overthrown and, on 9 November, Emperor Kaiser Wilhelm II was forced to abdicate. Chancellor Max von Baden handed the power over to Friedrich Ebert, the leader of the biggest parliamentary party, the social democrats (SPD), and the republic was proclaimed. A Council of Peoples' Representatives constituted the new government and found the support of the workers' and soldiers' soviets. The Council, however, became subject to an increasing influence of the imperial army who tried to work against any radical changes. Ebert and other moderate SPD leaders were willing to make concessions whereas the independent members of the Council aimed at profound socialist reforms. The resulting break-up of the Council in December 1918 led to a second revolutionary phase. The so-called January unrests were organized by a radical minority with the Spartakus group around Luxemburg and Liebknecht at its centre. Their aim lay beyond the establishment of a parliamentary democracy as they strove for a socialist state modelled on the Soviet Union. The governing social democrats called in volunteer corps, remnants of the imperial army with deep anti-socialist and anti-democratic sentiments, to fight the protesters and regain control. Apart from Berlin, the centres of the uprising lay in the Ruhr area, in Saxony and in Munich. There, the soviet republic was brutally dissolved by volunteer corps who marched into the city in May 1919. This event marked the end of the second revolutionary phase. A general election was held in January 1919, the national assembly constituted itself in February, and Germany became a parliamentary democracy. The WEIMAR REPUBLIC was born – although at a high price: the unsuccessful revolution had divided Germany's working class. (**Anselm Heinrich**)

Further reading

Bessel (1993). Haffner (1973). Despite its age this detailed study is still interesting and easy to read.

Richter, Gerhard Born 1932 Dresden. Painter and printmaker. Germany's pre-eminent painter since the death of Beuys. An eclectic artist renowned for abrupt shifts in style, he co-founded the 'capitalist realism' movement in 1963, and for a number of years painted pop-influenced photorealist canvases. A supreme technician, his output is cool and analytical, ranging from hyper-realism to luminous gestural abstraction on a grand scale. His subject matter has ranged from cityscapes, portraiture (*48 Portraits* of 1972 based on encyclopedia photographs), colour charts (from 1966) and grey monochromes to cloud and *memento mori* paintings and soft-focus landscapes based on his own photographs. (**Martin Brady**)

Riefenstahl, Leni Born 1902 Berlin. Film-maker and photographer. Documentary film-maker personally favoured by Hitler. Filmed the 1934 Nuremberg Party Convention (*Triumph des Willens, Triumph of the Will*) and 1936 Olympics. Went on to make critically acclaimed films on diving and Africa tribal cultures. (**Martin Brady**)

Röggla, Kathrin Born 1971 Salzburg. Author. Röggla first gained wider public attention with her collection of fiction *Niemand lacht rückwärts* (1995). Her first novel *Abrauschen* (1997) deals with the lives and frustrations of a young urban generation. Berlin, its periphery and the province are recurring themes in Röggla's work. In 2000 her collection of texts, *Irres Wetter*, was published. Kathrin Röggla has received various literary fellowships and prizes, such as the Alexander-Sacher-Masoch Prize or the Svevo-Literature Prize. (**Barbara Rassi**)

Rühmann, Heinz 1902 Essen–1994 Starnberg. Actor. Rühmann, son of an hotelier, was arguably the most famous German actor of the twentieth century. While his work did not transcend German language borders, nor perhaps moved to the very serious side of high culture, even today virtually any native German speaker is acquainted with his films. He was the incarnation of the 'little man' on the street, knocked about by life's vagrancies, but nevertheless refusing to give up his optimism and belief in the goodness of the world. Comedies such as *Die Drei von der Tankstelle* (1930) and his perhaps most famous role in *Die Feuerzangenbowle* (1944) assured his reach across generations. After the Second World War, it took him until the 1955 film *Charleys Tante* (*Charley's Aunt*) to regain his pre-war fame. In film after film, and also in the theatre, he continued to bring joy and self-recognition to his audiences. In later years, he would choose more sombre roles for himself, in plays such as Miller's *Death of a Salesman*, in Beckett's *Waiting for Godot* and many others. All of them, though, he would imbue with his very own notion of a human face. (**Holger Briel**)

Further reading

Sellin (2002).

LIVERPOOL JOHN MOORES UNIVERSITY
LEARNING & INFORMATION SERVICES

S

Sachs, Nelly   1891 Berlin–1970 Stockholm. Author. Sachs wrote poetry and drama and is regarded as one of the most important authors of HOLOCAUST literature. She grew up in a sheltered and wealthy household in Berlin, enjoying education at private schools and private tuition. She was very much interested in music and dance. Being Jewish, her life changed dramatically when Hitler seized power in 1933. Most of her relatives were murdered in concentration camps. With the help of the Swedish author Selma Lagerlöf, Nelly Sachs and her mother escaped to Sweden in 1940. Her writing, e.g *In den Wohnungen des Todes* (*In the Houses of Death*), was deeply affected by and dealt with the persecution of Jews and the Holocaust. In 1966 Nelly Sachs was awarded the Nobel Prize for Literature (together with Samuel Josef Agnon). (**Barbara Rassi**)

Schickedanz, Grete and Gustav   Grete 1911–1994, Gustav 1895–1977. Entrepreneurs. Grete Schickedanz was the second wife of the businessman Gustav Schickedanz, who in 1927 opened the mail order company Quelle in Fürth. By 1936, Quelle had one million customers. In the late 1950s, expanded into Austria. In competition with the Neckermann mail order company, but growth continued throughout the 1960s and 1970s. After Gustav Schickedanz's death, his wife took over the business and became one of the most recognized business tycoons in German-speaking countries. The Quelle catalogue became an annual institution and one of the most important symbols of the West German post-war economy, by 1985 amounting to more than 2000 pages. (**Holger Briel**)

Schlöndorff, Volker   Born 1939 Wiesbaden. Film-maker and producer. Leading director of the New German Cinema whose aim over four decades as film-maker and producer has been to establish an artistically credible, commercially successful art-house cinema in Germany. Distrusting his own talent as an author, he has concentrated on literary adaptation and collaboration, winning an Oscar in 1979 for *The Tin Drum, Die Blechtrommel* based on the novel by Günter GRASS. Subsequently turned increasingly to international co-production, adapting the works of non-German authors including Marcel Proust, Arthur Miller and Margaret Atwood. Managed the legendary Babelsberg film studios in Potsdam from 1992. (**Martin Brady**)

Schmidt, Arno   1914 Hamburg–1979 Celle. Author. Schmidt is widely viewed as one of the most innovative and exciting authors of the twentieth century. He began writing in 1932, but his first profound prose texts were not written until the beginning of the 1940s. From 1940 to 1945, Schmidt served as a soldier in the Second World War and was an English POW until the end of 1945. After the war he worked as a translator. In 1947, Schmidt decided to become a full-time writer. In 1949, *Leviathan* was published, but not to much acclaim. He kept afloat by writing radio essays. In 1955, his *Seelandschaft mit Pocahontas* was accused of containing blasphemy and pornography; but the accusation was squashed in 1956. His reputation as writer was growing, albeit within a very small circle. *Das steinerne Herz* was published in 1956, this time to wide acclaim. In 1958 he moved to Bargfeld near Celle, where he would remain for the rest of his life, far away from the hubs of German literary life. In 1964, he received the Fontane Prize; he began his translation of texts by Poe into German, and also started work on *Zettel's Traum,* his magnum opus, which was published in 1969. It consisted of 1334 A3 loose leaves, tightly written in his onomatopoeic German and interspersed with bricolage in various other languages. Critics have often compared him to James Joyce. In 1972 he published *Die Schule der Atheisten.* In 1973 he received the Goethe Prize. In 1975 his last complete text was published, *Abend mit Goldrand.* (**Holger Briel**)

Further reading

Krawehl (1982); Martynkewicz (1997).

Schmidt, Helmut Born 1918 Hamburg. Statesman. Entered the Bundestag for the SPD in 1953; *Innensenator* (interior minister) of Hamburg 1961–65. Chair of the SPD Bundestag fraction 1967; Minister of Defence 1969, economics and finance (later finance only) 1972; emerged as the safe option to succeed Willy BRANDT as *Bundeskanzler* 1974. Pursued a twin-track policy: military strength to discourage Soviet threats, and pronounced friendliness to East Germany. A pragmatic politician, known as the *Macher* (fixer), whose stance was generally well to the right of his party. Removed from office 1982 by withdrawal of FDP support and discontent on the left of the SPD, became publisher (since 1983), adviser and contributor on *Die ZEIT.* (**Alfred D. White**)

Further reading

Carr (1985). Best treatment of Schmidt's place in national life.

Schoenberg, Arnold 1874 Vienna–1951 Hollywood. Composer. One of the most influential classical composers of the twentieth century. Early works (including *Verklärte Nacht,* 1899) are late Romantic in style, with the *First String Quartet* (1904–5) marking a shift towards atonality, a revolutionary break with the harmonic rules of Western MUSIC. This culminated in the Expressionist songs of *Pierrot Lunaire* (1912). During the 1920s devised the serial (twelve-tone) method to reintroduce structure to longer compositions. Later works, combining rigorous construction and passionate emotion, include the *String Trio* and *A Survivor from Warsaw* (1946), a fierce lament for the victims of the HOLOCAUST. Championed by Theodor W. ADORNO, his music had a profound influence on post-war composers. (**Martin Brady**)

Scholl, Sophie 1921 Forchtenberg–1943 Munich. Together with her brother Hans and mutual friends, e.g. Christoph Probst and Alexander Schmorell, Scholl was a member of the students' resistance group *Weiße Rose* (*White Rose*). They produced leaflets appealing for people to resist National Socialism. In February 1943, Sophie Scholl and her brother were caught by the Gestapo when they were distributing leaflets at Munich University. Together with Christoph Probst they were put on trial and executed shortly afterwards. Further death sentences and prison sentences for other members of the resistance group followed. (**Barbara Rassi**)

Further reading

Leisner (2000). An interesting and informative insight into Sophie Scholl's life.

Schools and education In 1995 there were some 12.3 million pupils in 52 446 schools being taught by 777 600 trained teachers in the 16 states of the Federal Republic of Germany. The *Grundgesetz* (Basic Law) (Art. 7) has put the whole school system under the supervision of the state. However, because of the federal nature of Germany, the respective responsibilities for education are divided between the *Länder* and the federal authorities. Legislation regarding education and the administration of primary, secondary and tertiary education lies predominantly in the competence of the *Länder*.

This includes the spheres of further and adult education and its explanation can be found in the desire by the Western allies and statesmen in the new Germany, to remove education from the absolute control of the highest level of government and thus protect it against the kind of exploitation as a medium of indoctrination that was practised during the National Socialist dictatorship. Nonetheless, to ensure relative uniformity of standards and adequate provision for the relatively mobile population of Germany, the Permanent Conference of the Ministers of Education and Culture (PCMEC) of the states and the federation oversees the functioning and regulation of all aspects of the education system, in particular, mutual recognition of courses and qualifications given by schools, further and higher education institutions. In this way the co-operation between the states within the PCMEC has led to a wide-ranging uniformity and comparability in the education system.

At the age of 6 children in Germany enter the primary education system, graduating at the age of 10 to the next level which is intended to identify their suitability to pursue their education in one of several school types from the age of 12 on. These are: *Hauptschule*; *Realschule* (secondary modern); *Gymnasium* (grammar/sixth form/high school) and *Gesamtschule* (comprehensive). Pupils remain at these schools until age 16. Thereafter and until the age of 19 they progress to the second stage of secondary education. Depending on whether they are going down an academic or technical/commercial education route will determine which particular school type they will attend. Those at a *Gymnasium* (grades 5–12/13, depending on the individual state), will end their scholastic career with the Abitur which gives entry to higher education, while the other streams are divided into vocational school when their education is once again divided into school-based and work-place training or technical college and advanced technical college.

The higher and further education sector (tertiary sector) ranges all the way from university through teacher training, music academies and technological universities to institutions of higher education for administrative professions. Alongside these are what is known as the 'second-entry path' to higher education, i.e. colleges of technology and evening study courses leading to university entry qualifications.

In recent years, these have been increased by opportunities for retraining, 'topping-up' and so-called 'life-long learning' provisions for general and professional further and higher education in many and varied forms. (**John Taylor**)

Schröder, Gerhard   Born 1944 Mossenberg, near Detmold. Statesman. Active in SPD politics from 1969 in Lower Saxony, from 1978 nationally. After the SPD had exhausted itself in conflicts between centrists and purists, the stage was set for the emergence of the rather colourless Schröder, an expert on employment policy, administration, and policing, to become *Kanzlerkandidat* (candidate for Chancellorship) and lead the SPD to power as Federal Chancellor in 1998. A leading exponent of New Labour policies (*Der dritte Weg*, The Third Way) and of further European unification. (**Alfred D. White**)

Further reading

Hombach (2000). Insider's account of the German Third Way.
www.bundesregierung.de (website including a short personal and political biography, in German or English, and texts of his publications and interviews.)

Sebald, W.B.   1944 Wertach–2001 Norwich. Author. Although Sebald is best known as a writer of fiction, he was also a literary critic and poet, and held the post of Professor of Modern German Literature at the University of East Anglia. His death has led to the loss of a singular post-war literary talent. Sebald's writing explores the uncertain space between fiction and history with extreme delicacy. While his work was first written and published in German, it has achieved equal acclaim in translation. Perhaps his most successful contribution, *Die Ausgewanderten* (1993) (*The Emigrants*, 1996) tells the stories of four men whose lives have been marked by exile, trauma and loss. His fourth and final extended literary fiction *Austerlitz* (2001) condenses many of his earlier concerns. The account of the life of the central character in *Austerlitz* is a fictionalization of the experience of the *Kindertransport*, and of the delayed trauma of the Holocaust. Through his fiction Sebald has created a melancholic meditation on the catastrophes of recent European history. (**Benjamin Noys**)

Further reading

Wood (1999).

Second World War   The Second World War (1939–45) was the biggest military conflict in world history and cost the lives of 55 million people. The result of the Second World War was the division of Germany and Europe into two military and political blocs, which lasted for over 40 years.

The principal cause for the war was HITLER's aggressive and expansionist policy. Until 1938 he had achieved his goals without the use of military means largely due to the Allied appeasement policy. In September 1939, however, the German army (*Wehrmacht*) attacked Poland. Although England and France declared war on Germany, they did not take any military action. In a series of campaigns in spring 1940 the *Wehrmacht* invaded Denmark, Norway, Belgium, Holland, and France, and the British troops had to evacuate from Dunkirk. Italy joined the war against the Allies, and by summer 1940 Britain stood alone against the Axis powers. During the following Battle of Britain, however, the German air force proved unable to prepare the invasion. In spring 1941 Hitler turned against Northern Africa and occupied Yugoslavia and Greece while other countries such as Romania and Bulgaria joined the Axis powers. In June Hitler started the 'war of extermination' against the Soviet Union and by late autumn the *Wehrmacht* was only a few miles away from the Kremlin in Moscow. In December 1941 Japan attacked Pearl Harbor and brought the United States into the war, which now became another world conflict. From 1942 the initiative gradually passed to the Allies who successfully fought the German army in Northern Africa and prepared for the invasion of Italy. At sea, radar effectively helped to detect and destroy German U-boats, and in the air Allied bombing raids on German cities became increasingly severe. The defeat of the German Sixth Army at Stalingrad in February 1943 marked the turning point on the Eastern front where Stalin's Red Army began successful counter-attacks. The Allied invasion of Sicily in 1943 caused the downfall of Mussolini and led to the Italian armistice in September. In the Far East, naval battles stopped the Japanese advance in the Pacific and were followed by American counter-offensives. The Allied invasion in Normandy in 1944 meant the opening of another front and resulted in the liberation of France and Belgium, whereas the Soviets resumed their offensive in Eastern Europe. In March 1945 Allied armies crossed the Rhine, and in May Hitler committed suicide shortly before the Red Army entered Berlin. The *Wehrmacht* agreed to unconditional surrender on 9 May 1945. On 12 September, following the nuclear bomb attacks on Hiroshima and Nagasaki, Japan also capitulated.

The new dimension of the Second World War was marked by the HOLOCAUST, the mass extermination of the European Jews. This genocide was organized by the Nazis as one of Hitler's central war aims. Historians believe that over six million Jews were killed. (**Anselm Heinrich**)

Further reading

Overy (1995); Parker (1989).

SED (Socialist Unity Party)   The SED (*Sozialistische Einheitspartei Deutschlands*, Socialist Unity Party) was the ruling party in the GDR between 1949 and 1989. It was established on 22 April 1946 when the KPD (Communist Party of Germany) and SPD (Social Democratic Party) merged. The merger was only effective in the Soviet-occupied zone and was quickly reversed in the Western zone occupied by the Allies. In 1946, the SED had around 1.3 million members. Up until 1948, the SED was a mass socialist party whose offices were occupied equally by former KPD and SPD members. The first chairmen were Wilhelm Pieck and Otto GROTEWOHL. Under the leadership of Walter ULBRICHT, who was Party Chairman until 1971, the SED was restructured into a 'new type of party' in 1948 in response to pressure from the USSR and numerous members were expelled. From the establishment of the GDR on 7 October 1949, the SED was effectively the sole ruling party following instructions issued in the Soviet Union. Free and democratic ELECTIONS were not held. Election results were falsified if 99 per cent of votes were not cast in favour of the chosen candidates. All important economic and state positions were held by members of the SED. The highest party committees, called the 'Politbüro' (approximately 25 members) and the 'Central Committee' (approximately 150 members), made all the decisions taken in the GDR. In 1971, Erich Honecker, Chairman of the SED, brought the most important political powers under his control as Ulbricht had once done. A brief and slight economic boom was experienced in the GDR but nothing changed politically. A large section of the population was dissatisfied with the policies of the SED as is shown by the masses of people who fled to the Federal Republic before the Wall was built in August 1961 and the JUNE 1953 UPRISING. In the 1980s, the SED had 2.3 million members, approximately 20 per cent of the adult population of the GDR. Many positions within the economy and society could only be held by party members.

In autumn 1989, the SED lost its claim to power during the course of the peaceful revolution. Honecker and all the other important functionaries had to resign and stand trial. In December 1989, the SED was renamed the PDS and most of its former members left the party. (**Hendrik Berth**)

Further reading

Herbst *et al.* (1997). History, organization, politics. Gysi and Falkner (1990). Edited by Gregor Gysi, last leader of the SED, the book illustrates the events in 1989–90 and the development from SED to PDS. Mestrup (2000).

Seghers, Anna (Netty Reiling)   1900 Mainz–1983 (East) Berlin. Author. Seghers is regarded as one of the most outstanding female writers of contemporary German literature. She studied art history at Heidelberg and Cologne. In 1925 she married the

Hungarian exiled communist László Radványi. Her literary work has been published under the pseudonym Anna Seghers. Seghers linked literature and politics and saw her writing as a weapon in the class struggle. As a Jewish communist she and her family were forced to leave Germany once HITLER seized power. Despite the hardships of life in exile and the various changes of location (France, USA, Mexico), Anna Seghers' time as an émigré proved very productive: she wrote, gave talks and was in close contact with other exiled writers. Her novel *Das siebte Kreuz* (*The Seventh Cross*) was a best seller and was made into a Hollywood film. It treats escape from a concentration camp in pre-war Germany. In *Transit Visa* (*Transit*) Seghers explores the experiences of German refugees desperately trying to leave Vichy France for the USA. In 1947 Anna Seghers returned to (East) Berlin and later became the president of the Writers' Union of the GDR. Apart from novels she wrote essays, criticism and short stories. During her lifetime Seghers was awarded a number of prizes, such as the Kleist Prize and the Büchner Prize. While she is a greatly respected and important female author of twentieth-century German literature, she has also been regarded more critically because of her silence in the face of the repression of artists in the former GDR. (**Barbara Rassi**)

Further reading/listening

Seghers (2000). 2 CDs. Anna Seghers reads excerpts from selected novels and talks about the role of the author.

Social security   The social security system has long antecedents, with its roots in the Bismarck era legislation of the 1880s. This established the three compulsory forms of workers' insurance in health, accident and invalidity and old age insurance. The *Reichsversicherungsordnung* of 1911 added widows and orphans' pensions. The pension insurance system was established in 1927 and from 1938 craftsmen were included in the system. In the post-war period, 1957 saw the great pension reform which linked pension benefits to income growth ('dynamization'). Further pension reform followed in 1972, 1992, the mid-1990s and 2000–1. The social security net was transferred almost unchanged to the east in 1990. The social security system is wide-ranging, dense, generous and present transfers represent 35 per cent of GDP. One-third support pension insurance and one-fifth for health insurance. (Health insurance is described under HEALTH SERVICES). Pensions afford an adequate standard of living from the normal retirement age of 65 years for males and 60 years for females, although over time, the female retirement will equate with the male. Early retirement provisions are available. The *Eckrente* provides on average for a worker with 45 years of contributions, a benefit equalling 70 per cent of the net average income. The Blüm and Riester Reforms have sought to accommodate the pay-as-you-go system to the burden of an ageing population. Accident insurance in the FRG is paid for by employer contributions alone. UNEMPLOYMENT benefit is supported by joint employer/employee contributions and is income-linked: it offers benefit at 57 per cent of previous net income for married workers and 53 per cent for the single unemployed. Unemployment assistance and subsequently social assistance are available for the long-term unemployed. Social assistance is borne by the local authorities, is means-tested and includes income support for those with particular circumstances such as the handicapped or those needing long-term care. In 1995, long-term care insurance was introduced and recently child allowances and tax reliefs have been raised. (**Chris Flockton**)

Further reading

Bundesministerium für Arbeit und Sozialordnung. See advice and publications.

Soziale Marktwirtschaft   The concept of the social market economy (SMW) derives from the teachings of economists such as Böhm and Eucken of the Freiburg School in the early 1930s, and as transmitted by Müller-Armack who subsequently became economic adviser to Ludwig Erhard, under the Allied Control authorities in the early post-war years. The Freiburg School stressed the gains of competition, balanced budgets and the use of interest rates as a stabilizing tool in macroeconomic policy: it was then distinctly non-Keynesian in approach. Erhard's name is closely linked with the SMW and he was economics minister in CDU governments from 1949 to 1963 and, subsequently, federal Chancellor from 1963 to 1966. The SMW was introduced as a framework approach to economic management from 1948, with the linked currency reform, MARSHALL Aid and liberalization from wartime controls occurring in 1949. While based on a capitalist order, constituted by private property, competition, open markets and limited state intervention, nevertheless it accepted the need for state intervention in three broad areas: to promote active competition, to protect the weak and to correct to some extent the inequalities of income and wealth which arise under free markets. In practice, state intervention was denser than the SMW prescription. The role of the state in expenditure and taxation continued to grow at its historic tendency, a strong concentration of economic power re-arose, after US anti-trust measures, in the banks, the steel and chemicals industries and heavy subsidization continued in areas such as AGRICULTURE, coal-mining and shipbuilding, housing and TRANSPORT. Finally, protective measures were taken in 1950. The Growth and Stability Law of 1967 introduced Keynesian instruments and during the 1970s, there was a jump in state activities and in regulation of the labour market. Economic liberals date the major transgressions to this period and later. (**Chris Flockton**)

Further reading

Abelshauser (1983); Wallich (1955).

SPD (Social Democratic Party of Germany)   The Social Democratic Party of Germany (*Sozialdemokratische Partei Deutschlands*, SPD) can trace its roots back to the beginning of the German Labour Movement in the mid-nineteenth century. In

1875, under the leadership of Ferdinand Lassalle, August Bebel and Wilhelm Liebknecht the *Sozialistische Arbeiterpartei Deutschlands* (Socialist Labour Party of Germany) was founded. From 1890 the party was known as the SPD. It followed a Marxist world-view and worked towards a thorough reform of the economic, social and political conditions in Germany. The party soon became a strong political force in German politics. Friedrich Ebert of the SPD became Germany's first republican President after the demise of the monarchy in 1918. With HITLER's accession to power in 1933 social democrats – who were the only ones to vote against Hitler's emergency legislation (*Ermächtigungsgesetz*) – became the target of a relentless policy of political repression. Many party activists perished in concentration camps and Nazi prisons.

After the Second World War the SPD regrouped in a divided Germany. In the Soviet occupied zone the SPD was forced into an alliance with the Communist Party to form the *Sozialistische Einheitspartei* (Socialist Unity Party, SED). In West Germany, the SPD reformed at its party congress in Bad Godesberg in 1959 from a Marxist-oriented political force to a modern social democratic party. By moving to the centre ground the SPD gained enough votes to take office at the federal level in 1969 under Chancellor Willy BRANDT. With Brandt's famous *Ostpolitik*, the SPD made a significant contribution to Cold War détente and to German unification. Helmut SCHMIDT, Brandt's successor as Chancellor in 1974, stood for a pragmatic policy of economic growth and social justice coupled with a determined reaction against the upcoming far-left TERRORISM in Germany.

In 1982, the SPD was forced into opposition by the conservative Helmut KOHL. The party was forced to adapt to the new political realities that had emerged with the end of the Cold War and German unification. It won the 1998 parliamentary ELECTION under the leadership of Gerhard SCHRÖDER. (**Manuel Gull**)

Further reading

Braunthal (1996).
www.spd.de (website with SPD party programmes and historic documents)

Spiegel, der   Weekly (Monday) news magazine, founded in 1946, whose publisher since 1947 has been Rudolf Augstein. Modelled on American organs (*Time*), it became required reading for the intelligentsia through wide-ranging, snappy reporting, easy-to-read personalized writing, penetrating interviews (*Spiegel*-Gespräch), investigative work, liberal attitudes and insistence on democratic rights (giving space to views of leftist radicals around 1968 and 1977). Correspondingly unpopular with early federal governments (*Spiegel-Affäre* 1962, started when Defence Minister F.-J. Strauß, seeking the source of an injurious scoop, ordered illegal searches – see STRAUß-AFFAIR). As, aided by massive ADVERTISING revenues, *Spiegel* grew to intimidating size, readers tended to move to thinner magazines. However, its contents still often determine Germany's weekly political and journalistic agenda. (**Alfred D. White**) www.spiegel.de (website with daily updated news and features, contents of current issue, English summaries, archive, and programme listings of related *Spiegel-TV.*)

Sports   Sports play an important part in German life. Even at the beginning of the twentieth century, a strong naturalist movement urged Germans to be sporty and healthy, take exercise and eat healthy FOOD. During the HITLER era, Germans were organized into sports unions and made to exercise for the *Vaterland* (Fatherland). In West Germany, sports were organized in and through VEREINE (sports associations), which, unlike in Anglo-American countries, were independent of schools and universities. Communal, state and federal institutions have always taken a proactive approach to sports; almost every city and large village has at least one public indoor and/or outdoor swimming pool, medicinal saunas are everywhere, and especially in the 1970s, *Trimm-dich-Pfade* (outdoors get-fit-circuits) were the rage. In the GDR, sports were centrally organized, and children were tested for talent very early on. With its stringent sports programmes, GDR sports became very successful, with athletes such as Udo Beyer (shot putter) and Katharina Witt (ice skater) enjoying success on both sides of the Wall. It was only after unification, when revelations began to appear about systematic doping in GDR sports, that many of its successes became somewhat tainted. In West Germany, fitness centres began to appear as early as the late 1970s. They have been enjoying exponential subscriber rates. Newer sports such as inline skating, mountain biking, climbing and hang gliding enjoy growing popularity. Nevertheless, the biggest sport in Germany remains FOOTBALL, followed closely by tennis, gymnastics, shooting associations, handball, table tennis, equestrianism, skiing, swimming and golf. While the predominance of football has never been challenged, the relative popularity of other sports is always associated with one or several seminal practitioners; over the last decades, those were Rosi Mittermaier for skiing, Boris Becker and Steffi Graf for tennis, Jan Ullrich for cycling, Bernhard Langer for golf, Michael and Ralf Schumacher for Formula 1 racing and Martin Schmidt and Sven Hannawald for ski jumping. (**Holger Briel**)

Further reading

www.dsb.de (official webpage of the *Deutscher Sportbund,* German Sports Federation.)

Staeck, Klaus   Born 1938 Bitterfeld. Graphic artist and publisher. Heidelberg-based montage artist in the tradition of John Heartfield. Renowned and vilified for his hard-hitting socialist posters, collages, postcards and publishing work. (**Martin Brady**)

Stasi (Staatssicherheit)   The *Stasi* (the East German Ministry for State Security) was without doubt the most insidious element of the GDR's security system. Founded in February 1950, it was designed to be the 'sword and shield' of the SED, the GDR's ruling party, with the function of 'preventing or throttling at the earliest stages – using whatever means and methods may be necessary – all attempts to delay or hinder the victory of socialism'. It was led by the Minister for State Security, Erich Mielke, and was a huge and complex entity with 13 main departments and over 20 other sections involved in monitoring events both inside and outside the GDR.

Abroad it operated just like any other national secret service, comparable with MI5 or the CIA. In this capacity it was particularly effective, as was shown, for example, by the fact that it managed to plant a spy within the advisory staff of the BRANDT administration. However, since the collapse of the GDR it is the internal activities of the organization that have become the main focus of attention and in particular the massive network of unofficial collaborators (*Inoffizielle Mitarbeiter* or IM) it employed. IMs were to be found in all aspects of life in the GDR, functioning as the eyes and ears of the service and making regular reports to their *Stasi* handlers. This information could then be used in the *Stasi*'s campaigns of psychological warfare against individual citizens deemed by the authorities to be a danger to the state. Dealing with IMs has been a major problem in POST-UNIFICATION Germany. Gradually, the view that anyone connected with the *Stasi* should be treated simply as a perpetrator of oppression has been replaced by a more differentiated approach which takes into account the fact that many IMs were actually press-ganged into co-operation and can themselves be seen as victims of the SED. (**Paul Cooke**)

Further reading

Fricke, (1991). The standard German work on the subject. Childs and Popplewell (1996). An accessible overview of the *Stasi*'s activities.

Staudte, Wolfgang　1906 Saarbrücken–1984 Zigarski Vrh, Slovenia. Film-maker. Directed his first films during the THIRD REICH. A co-founder of DEFA, the GDR film production company, he worked in East and West until 1955 when he settled in the FRG. *The Murderers are Among Us* (*Die Mörder sind unter uns*, 1946), the first postwar German feature film, tackled the aftermath of National Socialism in an Expressionist style and starred Hildegard Knef. German history remained a theme in Staudte's subsequent film and television work, including children's films, thrillers and literary adaptations (notably *The Underdog* (*Der Untertan*, 1951). (**Martin Brady**)

Stock Exchange　There has been a sea change in the 1990s in attitudes within Germany to stock exchange investments and to raising capital through share issues: PRIVATIZATION issues, cheaper capital-raising and EU liberalization directives help explain this shift. By the end of 2000, 20 per cent of the population owned shares, compared with one-half that in 1997, though there are only 680 joint-stock companies listed and stock exchange capitalization represents only 27 per cent of GDP, compared with 130 per cent in the UK. Historically, the Bundesbank (see BANKING AND THE

Deutsche Bundesbank) had opposed many capital market reforms, but there has been a profound reform of securities markets, partly under the threat of UK and French competition. The Bundesbank began to introduce reforms first in the mid-1980s to help bring part of the DM Eurobond business back to Germany and later, in conjunction with the Federal Finance Ministry set out a programme to promote 'Finanzplatz Deutschland'. After the creation of the Federation of German Stock Exchanges in 1987 and the creation of the unified DAX index in 1988, the regional stock exchanges were all brought under the central control of the Deutsche Börse AG in Frankfurt in 1992. In 1989, the DTB (*Deutsche Terminbörse*) was created and has since won a key position in futures contracts on the Bund and Euro interest rate futures. A common electronic trading platform, the IBIS system, then the advanced Xetra trading system from 1998 unified the DTB futures markets (now called Eurex), the Neuer Markt for small, high growth companies, the *Kassenverein* clearing system and the cash exchanges all within one platform, so permitting share trading, futures hedging and clearance and settlement all to take place from a single computer platform. A succession of financial market promotion laws abolished the stock exchange turnover tax, reformed supervision so as to forbid, for example, insider trading, and finally, at a late date, implemented the EU Directive on Investment Services. In spite of planned mergers with first Paris and then London stock exchanges, nothing definite has taken place so far. (**Chris Flockton**)

Further reading

www.ip.exchange.de (*Deutsche Börse* website, for publications and reports.)

Stockhausen, Karlheinz   Born 1928 Burg Mödrath. Highly influential composer whose impact on popular music (Krautrock in particular) is as significant as his legendary status in new music history. Featured on the cover of the Beatles' *Sergeant Pepper*. Early works expand the serial composition techniques of Schoenberg and Webern (*Kreuzspiel*, 1951). Experiments with complex sounds, graphic notation and electronics, culminate in the tape piece *Gesang der Jünglinge* (1955–56) and *Kontakte* for piano, percussion and tape (1958–60). Subsequent works frequently include theatrical elements, feeding into the long-term *Licht* project (from 1977) to compose an opera for each day of the week. (**Martin Brady**)

Strauss, Botho   Born 1944 Naumburg. Author and playwright. Strauss is one of the most prolific and controversial writers of present-day Germany. He started his writing career at the theatre, working for Peter Stein at the *Schaubühne* in Berlin. His plays chart the loss of identity in the mechanical and cold German world of the 1960s and 1970s. Typical for his method is *Der Park* (1983), in which he confronts the modern individual with a mythological assemblage of characters from Shakespeare's *A Midsummer Night's Dream*. For Strauss, the modern characters lose out, having given up on human urges in favour of an administered world. In his prose texts, such as *Paare, Passanten* (1981), he projects his pessimistic world-view upon individuals caught up in destructive relationships. His disjointed, scrapbook style of writing reflects his sentiments also on a formal level. In 1993 Strauss published an essay in the magazine Spiegel, entitled *Anschwellender Bocksgesang*, a literal translation of the Greek word for tragedy. There he charges politicians with capitalizing and de-mythologizing society and predicts the demise of the democratic system. He includes the left in this demise, as it has no moral or philosophical fibre left with which to fight. The essay called forth a huge echo in the press, once again underlining Strauss' potential to provoke. (**Holger Briel**)

Further reading

Willer (2000).

Strauß-Affair   The *Strauß-Affair*, or *Spiegel-Affair* as it is also referred to, was a watershed in the development of West German political culture. Franz Josef Strauß (1915–88) had helped found the Bavarian Christian Social Union (CSU) in 1945 and became its long-time leader in 1961. He was appointed minister for atomic affairs and deputy chairman of the Defence Council in 1953. In October 1956 Chancellor Konrad Adenauer appointed him Minister of Defence. As such, Strauß was largely responsible for the rearmament of West Germany and the building of her armed forces, the Bundeswehr. He also strongly favoured the acquisition of nuclear forces. When the weekly news magazine *Der Spiegel*, which had on previous occasions criticized his policy, published an article on a NATO exercise in October 1962, its editor Rudolf Augstein and the reporter Conrad Ahlers were arrested on suspicion of treason. In a police action, which was not legally justified, the magazine's offices were searched and temporarily closed. The police action, including the arrest of Ahlers and his wife in Spain following Strauß' personal intervention, severely shook public opinion in West Germany. For many it revealed the authoritarian and anti-democratic character of parts of the late Adenauer cabinet and provoked increasing public opposition against an open attack on the freedom of the press. Finally, the oppositional SPD took up the case. When the FDP ministers of the cabinet resigned, Strauß was forced to step down as minister. The affair's impact on the changing political climate can hardly be overestimated; it demonstrated the growth of public and political opposition against the 'restorative' character of state and society in the early 1960s which came to be symbolized by Strauß in the eyes of many contemporaries. The crisis did not end, as so often in previous German history, with a 'victorious' state, but strengthened the role of the critical public in West German society. (**Jörn Leonhard**)

Further reading

Bark and Grees (1993). A detailed and readable history of West Germany's internal development. Nicholls (1997). A concise and well-written account of West Germany.

Swiss literature   Unlike French-language Swiss literature, which has always been marginal, German-language Swiss literature is an integral part of German culture. Indeed, a Swiss writer is not successful until he or she has a publisher in Germany. Conversely, at various times German writers have sought refuge in Switzerland from the oppressive regimes of their homes, or simply preferred to live there: Hesse for a long time, Expressionists and Dadaists during the First World War, Jewish writers such as Else Lasker-Schüler after 1933, Brecht fleetingly as a half-way house to returning to Germany after 1945, Musil and Thomas Mann more permanently. Native German-Swiss writing includes the progressive nature-oriented work of Haller, Bodmer and Breitinger and the naïve autobiography of Bräker in the eighteenth century, and has high points in the nineteenth: the rural novels of Gotthelf with their evocative DIALECT, the short stories of Keller with their light satirical barbs on the life of sleepy Zurich, those of his contemporary Meyer with their psychological investigations of history, and Meyer's haunting poems. The reputation of Spitteler and other writers of the early twentieth century has faded. The detective novel was developed by Glauser, narratives with a specific Swiss ethos by Inglin and Zollinger, but a tendency to inward-looking smugness is identifiable – broken by a crisis of confidence when Germany and Austria succumbed to Hitler, leaving Switzerland embarrassingly opposing one nationalist and racist ideology with another. After 1945 Swiss letters were brilliantly led out of isolation by Frisch and Dürrenmatt; further generations of authors such as Bichsel, Erica Pedretti, Diggelmann and Muschg gathered self-confidence from their example. (**Alfred D. White**)

Further reading

Watanabe-O'Kelly (1997). Short treatment of 1960–88 in particular (pp. 503–5); further reading (p. 582). Pezold *et al.* (1991). Fair summary of developments.

Syberberg, Hans Jürgen   Born 1935 Nossendorf. Film-maker, theatre director and author. A visionary director celebrated and reviled for his dramatic explorations of the German psyche. Combining the dramatic estrangements of Brecht with the operatic extravagance of Wagner, his eight-hour *Hitler, ein Film aus Deutschland* (*Hitler: A Film from Germany*, 1977) is a monumental collage of styles, images and ideas. Unshakable in his belief that Germany must overcome its past and be a guiding force in Europe, he celebrated its cultural heritage in a series of stately monologue films with the actress Edith Clever using texts by Kleist and Goethe (1984–94). (**Martin Brady**)

T

Telecommunications   On 1 January 1998 the German telecommunications market was liberalized, thus changing the number of telephony suppliers from one to 180 at the beginning of 2001. Prior to liberalization the market was monopolized by Deutsche Telekom AG.

The German telecommunications market was liberated by three post/telecommunications reforms, culminating in the German Telecommunications Act, 1996 (*das Telekommunikationsgesetz* – TKG). The Act defines the legal framework of German telecommunications law and was established on the enabling basis of Article 87f of the German Constitution (*Grundgesetz*) which in turn guarantees the availability of adequate and appropriate telecommunications services throughout Germany and permits competition in this market. The liberalization process was initiated by the European Union and can be interpreted as an objective of the Treaty of Rome, namely, to create an internal market.

Customers have benefited from market deregulation in various ways including cheaper calls, improved technology and greater choice in terms of services and providers. Between 1998 and 2001 call charges have been reduced by up to 92 per cent for daytime local and national calls. Furthermore, there are now more than 1900 telecoms service providers registered with the regulatory authority, *Regulierungsbehörde für Telekommunikation und Post* (Reg TP) as required by Section 4 TKG. Internet access and voice telephony are the services predominantly offered by these providers.

Reg TP is responsible for all telecommunications regulatory activities including ensuring that regulatory aims are met and helping consumers with any queries and concerns that they may have regarding telecommunication. German universal service legislation provides that everyone in Germany should have access to a minimum set and standard of telecommunication services.

The immense size of the German telecommunications market is highlighted by the fact that 239 000 people were working within the telecommunications market in Germany by the end of 2000 and telecoms revenues exceeded DM100 bn. (**Enida Ighodaro**)

Further reading

Schäfer (1998). The book contains a collection of the main pieces of legislation relating to German telecommunications law, as well as a useful introduction and terminology section providing translations of specialist vocabulary.

Television   Television is the number one leisure activity in Germany. Its history can be traced back to the early 1920s, when experimental television shows were broadcast from public institutes. During the Nazi era, it was tightly regulated through GOEBBELS' *Reichspropagandaministerium,* as was the case with all broadcasting and the PUBLISHING industry. An important televisual event was the broadcasting of the 1936 Olympics. With the beginning of the Second World War, however, television broadcasting ceased, with RADIO once again taking over the airwaves. After the Second World War, television broadcasting began anew; programmes were aired from 1952 onward in the Federal Republic; early highlights included the coronation of Queen Elizabeth II of England and the FOOTBALL World Cup Finals of 1954, which were won by Germany. For fear of repeating the ideologically dangerous route of centralizing broadcasting (as would be the case again in the GDR), in the Federal Republic, television and radio was put under the jurisdiction of the individual *Länder* (states); all of them worked together in the ARD, also called *Das Erste* (Channel One). The broadcasting system would become known as *öffentlich-rechtliches Fernsehen* (public broadcasting), with all major segments of society such as politicians, clergy, industry, etc. involved in programming and production decisions via their representatives in the *Rundfunkrat* (Broadcasting Council). A second channel, the ZDF, was introduced in 1963. In the mid-1960s regional third channels would follow. In the GDR, state television did not play as much of a social role as it did in the Federal Republic. However, almost everywhere in the GDR, West German television could be received. It was much in demand, as it offered more entertainment than the local stations. Some historians and media researchers believe that CONSUMPTION-oriented West German broadcasting played an important part in creating the desire within the East German population to participate in this consumption process, eventually contributing to the moves which would lead to UNIFICATION. During the 1980s, private satellite and cable television were introduced, against heavy resistance from the left. Stations such as SAT1, RTL and PRO7 have managed to capture high audience figures. Today, Germany has close to 100 TV broadcasters, the overwhelming majority of which remain committed Free TV stations. (**Holger Briel**)

Further reading

Briel (1998). Faulstich (1999). The standard text on media in Germany. Humphreys (1994). Still the standard text on German media in English. Kreuzer and Thomson (1993–94). Extensive study of German television.

Terrorism   In the Federal Republic, left-wing terrorism had its roots in the student revolt of the 1960s (see GENERATION OF 1968, 68ERS). Several of its more radical members, including Andreas Baader, Gudrun Ensslin and Ulrike Meinhof decided that *Gewalt gegen Sachen* (violence against objects) was not enough to induce revolution, and therefore began a terrorist campaign against key figures of the 'system'. Known as the *Baader-Meinhof-Gang* or *Group* or *Rote Armee Fraktion* (RAF, Red Army faction), their victims included Hanns-Martin Schleyer (President of the Employers' Federation), Karsten Rohwedder (President of the *Treuhand*), Jürgen Ponto (CEO of the Deutsche Bank), and Alfred Herrnhausen, another banking official. The RAF was part of an international network of leftist terrorism, training with the more radical elements of the Palestine Liberation Organization, and liaising with the French *Action Directe* and the Italian *Brigade Rosso*. Matters came to a head in 1977, when members of the RAF hijacked a commercial aeroplane in order to free their imprisoned leaders. The hijacking ended unsuccessfully, whereupon Baader, Ensslin and Raspe were found dead under suspicious circumstances in their prison cells in the high-security area of the Stuttgart-Stammheim prison complex. It was judged that they had committed suicide. After UNIFICATION, several of its members, who had sought clandestine asylum in the GDR, were apprehended. In 1998, the RAF officially disbanded, after several of its imprisoned members had already been granted clemency. (**Holger Briel**)

Further reading

Aust (1998); Butz (1993).

Theatre festivals   Among the theatre festivals that focus on *Sprechtheater*, i.e. theatre that is not sung or danced but only spoken, are the *Salzburger Festspiele* in Austria that take place every summer between July and August. They were established in 1890 and strongly influenced by Hugo von Hofmannsthal and Max Reinhardt. Mostly German-language plays from Germany, Austria, and other European countries are invited to Salzburg with few exceptions in other languages. Since 1963, the *Berliner Theatertreffen* that takes place every May in Berlin has offered the more experimental performances in German theatre. In Berlin, prizes are awarded to ensembles for the best performances. Since 1976, the *Mülheimer Theatertage* are held in Mülheim, North-Rhine Westphalia, between May and June every year. Only contemporary German plays are invited and the playwrights are recognized with awards rather than the productions. The *Ruhrfestspiele* that are held in Recklinghausen, North-Rhine Westphalia, emphasize their character as a European theatre festival that reaches out to West and East European performances; it was established in 1946. The *Theater der Welt* (theatre of the world) is another theatre festival in Berlin between July and August that invites international ensembles from all continents. This festival focuses on theatre, dance, and performance in general. There are also regional festivals such as the *Bayrische Theatertage* or the *Nordrhein-Westfälische Theatertreffen*. Another important festival that focuses on music theatre, particularly operas, is the *Bayreuther Festspiele* that takes place annually between July and August in Bavaria. Richard Wagner established the festival in 1876 because he needed a stage for his operas that require such a large number of actors and actresses that many houses in Munich at that time were not suitable for Wagner's needs. (**Britta Kallin**)

Further reading

Gallup (1987); Spotts (1994).

Theatres   In general one differentiates between *Sprechtheater* (traditional theatre), *Tanztheater* (dance theatre, pantomime, and ballet), as well as *Musiktheater* (musicals and opera). In Germany, theatre has been strongly influenced by the *Commedia dell' arte*, Italian troupes that toured the continent in the sixteenth century. Touring theatre troupes in Germany developed further in the seventeenth and eighteenth centuries under the influence of British troupes staging plays by Shakespeare and other British authors. Kings and courts started requesting performances by the groups that toured the continent and thus helped slowly establish a *Hof-Theater* (court theatre) with its own ensemble. The *Hof-Theater* was the precursor of the *Staats-* and *Nationaltheater* (state and national theatres) that were later established to educate the people through shows. The development of theatre changed dramatically in the eighteenth century with Johann Christoph Gottsched's and Gotthold Ephraim Lessing's reforms that changed the theatre from its mainly entertaining function to a more educated art form. The period of *Sturm und Drang* (Storm and Stress) as well as the *Klassik* (classicism) in German literature (with Goethe and Schiller as their best known representatives) made a vital impact on the stages in Germany. The theatre became an essential part of bourgeois life and it became a habit for the lower to upper classes to attend performances, which did not change throughout the nineteenth century. A revival of political theatre occurred in the first part of the twentieth century with influences of naturalism, Expressionism as well as BRECHT's *Epic Theatre* and its goal of educating the proletariat. After the Second World War, the highly subsidized German theatre tried to regain its powerful position but could not compete with other media such as TELEVISION and movies. Since the 1970s there has been a tendency towards a *Regisseurtheater* (director's theatre) that is distinctly different from other countries because the director of the play and the production became the focus of attention and not the play itself. Puppet theatre and theatre for children are important institutions in German cultural life. Experimental theatre has been one of the mechanisms of social critique in Germany. (**Britta Kallin**)

Further reading

Patterson (1996); Yates (1996).

Third Reich (*Das Dritte Reich*)   The Third Reich describes the time of National Socialist rule in Germany between 1933 and 1945, during which the Nazis established a total dictatorship, persecuted political opponents and started the Second World War. The singularity of the Nazi dictatorship is marked by the HOLOCAUST, the systematic mass extermination of the European Jews.

The Third Reich began on 30 January 1933 when President Hindenburg appointed Adolf HITLER, the leader of the National Socialist German Workers' Party (NSDAP), Chancellor of a nationalist government. Although the Nazis neither had the majority within the government nor the majority of the German vote they managed to establish a one-party dictatorship within a few months. They forbade other political parties and trade unions, they forced the *Länder* and formerly independent organizations into line and suppressed criticism with reckless terror. This process of Gleichschaltung aimed at the total orientation of Germany's public life towards the NSDAP and Hitler himself, who, after the death of President Hindenburg in August 1934, assumed the title of *Führer* and state Chancellor. From the beginning of their rule the Nazis persecuted the Jews. With the 1935 Nuremberg Laws the Jews were deprived of virtually all civil rights. Their persecution reached an early climax with the pogrom of 1938, until in 1941 the systematic extermination started. In foreign politics Hitler tried to stress the peace-loving character of the new regime despite initiating a large-scale rearmament programme. A four-year plan was set up to prepare Germany for war by 1940. After the Allied appeasement policy had tolerated the annexation of Austria and the Sudetenland in 1938, Hitler's aggressive politics became obvious when he invaded Czechoslovakia. The Allies declared war on Germany when Hitler's troops marched into Poland in September 1939. After the first *Blitzkrieg* victories Hitler stood at the height of his power, but with the invasion of his great ideological enemy, the Soviet Union, the situation gradually changed. After 1942 the impact of the war came to be felt sharply, and with the declaration of 'total war' in 1943 Germans experienced total mobilization. Additionally, Allied bombing became more extensive. However, many Germans believed in the *Führer* until the end. In May 1945 the Third Reich collapsed with the German surrender and Hitler's suicide. (**Anselm Heinrich**)

Further reading

Burleigh (2000). Noakes and Pridham (1983–98). Documents interwoven with a fascinating analytical narrative. Fest (1970). Still brilliant. With biographies of the most important Nazi leaders. Thamer (1994). The most significant recent German study about the history of the Third Reich.

Transport The western *Länder* have long benefited from a modern, comprehensive and high quality transport infrastructure, including a dense rail network with high-speed inter-city connections, as well as generally excellent local bus services, often heavily subsidized by the municipalities. In the east, by contrast, major and costly improvements have been made, both of *Autobahnen* and *Bundesstrassen*, but transport connections are generally regarded as in need of significant upgrading. Of the 231 000 km of classified roads, 11 310 km were *Autobahnen*. The RAILWAY organizations of east and west were amalgamated and fundamentally re-organized by the December 1993 merger of the Bundesbahn and the Deutsche Reichsbahn. The legislation, in line with an EU liberalization directive, separated the rail network as an independent subsidiary and divided the merged organization, the Deutsche Bahn AG into three operating subsidiaries, the long-distance passenger, regional passenger and freight services. Long-distance services are expected to be profit-making while regional and local train services require heavy subsidy from the states and localities. DB plans to separate off into 38 operating companies 18 000 km of local track, while maintaining 20 000 km as the core network. Already one-quarter of the workforce, or 100 000 jobs, have been shed since 1994 without redundancy. Private shareholdings in Deutsche Bahn AG are scheduled for 2004/5, but a thoroughgoing financial restructuring is required. For waterborne freight, the major port is Rotterdam, but one-third of all water freight shipped passes through Hamburg, with Oldenburg, Bremerhaven, Lübeck, Rostock also having important freight terminals. The Deutsche Lufthansa AG was privatized in the first half of the 1990s and has successfully maintained its pre-eminence domestically in the face of budget carriers. Domestic airfares remain high, due principally to airport congestion and market dominance, with the Frankfurt–Berlin route having the most expensive per km fares in the world. The PRIVATIZATION of airports by the *Länder* and municipalities gained pace at the turn of the century. (**Chris Flockton**)

Further reading

Statistisches Bundesamt, *Statistisches Jahrbuch*, annual.

UFA UFA (Universum Film AG) was founded in 1917. It united several FILM production companies that had been purchased by the state and by uniting production, distribution and film theatres. UFA was the largest German film company. In 1921 it purchased a production company called Decla-Bioscop, thereby taking over the famous studios at Potsdam-Babelsberg. Until 1928 UFA produced only silent films – among them internationally acclaimed works like *Nosferatu* by Friedrich Wilhelm Murnau and *Metropolis* by Fritz LANG (adapted from the novel by Thea von Harbou). Among UFA's first sound-films were *Der blaue Engel* (director: Joseph von Sternberg, lead: Marlene DIETRICH) and *M – Eine Stadt sucht einen Mörder* (director: Fritz Lang, lead: Peter Lorre).

In March 1933, shortly after HITLER had become *Reichskanzler*, the propaganda ministry 'asked' UFA to dismiss employees for 'racial reasons'. This was mainly directed against Jewish and part-Jewish members of staff. UFA complied very readily and dismissed its chief producer, its chief press officer, several directors and many others. Foreign countries lost interest in German films which were now under state censorship. Exports decreased about 80 per cent in 1933. In the following years only huge state investments saved UFA.

After the Second World War had ended, the Soviets founded the DEFA, a new state owned film company, as UFA's successor. Complying with the Allied forces' demands, the first West German government split UFA in West Germany into three companies, but then sold them all to the Deutsche Bank. Nevertheless, UFA did not do well. After bankruptcy proceedings and several sales the West German government established the Friedrich-Wilhelm-Murnau foundation and bought the old UFA film library. The media giant Bertelsmann purchased 'the rest' and in 1984 it established the *UFA Film und Fernseh-GmbH*, which mainly produces films for TV. (**Corinna J. Heipcke**)

Further reading

Borgelt (1993). The UFA story from its beginnings to its sale. Conversations with former UFA members are of special interest.

Ulbricht, Walter 1893 Leipzig–1973 Döllnsee. Politician, GDR. As head of state he was responsible for the suppression of the GDR JUNE 1953 UPRISING and the erection of the Berlin Wall in 1961. Ulbricht was a professional carpenter; he was married twice (1920, 1953). In the First World War he served as a soldier. He became a member of the SPD (Social Democratic Party of Germany) in 1912, and he was one of the founders of the KPD (German Communist party) in 1919. In 1933 he emigrated to Paris;

1938–45 he lived and worked in Moscow. Since 1946 Ulbricht was a member of the *Zentralkomitee* of the SED (Central Committee of the Socialist Unity Party of Germany, the most important political institution in GDR), he held several leading functions. (1950–73 Member of *Volkskammer* of the GDR (parliament of the GDR), 1953–71 First Secretary of the *Zentralkomitee* of SED (leader of Social Unity Party, replaced by Erich Honecker), 1960–71 chairman of the *Nationaler Verteidigungsrat* (National Defence Council), 1960–73 chairman of the *Staatsrat* (Council of State).) (**Hendrik Berth**)

Further reading

Müller-Enbergs *et al.* (2000); Frank (2001); Stern (1963). First biography of Walter Ulbricht.

Unemployment   Federal German unemployment statistics use the civilian population as the base and therefore overstate somewhat the proportion of unemployed. In east Germany, the causes of chronic unemployment are structural relating to economic transformation, and in west Germany, frictional, structural and 'Keynesian' unemployment coexist. Frictional unemployment arises as workers are voluntarily changing jobs. Keynesian unemployment arises with deficiency of aggregate demand, such as low private investment or state expenditure cutbacks, and structural unemployment arises through rigidities of various origins, whether poor wage adjustment or skill and geographical mismatches. In the Federal Republic of the post-oil crises period, unemployment has typically been of the structural kind, overlain by a Keynesian unemployment, as governments have depressed demand to contain INFLATION. From an unemployment rate of 10.4 per cent in 1950, West Germany absorbed both the unemployed and the influx of 11 million refugees and expellees to produce an unemployment rate of only 0.7 per cent in 1962. The large influx of GASTARBEITER in the period 1965–73 acted to meet the labour shortage of the time. Germany weathered the oil crises relatively well, although sustaining an unemployment rate which never fell below 4.3 per cent. After the second oil crisis and with the austerity packages of the first KOHL government from 1982, unemployment in the West rose to 2.25 million and could not be brought down, except in the boom at the end of the 1980s. Since unification, unemployment rates of 8 per cent have been experienced in the west and of up to 18 per cent in the east, although here labour market measures such as early retirement, job creation and retraining measures help relieve the mass unemployment. Critics point to poor adjustment in the German economy, whether the high levels of job protection, the favourable SOCIAL SECURITY net or the all-encompassing collective wage agreements, which effectively set a wage floor and provide little wage differentiation by branch, region or by firm. (**Chris Flockton**)

Further reading

Deutsche Bundesbank, *Monatsbericht*, monthly.

Valentin, Karl   1882 Munich–1948 Munich. Actor, writer and film-maker. Germany's foremost stage, film and radio comedian of the inter-war years. Admired by fellow Bavarian BRECHT, with whom he briefly collaborated. (**Martin Brady**)

Further reading

Bronnen (1998).

Vereine   Although *Verein* can often be translated as 'organization' or 'club', there is a lot more life in this little German word than meets the eye. Traditional British student societies would be *Studentenvereine*, but the term 'e.V.' (*eingetragener Verein*) is also found in the name of FOOTBALL clubs such as '1. FC Köln e.V.'. The fact that Germans often use the pejorative term '*Vereinsmeier*' (person who lives for the clubs of which they are executive members) points to the fact that a *Verein* may well take over a zealot's life.

Article 9 of the *Grundgesetz* (Basic Law) states that German citizens are entitled to join or establish a *Verein*: natural or legal bodies may join forces over a relatively long period of time for a common aim, by giving themselves an appropriate name. In the Federal Republic of Germany, the public law on these (*Vereinsrecht*) is laid down in the Act of 1964; private organizations are covered by Articles 21–79 of the BGB (*Bundesgesetzbuch* = Federal written law). A *Verein* may not pursue illegal aims nor may its members act in an unlawful manner; it must not contravene the *Grundgesetz* and must not be directed against the idea of international friendship of the peoples of the earth (§ 3 *Vereinsgesetz*: *Gedanke der Völkerverständigung*).

Most *Vereine* are non-profit-making organizations and therefore exempt from paying taxes. International organizations such as Greenpeace or Amnesty International carry the 'e.V.' in their official names. In these days of increased interest in volunteering, this type of organization is beginning to play a much greater role in civil society and the image of traditional *Vereine* is bound to change with them. (**Astrid Küllmann-Lee**)

Further reading

Zimmer (1996).

Vergangenheitsbewältigung   (Literally, overcoming the past.) A wide-spread term used in relation to dealing with the past of the Nazi era and especially the HOLOCAUST. Much of the search for German post-war IDENTITY has been entwined with this process.

However, some critics rightly point out that what is needed is not an *overcoming* of the past, but rather a *working through*, a continuous effort. Unification and its inherent problems in particular have begun to move the intra-German focus away from the THIRD REICH, with a new sense of nationalist pride appearing. Furthermore, this nationalism is particularly problematic if fostered from East Germany, as attempts at *Vergangenheitsbewältigung* were officially deemed a problem of the West only. (**Holger Briel**)

Volkshochschule   Continuing education is the largest education sector in Germany, with an annual turnover of more than Euro 35 bn, split between federal, state and private funding initiatives. (See SCHOOLS AND EDUCATION). *Volkshochschulen* (so-called 'people's universities' or VHS) are one of the main providers of continuing education and offer a wide range of courses. They are non-profit-making organizations that define themselves as centres of learning, discussion, health and culture. Their workshops and courses are open to all age groups and sections of the population. Classes can be attended during the day and/or in the evenings. VHS provide a great variety of courses: from languages to history, philosophy and politics, from classes in art and handicraft to vocational and A-level courses. (**Barbara Rassi**)

Further reading

Bisovsky and Stifter (1996). Various contributions dealing with continuing education in a democracy and the role *Volkshochschulen* play within this scheme.

von Trotta, Margarethe   Born 1942 Berlin. Film-maker, screenplay author. Began her career as an actress on stage and screen and as co-director with her then partner Volker SCHLÖNDORFF. Directed her first film in 1977 and soon gained an international reputation for socially critical dramas with strong female protagonists and straightforward narratives. *The German Sisters (Die bleierne Zeit*, 1982) is her most celebrated work and typical in its sister–sister relationship and topical themes (Baader-Meinhof TERRORISM, state oppression, and FEMINISM). Unduly attacked at home from both left and right, she began making films in Italy after the biopic *Rosa Luxemburg* (1985). (**Martin Brady**)

Walraff, Günter   Born 1942 Burscheid. Author. Walraff, the son of a worker for Ford Cologne finished an apprenticeship at a bookshop before he was drafted into the BUNDESWEHR, the German army. His failed struggle to be acknowledged as a conscientious objector would find its way into his diaries of his military service days. After studying journalism, and incorporating his earlier documentary mode of writing practised in the diaries, Walraff would work undercover in large German companies and report on the subjugation of German industrial workers. His breakthrough came via the literary-documentary report at the time he was working undercover at the *Bild-Zeitung*, published as *Der Aufmacher: Der Mann, der bei* Bild *Hans Esser war* (1977). Here, Walraff exposes the cynicism, the manipulation of facts and political rightist partiality rampant at Germany's largest tabloid. He achieved even greater success with the publication of *Ganz Unten*, the book of his exploits while posing as a Turkish GASTARBEITER (guest worker). The book, translated into several other languages, became a runaway success throughout Germany and was instrumental in revitalizing the debate about the horrific treatment meted out to foreigners in Germany. (**Holger Briel**)

Further reading

Berger (1988).

Walser, Martin   Born 1927 Wasserburg. Author. Walser is considered to be one of the most important and prolific German writers of the past 40 years or so. Beginning with *Ehen in Philippsburg* (1957), the chronicle of the WIRTSCHAFTSWUNDER years and the (inter-)personal price to pay for them, his books and plays have consistently accompanied the realities of the FRG. Walser honed his particular critique of reality by writing his PhD on Kafka, and the sad irony of the fact that the individual will always lose (his/her soul) to the irrational mechanization of modern-day life was never lost on him, nor on his writing. His texts are narrated from the perspective of individuals caught up in these broken promises of the quest for a fulfilled, better- than middleclass lifestyle. His novel *Halbzeit* (1960) would see the introduction of the anti-hero Anselm Christlein, who would reappear several times in Walser's books, for instance in *Das Einhorn* (1966). Other characters would also make repeat entrances, Walser deepening and continuing their stories as they drift towards middle age and beyond (*Ein fliehendes Pferd*, 1978; *Brandung*, 1985; *Die Jagd*, 1988; *Ein springender Brunnen*, 2000; *Der Lebenslauf der Liebe*, 2001). In recent years, Walser has become increasingly involved in the debate on German IDENTITY (*Über Deutschland reden*, 1988). His controversial remarks during his acceptance speech for the *Friedenspreis des Deutschen Buchhandels* have prompted harsh critiques from the left. (**Holger Briel**)

Further reading

Fetz (1997).

Webern, Anton (Friedrich Wihelm von) 1883 Vienna–1945 Mittersill. Composer. A pupil of Arnold SCHOENBERG, with whom he took private lessons from 1904 (along with fellow Austrian Anton Berg). First experimented with atonality in settings of poems by Stefan George (1907–9). These were followed by some of his most celebrated works – extremely brief and intense instrumental studies, including the *Six Bagatelles for String Quartet* (1913), masterpieces in concision which, according to his former teacher, express 'an entire novel in a single gesture'. Adopted Schoenberg's serialism during the 1920s and set numerous poems by Hildegard Jone. (**Martin Brady**)

Weimar Republic   The first German republic was proclaimed on 9 November 1918 after imperial Germany had lost the First World War. The constitution was passed in 1919, and the first general election resulted in a clear victory of the republican parties. The representatives of the corporate society, which had dominated Wilhelmine Germany, however, still held key positions in industry, commerce, the administration, the judiciary, and the army. The new democracy was also dealt a severe blow by the Versailles Peace Treaty in 1919, which required Germany to pay huge reparations and to give up considerable territories. Crucially, the republic kept being assigned to the 'disgrace of Versailles'. Until the end of 1923, Germany was also shaken by economic problems, such as the high INFLATION, and political radicalism. The government eventually beat the inflation, and in 1924 a time of relative stability began. With the help of substantial financial assistance – mostly in form of loans – from the United States the economy recovered slowly while the Dawes Plan regulated Germany's reparation payments. Politically it was thanks to Foreign Secretary Stresemann that Germany became a respected member of the League of Nations, and with the Locarno Treaty in 1925 the rehabilitation seemed complete. Germany's cultural life flourished, too, and Berlin became Europe's artistic capital.

The period of relative stability ended with the Wall Street Crash in 1929. The elaborate system of international loans collapsed and so did Germany's economy with an UNEMPLOYMENT rate of 31 per cent in February 1932. Radical parties such as the Communists and the Nazis gained ground, the conservative classes and the industry increasingly favoured dictatorial solutions, and the democratic parties seemed incapable of solving the problems. Support for the Weimar Republic decreased significantly. From 1930 presidential cabinets ruled with the sole backing of the arch-conservative President Hindenburg. They incorporated dictatorial elements although they were still formally based on the Constitution. The presidential cabinets of Brüning (1930–32), Papen (1932) and Schleicher (1932–33) prepared the ground for HITLER's seizure of power. When Hindenburg conferred the power on a nationalist cabinet headed by Hitler on 30 January 1933 the Weimar Republic ceased to exist. (**Anselm Heinrich**)

Further reading

Kaes *et al.* (1994); Kolb (1998); Nicholls (1991); Schulze (1994).

Weiss, Peter 1916 Nowawes–1982 Stockholm. Author. Weiss, the son of a Jewish factory owner emigrated in 1934 to London, Prague and then settled in Sweden. Although he had been writing already during the 1950s, he only became known in Germany during the 1960s. While his early prose attracted some attention, it was his plays which created the most publicity. His *Marat/Sade* (1964) analyses the power structures inherent in political revolutions, contrasting the historic and ideologically fixed figure of the revolutionary Jean Marat with the anarchist tendencies of the Marquis de Sade. The play is broken up into various parts, using Brechtian methodologies. His next play, *Die Ermittlung* (*The Inquiry*), works through the protocols of the 1963–65 court case against some of the guards of the Auschwitz concentration camp. Again, his documentary style does much to highlight the 'banality of evil' (ARENDT). In 1981, the last of the three volumes of his *Ästhetik des Widerstands* (*The Aesthetics of Resistance*) was published, volume one and two having been published in 1975 and 1978, respectively. It is an expansive novel, telling the fictitious/autobiographical story of (aesthetic) resistance against fascism, starting in 1937 and finishing in the late 1970s, with a more or less positive assessment of the protagonist's/author's lifetime struggle. (**Holger Briel**)

Further reading

Falkenstein (1996).

Wenders, Wim Born 1945 Düsseldorf. Film director. Wenders is a leading film director who has worked in Germany and the USA. He contributed to the creation of the 'New German Cinema' and today is highly regarded by critics and fellow filmmakers. Generally speaking, his œuvre offers an original combination of poetic fantasy and social realism, with a frequent disregard for narrative pace or plot development. Among some forty pictures, his most important contributions include *Der Amerikanische Freund* (*The American Friend*, 1977), *Paris, Texas* (1984) and *Der Himmel über Berlin* (*Wings of Desire*, 1987). The latter is perhaps the most famous portrait of Berlin in recent film history. Wenders is a prolific director and perhaps this has led to an uneven quality of work in the 1990s. However, his Cuban music piece, *The Buena Vista Social Club* (1999), was a popular triumph. (**Hugo Frey**)

Further reading

Wenders (1986, 1988 and 1992). These three volumes are an excellent insider's view of the director's life and work.

West German identity   Collective IDENTITY can be explained by the experiences of a nation. West German identity is determined in a different way from the EAST GERMAN IDENTITY; by the political and economic success of the Federal Republic. During the economic boom of the 1950s and 1960s, it only seemed natural that people should want to help their 'poor brothers and sisters in the Soviet zone' and there has therefore always been a clear majority of people with a declared belief in the reunification of Germany. The movement of 68 (see GENERATION OF 1968, 68ERS) was an important identity-forming factor. The intense collective reappraisal of the country's National Socialist past and most importantly, the freedom of the individual and the right to self-realization were heavily stressed and still represent key values today. Emphasis was placed on FEMINISM and emancipation of women. Importance was also assigned to ecology and environmental protection, as can be seen for example through the formation and success of a Green Party (see GRÜNEN) or the protests staged against the nuclear industry. There were no such comparable movements in the GDR – even during the peaceful revolution of 1989–90. The present West German identity is therefore often viewed as a contrast to the East German identity. Unlike that of the East Germans, West German identity has hardly changed during the course of German WIEDERVEREINIGUNG (reunification) and has been spared the shock of modernization as experienced by East Germans. The influx of GASTARBEITER (guest workers) since the 1950s has resulted in calmer dealings with foreigners in the Federal Republic and also greater tolerance within society. In opinion polls, West Germans first of all consider themselves as 'Germans' and not 'West Germans', they stress their identity as 'Europeans' much more than Germans from the East. The development of Europe can also be considered an opportunity for the development of an inner German unity. Germans in the east and west both value, e.g. the desire for security, material prosperity, the high regard they have for MARRIAGE and the family and their support of democracy. (**Hendrik Berth**)

Further reading

Meulemann (1996). Describes the development of East and West German identity and developments after unification. Thomas and Weidenfeld (1999).

West German literature   The literature of the West during the partition of Germany was rich in fruitful conflicts. Immediately after 1945, while right-wing authors continued to sell well, some writers tried a pared-down style (*Kahlschlag*), contrasting with the excesses of Nazi rhetoric and euphemism. Older writers had their comebacks (Benn); younger ones flirted with Existentialism, described their war experiences, or viewed the recent past in philosophical or religious terms. Outside influences were welcome in general: foreign writing unavailable before 1945, Austrian and German-speaking Swiss writers, East German literature.

A jaundiced view of the new Republic and its economic miracle, seen as a cheap distraction from doing penance for the past, was soon apparent (Böll). The novel was the leading genre (Böll, Koeppen, S. Lenz, Arno Schmidt, Grass, Johnson and others) and tackled the Nazi inheritance. Poetry had its phase of apolitical so-called magic realism, seeking transcendent significance in natural phenomena, as well as lamenting the shoah (the holocaust) (Nelly Sachs), but soon turned to gritty political relevance (Enzensberger) and deadpan recreation of reality (Brinkmann). Radio plays flourished just after the war (Eich). The documentary wave of the early 1960s revivified stage drama; Handke staged his committed critiques of the language of affluence. Events of 1968 led Enzensberger and others to conclude that aesthetic writing (*schöne Literatur*) was dead: only committed, operative writing could survive. Authors argued incessantly about moderate or extreme socialism; the political song (Degenhardt) and social drama (Kroetz) flowered briefly. Against this was set the *Neue Innerlichkeit* of the 1970s.

Increasingly the writing of the late Bonn Republic was postmodern, abandoning the overarching ideals of modernism in favour of explorations of difference – eccentric fates (B. Strauss), homosexuality (H. Fichte), women's issues and the like – bringing in theory (Kirchhoff), rejecting causal models (Brigitte Kronauer) or blurring the distinction of literary and non-literary writing (travel writing, essay, diary, autobiography). Slowly a new grouping of migrants' literature, by authors from different cultures but writing in German, crystallized. (**Alfred D. White**)

Further reading

Watanabe-O'Kelly (1997). Full survey (pp. 440–500). Fischer (1986). Authoritative and wide-ranging presentation. Briegleb and Weigel (1987). In the same series as the previous item, this continues the story after 1968.

Wiedervereinigung   The division of Germany, dating back to 1945, was ended on 3 October 1990 with reunification. The economic and political dissatisfaction of large parts of the GDR population had been growing continuously up until 1989. Opposition groups mostly met in churches but were brutally suppressed. The process of Perestroika, initiated by Gorbachev in the USSR, was not adopted by the dictators in the GDR. Although Honecker announced in January 1989 that the Wall would still be standing in 100 years, it came down on 9 November 1989. The fall of the wall was preceded by masses of GDR citizens flooding, via the embassies of the Federal Republic of Germany, into Prague, Warsaw, Budapest, East Berlin and over the Austria–Hungary border in the summer of 1989. During local elections in May, the civil rights campaigners were able to uncover and publicize election fraud committed by the SED. On 4 September 1989, following a prayer for peace in the St Nicolas Church, the first 'Monday demonstration' was held in Leipzig. From this time onwards, demonstrations were held on a regular basis with up to 250 000 participants. The East German dictators celebrated the 40th anniversary of the GDR on 7 October as if nothing had changed whereas citizens wanting change demonstrated in many towns where there were numerous arrests and attacks. Honecker resigned on 18 October as a result of ever increasing pressure and by December all key state and government figures of the GDR had followed him. On 4 November, over one million people demonstrated in Berlin, on 9 November, the Wall came down. The first 'round-table talks' were held on 7 December during which the opposition and SED jointly discussed the future. The first and only ever free elections to the *Volkskammer* (People's Chamber) of the GDR were held on 18 March 1990 and were won by the CDU (40.8 per cent) which was promising rapid reunification. The treaty governing the creation of an economic, currency and social union was signed in May and the DEUTSCHE MARK became the official form of payments in the GDR on 1 July. The victorious powers of the Second World War and the two German states negotiated the conditions of reunification in the Two-plus-Four talks and the reunification treaty was signed on 12 September 1990. Reunification was completed on 3 October 1990 when the GDR joined the geographical area officially subject to the Basic Law of the Federal Republic of Germany. In December the CDU under Helmut KOHL won the subsequent first ever all-German elections. (**Hendrik Berth**)

Further reading

Leiby (1999). Paterson and Spence (2000). Two recently published books illustrating different aspects of German reunification.
www.wiedervereinigung.de (online bibliographical database with more than 30 000 references about all aspects of German reunification – law, education, politics, social issues, etc.)

Wiener Kreis A group of about 30 natural scientists, social scientists, philosophers and mathematicians met regularly in Vienna during the 1920s and 1930s. The manifesto of the Vienna Circle, *Wissenschaftliche Weltauffassung: Der Wiener Kreis* (1929) called for a unified physicalist world-view, i.e. an explanation of nature and human behaviour according to the methods and principles of the natural sciences. At its centre lies the assumption that science and philosophical thought cannot be separated, but that they are dependent on each other. This approach can best be described as 'logical positivism' or 'logical empiricism'. It continued to influence philosophy outside Germany (especially in North America) until the last decades of the twentieth century and is often regarded as the historical starting point of analytical philosophy of science. Its most prominent members were R. Carnap, O. Neurath, M. Schlick and the mathematician K. Gödel, and over the years it attracted some of the most important philosophers of the twentieth century: H. Reichenbach, A. Ayer, E. Nagel, W. Van

Orman Quine, A. Tarski, L. WITTGENSTEIN, J. v. Neumann, and K. Popper. (**Christian J. Emden**)

Further reading

Ayer (1979). Contains several papers which originated in the Vienna Circle and which outline the doctrines of 'logical positivism' and 'logical empiricism'. This volume also highlights the influence of the Vienna Circle on analytical philosophy in Great Britain and North America. Carnap *et al.* (1973). An English translation of the manifesto of the Vienna Circle, which outlines its main theoretical tenets. Originally written for a wider audience and therefore very accessible. Gaier (1992). A very short introduction with many photographs. Includes biographical information and outlines the main philosophical arguments. An ideal starting point for a first orientation, but not detailed enough with regard to the philosophical discussions of the Vienna Circle. Haller (1993). A short and accessible introduction to the philosophy of the Vienna Circle. Well written and informative, this book provides a more serious account of the different philosophical positions which can be found among the members of the Vienna Circle. Stadler (1997). Comprehensive and detailed philosophical account of the Vienna Circle, which also discusses its influence on more contemporary philosophical positions. Difficult to read for beginners, but important for further study.

Wiesenthal, Simon   Born 1908 Buchach, now Ukraine. Architect and activist. During the Red Purge of Jewish professionals at the beginning of the Second World War, Wiesenthal and his family suffered persecution from the hands of Soviet occupation forces. Wiesenthal had to close his business and consequently earned his living as a mechanic in a bedspring factory. In 1941 Lvov came under the control of National Socialist Germany. Simon Wiesenthal and his wife Cyla were forced into a labour camp; later on Wiesenthal was transferred to several concentration camps. He was one of the few to survive and was rescued when US soldiers liberated Mauthausen concentration camp (Austria). Most of his and his wife's relatives had been murdered in the HOLOCAUST. Wiesenthal made a promise to himself never to forget the atrocities committed in this genocide. He has since dedicated his life to tracing war criminals responsible for the 'Final Solution', the official and organized mass killing of Jews.

Simon and Cyla Wiesenthal live in Vienna where much of their energy has been spent on identifying and locating National Socialist persecutors. To this end Wiesenthal established the Jewish Documentation Centre. An international network of friends and sympathizers contributes to the work of the Centre. Despite hate mail, threats and even a bomb attack, Simon Wiesenthal has not lost his determination to bring National Socialist war criminals to court. Simon Wiesenthal has received various international honours. A centre for Holocaust studies, based in Los Angeles and with offices in Israel and France, bears his name. (**Barbara Rassi**)

Further reading

www.wiesenthal.com (informative and well-designed website of the Simon Wiesenthal Center, Los Angeles, offering biographical material, photos and quotes from Simon Wiesenthal.)

Wirtschaftswunder   Due to the unexpectedly high growth experienced by West Germany in the post-war period it became known as the country of the 'economic miracle', or *Wirtschaftswunder*. *The Times* coined this term in 1950 following the first economic upswing after a gloomy outlook in 1945 when the country's economic potential appeared shattered. Yet, by the mid-1950s, output had recovered to pre-war levels and West Germans had achieved a sustained and rapid growth in their real per capita income. The term, *Wirtschaftswunder*, therefore, quickly became synonymous for this success story around the world.

Credit for this success was widely attributed to the introduction of the DEUTSCHE MARK and the lifting of most price controls in 1948. Indeed, by reconstituting coherent incentives, these reforms created conditions under which production could, at first, continue to recover within the bounds of existing supply-side potential and then, increasingly, undergo sustained growth due to ample investment opportunities, unanticipated high productivity growth and falling real labour costs.

Opinions differ, however, concerning the interpretation of West Germany's economic performance. Neo-liberal economists regard the Federal Republic's apparently outstanding early economic performance not as a 'miracle', but as the result of the SOZIALE MARKTWIRTSCHAFT implemented by the then economics minister, Ludwig Erhard. In this view, the retardation of economic growth experienced by West Germany after the first oil price crisis in 1973 as well as rising UNEMPLOYMENT are the consequences of institutional changes that have focused too much on the word 'social' and that have hampered economic activity. In contrast, economic historians regard the early post-war period as exceptional, because the growth process drew mainly on non-utilized resources, technical 'catching up', and policies that were pursued in West Germany that were less INFLATIONary than those pursued abroad. Finally, they argue, West Germany's early economic achievements were not unique. Austria and Italy, for example, also experienced 'miracles'. They, like West Germany, benefited from high levels of growth during the 'Great Boom' from 1950 until 1973 – albeit without having introduced a West German-style 'social market economy'. (**Lothar Funk**)

Further reading

Schulze (1999). An important collection of essays, including excellent surveys of post-war comparative economic history.

Wittgenstein, Ludwig Josef Johann   1889 Vienna–1951 Cambridge. Philosopher and architect. Pre-eminent analytical philosopher of language, logic, psychology and mathematics. Publications: *Tractatus Logico-Philosophicus* (1921), *Philosophical Investigations* (1953). (**Martin Brady**)

Further reading

Von Wright (1990); Vossenkuhl (1995).

Wolf, Christa   Born 1929 Landsberg, Warthe, Germany, now Poland. Novelist and essayist. Began in the manner of 'Socialist Realism' by publishing the *Moskauer*

Novelle (*The Moscow Novella*, 1961). Developed successively her concept of 'subjective authenticity', which includes the author's personal experience, his or her 'dimension'. Wolf was praised highly in Western Germany for her supposedly critical attitude towards the GDR, but the novella *Was bleibt* (*What Remains*, 1990) and her opposition towards REUNIFICATION fed the *Literaturstreit*, a critical debate about if and to what effect East German INTELLECTUALS supported or defied the regime. Main texts: *Der geteilte Himmel* (*Divided Heaven*, 1963), *Nachdenken über Christa T.* (*The Quest for Christa T.*, 1968), *Kindheitsmuster* (*A Model Childhood*, 1976), *Kassandra* (1983). (**Markus Oliver Spitz**)

Further reading

Finney (1999).

Wolf, Konrad 1925 Hechingen–1982 East Berlin. Film-maker. A decorated Lieutenant in the Red Army during the Second World War, Wolf established an international reputation with a series of feature films dealing with the THIRD REICH, including *Stars* (*Sterne*, 1959) which tackled the taboo subject of the persecution of the Jews. The most renowned East German director of his generation, his wide-ranging œuvre encompassed literary adaptations (*The Divided Sky, Der geteilte Himmel,* 1964, based on the novel by Christa WOLF) and popular successes such as *Solo Sunny*, the bittersweet story of an aspiring GDR pop singer. (**Martin Brady**)

Working time   German employees have one of the shortest working years in the world, if one aggregates the 35-hour week, HOLIDAY time and sick leave (with this latter approaching several weeks on average per employee-year). This is a prime influence on unit labour costs, and capital productivity is restrained because of the shorter running times for machinery. The issue of the 35-hour week, as a prime objective of trade union negotiating agendas, arose in 1984, when it became clear to unions that the KOHL government would not practise Keynesian demand-management policies to help counter high UNEMPLOYMENT. Unions argued that a cut of the working week from 40 hours to 35 hours would absorb, mechanically, the 2.25 million unemployed at the time. The IG Metall fought a bitter strike to achieve the principle of working time reduction and won employer agreement for a phased move to 35 hours by 1994. The IG Druck and other unions followed. In MANUFACTURING, the cut in time has been accompanied by changes in shift systems, by Saturday working and by agreements which allow contract and part-time staff to be employed to bridge the gaps in the shift system. Machine-running times have improved significantly and so the hours reduction has partly paid for itself, given that the unions would not countenance any cut in gross pay regardless of the fewer hours worked. Clearly, in service industries and office activities, such a reorganization of time is harder to achieve and costs cannot be so contained. Employees on flexible working systems can work longer than 35 hours weekly and this is then averaged over a longer period. The introduction of hours cuts has been accompanied by a boom in overtime worked. Evidence is meagre, and there is no theoretical underpinning, that the cut has reduced unemployment. (**Chris Flockton**)

Further reading

Owen Smith (1994); Sachverständigenrat zur Begutachtung der gesamtwirtschaftlichen Entwicklung, *Jahresgutachten*, annual.

Youth culture   While youth has always been around, as a phenomenon of mass culture and CONSUMPTION, it has only been thematized in recent times. During the Nazi era, several groupings existed which aimed at collectivizing youths, such as the *Deutsche Jungvolk* or the *Bund Deutscher Mädel*. After the Second World War, largely due to the American influence, youths publicly began to take on a strong separate IDENTITY from their parent generation. Psychologists and sociologists have attempted to explain this fact with German post-war youths growing up without (often literally) a strong father generation. Electronic media, such as cinema, radio and TV helped to shape/create a new uniform image, going beyond national borders. Blue jeans became one of the must-haves of the 1950s and 1960s. During the 1960s revolution (see GENERATION OF 1968, 68ERS), politics became an important element and instrument of protest, manifesting itself in large-scale demonstrations against the Vietnam War and insufficient and outdated university resources. Private life practices were also scrutinized. Commune living, such as in the infamous *Kommune K-1* in Berlin, 'free' love, rock 'n' roll music and drugs became desirables among the young. In the GDR, similar developments could be observed. Especially Ulrich PLENZDORF's *Die Neuen Leiden des Jungen W* (1972), an account of romantic youth rebellion and love under GDR socialism, seemed to express the sentiments of a whole generation. In the West, while the hopes for a revolution remained unfulfilled, in the 1970s the changed lifestyles remained. Furthermore, the voting age had recently been lowered to 18, and at least in communal ELECTIONS, the age of eligibility is likely to become 16 in the near future, giving youths a much greater say in social decisions. The 1980s and 1990s brought a change in focus for youthful living. Political activism had been institutionalized through the Greens (see GRÜNEN), Greenpeace and other organizations and no longer lent itself to rebellious movements; rather, personal fulfilment was more and more sought through conspicuous consumption (*Yuppies*), earning that generation the monikers of *Generation Golf* (according to their preferred automobile), *MTV generation* or just *Fun-Generation*. What could also be observed was a further tribalization of youth culture(s), mostly instigated through musical and FASHION tastes, with punks, hiphoppers, *grufties*, skins, ravers, etc. all sharing part of the (youth) pie. These developments seem to be ongoing. (**Holger Briel**)

Further reading

Baacke (1999). Comprehensive discussion. Farin (2001). Hafeneger and Jansen (2001). Study of youths, rightist skinheads and neo-Nazism. Poell (1996). Roth and Rucht (2000). Zötsch (1999). Study of the role of women in youth culture.

Z

ZDF (*Zweites Deutsches Fernsehen*)   Established in 1963, the ZDF with its head-quarters in Mainz, was conceived by the CDU government to provide a more conservative counterweight to the ARD. Unlike the ARD, which followed the BBC model, the ZDF was allowed a certain amount of ADVERTISING (later on, the ARD would follow suit) and a more entertainment-oriented programming structure. Nevertheless, the ARD and ZDF, both public broadcasting stations and financed through licensing fees, continue to co-operate in many areas, such as jointly securing the rights for major sporting events, making sure that their programming structures are compatible and not overly competitive, etc. (**Holger Briel**)

Further reading

Humphreys (1994). Well-researched and comprehensive account of German media. Kreuzer and Thomson (1993–94). Extensive study of German television.

Zeit, Die   Weekly (Thursday) newspaper founded in Hamburg in 1946 by G. Bucerius, the leading weekly broadsheet with national circulation. Not seeking to imitate the mobility and range of its neighbour *Der Spiegel*, or to compete with the daily press, it prefers in-depth reporting (a special thematic 'Dossier' in each issue), investigative work with an eye to issues rather than personalities, political comment from a liberal viewpoint, a strong cultural component and intelligent entertainment sections. *Zeit* features its writers; loyalty to the paper has been fostered at various times by the work of Marion Gräfin Dönhoff (columnist), Helmut Schmidt (political commentator) – these two now figuring as publishers – Fritz Raddatz (literary editor) and the like. (**Alfred D. White**)

Further reading

www.zeit.de (website with contents of and selected articles from current issue, and archive.)

Zetkin, Clara   1857 Wiederau–1933 Moscow. Politician and campaigner. From 1890 onwards Zetkin (maiden name Eißner) became a leading figure of the Social Democrat women's movement in Germany. Zetkin fought for the right of women to work and equally for the improvement of women's working conditions. She edited the magazine *Die Gleichheit* (*Equality*), voicing the interests of working-class women. She demanded women's suffrage and campaigned against war. After the First World War Zetkin became a member of the German Communist Party. Despite her appeal for resistance against fascism she had to witness the rise of National Socialism in Germany. (**Barbara Rassi**)

LIVERPOOL JOHN MOORES UNIVERSITY
LEARNING & INFORMATION SERVICES

Further reading

Badia (1994). An in-depth biography covering Zetkin's political and private life.

Zweig, Stefan   1881 Vienna–1942 Petropolis, Brazil. Austrian writer (narrative prose, biographies, plays, poetry, essays, translations). In the 1920s and 1930s he was the most widely read and translated German-speaking author. Born into a Jewish upper-class family, he grew up in the culturally fertile atmosphere of turn-of-the-century Vienna. After his studies feature writer for the leading Austrian newspaper, the liberal *Neue Freie Presse*. During the First World War, he served in the Vienna war archives, but turned to pacifism which in conjunction with the idea of a united Europe founded on common cultural values he promoted in a series of lectures throughout Europe. In 1933 his books were burned by the Nazis (together with works by other victims of political or racial persecution). In 1934 Zweig left Salzburg to go into exile in London (he took British nationality in 1940) and then to Petropolis (Brazil) where he and his second wife Lotte committed suicide. A lyric poet at first, he increasingly turned to novella-like prose, particularly dealing with characters in emotionally exceptional situations and dominated by destructive (often erotic) passions.

S. Freud's psychoanalysis and A. Schnitzler's psychological writing influence his works. Among the more successful ones were *Amok. Novellen einer Leidenschaft* (*Amok*, 1922), *Verwirrung der Gefühle* (*The Confusion of Sentiments*, 1927) and *Ungeduld des Herzens* (*Beware of Pity*, 1939). In his extremely successful historical and biographical studies, he illustrates the inner life and driving motives of characters in history, who in defeat are often the truly victorious (*Triumph und Tragik des Erasmus von Rotterdam; Erasmus*, 1934); influential figures in art and science (*Baumeister der Welt; Master Builders*, 1920–28), containing portraits of Dickens, Nietzsche, Tolstoy among others; and the best-selling *Sternstunden der Menschheit* (*The Tide of Fortune: Twelve Historical Miniatures*, 1927) containing essays about junctions considered to be decisive for mankind (e.g., the Battle of Waterloo, Handel's inspiration for the *Messiah*, Scott at the South Pole . . .). Tragically, the apolitical pacifist, bourgeois humanist and cultural mediator Zweig had to witness Europe – which he, in an idealized manner, had described in his autobiography *Die Welt von gestern. Erinnerungen eines Europäers* (*The World of Yesterday: An Autobiography*, 1941) – going to pieces, an impression at least partially responsible for his suicide. (**Stefan Hauser**)

Bibliography

Abelshauser, W. (1983) *Wirtschaftsgeschichte der Bundesrepublik Deutschland, 1945–1980*, Frankfurt: Suhrkamp.

Abrams, L. and Harvey, E. (eds) (1996) *Gender Relations in German History: Power, Agency and Experience from the Sixteenth to the Twentieth Century*, London: UCL Press.

Ackermann, I. (ed.) (1996) *Fremde Augenblicke: Mehrkulturelle Literatur in Deutschland*, Bonn: InterNationes.

Adorno, T.W. (1974) *Noten zur Literatur*, Frankfurt: Suhrkamp.

Adorno, T.W. and Horkheimer, M. (1972) *Dialectic of Enlightenment*, first English translation, New York: Herder & Herder.

Ammon, U. (1995) *Die deutsche Sprache in Deutschland, Österreich und der Schweiz*, Berlin: de Gruyter.

Anderson, J. (1999) *German Unification and the Union of Europe: The Domestic Politics of Integration Policy*, Cambridge and New York: Cambridge University Press.

Ardagh, J. (1991) *Germany and the Germans: After Unification*, new revised edn, London: Penguin.

Arendt, H. (1951) *The Origins of Totalitarianism*, New York: Harcourt, Brace.

Arnold, H-L. (ed.) (1983) *Lion Feuchtwanger* (*Text und Kritik*, vol. 79/80), Munich: Edition text + kritik.

Arnold, H-L. (ed.) (1999) *Peter Handke* (*Text und Kritik*, vol. 24), Munich: Edition text + kritik.

Aust, S. (1998) *Der Baader Meinhof Komplex*, Munich: Goldmann.

Ayer, A.J. (ed.) (1979) *Logical Positivism*, New York: Free Press.

Baacke, D. (1999) *Jugend und Jugendkulturen Darstellung und Deutung*, Weinheim: Juventa.

Bach, S. (2000) *'Die Wahrheit über mich gehört mir': Marlene Dietrich*, Munich: Econ.

Bachmann, I. (1995) *The Thirtieth Year*, New York: Holmes & Meier.

Badia, G. (1994) *Clara Zetkin*, Berlin: Dietz Verlag.

Bakhtin, M. (1984) *Rabelais and his World*, Bloomington: Indiana University Press.

Balzer, B. (1997) *Das literarische Werk Heinrich Bölls: Einführung und Kommentare* (dtv, 30650), Munich: Deutscher Taschenbuch Verlag.

Barbour, S. and Stevenson, P. (1990) *Variation in German*, Cambridge: Cambridge University Press.

Baring, A. (1972) *Uprising in East Germany: June 17, 1953*, trans. Gerald Onn, Ithaca, NY and London: Cornell University Press.

Bark, D.L. and Grees, D.R. (1993) *A History of West Germany:* vol. 1: *From Shadow to Substance, 1945–1963;* vol. 2: *Democracy and its Discontents, 1963–1988*, 2nd edn, Oxford: Blackwell.

Beinssen-Hesse, S. and Rigby, K. (1996) *Out of the Shadows: Contemporary German Feminism*. Carlton, Victoria: Melbourne University Press.

Benjamin, W. (1996ff.) *Selected Writings*, ed. M. Bullock and M.W. Jennings, Cambridge, MA: Belknap Press.

Benjamin, W. (1998) *The Origin of the German Tragic Drama*, trans. J. Osborne, London: Verso.

Benjamin, W. (1999) *The Arcades Project*, trans. H. Eiland and K. McLaughlin, Cambridge, MA: Belknap Press.

Berdahl, D. (1999) *Where the World Ended: Re-unification and Identity in the German Borderland*, Berkeley, CA: University of California Press.

Berger, F. (1988) *Thyssen gegen Walraff*, Göttingen: Vandenhoek und Ruprecht.

Berrong, R. (1986) *Rabelais and Bakhtin: Popular Culture in Gargantua and Pantagruel*, Lincoln: University of Nebraska Press.

Berth, H. and Brähler, E. (eds) (1999) *Deutsch-deutsche Vergleiche: Psychologische Untersuchungen 10 Jahre nach dem Mauerfall*, Berlin: Verlag für Wissenschaft und Forschung.

Bessel, R. (1993) *Germany after the First World War*, Oxford: Oxford University Press.

Beyer, F. (2001) *Wenn der Wind sich dreht. Meine Filme, mein Leben*, Munich: Econ.

Biermann, W. and Pleitgen, F. (2001) *Die Ausbürgerung. Anfang vom Ende der DDR*, Berlin: Ullstein Quadriga.

Bisovsky, G. and Stifter, C. (eds) (1996) *Wissen für alle*, Vienna: Edition Volkshochschule.

Blubacher, T. (1999) *Gustaf Gründgens*, Berlin: Spiess.

Böhnke, P. (1999) *Lebensstandard und Armut im vereinten Deutschland*, Berlin: Wissenschaftszentrum Berlin.

Borgelt, H. (1993) *Die UFA – ein Traum: hundert Jahre deutscher Film; Ereignisse und Erlebnisse*, Berlin: Edition q.

Borries, M. (1995) 'Deutschsprachige "Ausländerliteratur": Theoretische Überlegungen und unterrichtspraktische Vorschläge', *Die Unterrichtspraxis – Teaching German*, vol. 28, no. 1, pp. 19–28.

Bracher, K.D. (1970) *The German Dictatorship: The Origins, Structure, and Effects of National Socialism*, New York: Praeger.

Brady, M. and Hughes, H. (1998) 'German cinema', in *The Cambridge Companion to Modern German Culture*, Cambridge: Cambridge University Press, pp. 302–21.

Brandt, W. (1997) *Erinnerungen*, Berlin: Ullstein.

Braunthal, G. (1996) *Parties and Politics in Modern Germany*, Boulder, CO: Westview Press.

Briegleb, K. and Weigel, S. (eds) (1987) *Gegenwartsliteratur*, Munich: Hanser.

Briel, H. (1991) *Adorno und Derrida, oder wo liegt das Ende der Moderne?*, Frankfurt: Lang.

Briel, H. (1998) 'The media of mass communication: the press, radio and television', in Kolinsky, E. and Van der Will, W. (eds) *Modern German Culture*, Cambridge: Cambridge University Press, pp. 322–37.

Briner, A. *et al.* (1988) *Paul Hindemith*, Mainz: Schott.

Brockmann, S. (1999) *Literature and German Reunification*, Cambridge: Cambridge University Press.

Bronnen, B. (1998) *Karl Valentin und Liesl Karlstadt: Blödsinnkönig und Blödsinnkönigin*, Reinbek: Rowohlt.

Broszat, M. (1981) *The Hitler State: The Foundation and Development of the Internal Structure of the Third Reich*, London: Longman.

Buck-Morss, S. (1991) *The Dialectics of Seeing: Walter Benjamin and the Arcades Project*, Cambridge, MA: MIT Press.

Bund Deutscher Industrie publications.

Bundesministerium für Arbeit und Sozialordnung (eds) (n.d.) *Lebenslagen in Deutschland: der erste Armuts- und Reichstumsbericht der Bundesregierung*, Berlin.

Bundesministerium für Familie, Senioren, Frauen und Jugend (1998) *Die Familie im Spiegel der amtlichen Statistik*, 4th edn, Bonn.

Bundesministerium für Umwelt, *Umweltbericht*, annual.

Bundesministerium für Verbraucherschutz, Landwirtschaft, Ernährung und Forsten, *Grüner Bericht*, biennial.

Bürger, P. (1984) *Theory of the Avant-Garde*, Minneapolis: University of Minnesota Press.

Burke, P. (1978) *Popular Culture in Early Modern Europe*, New York: New York University Press.

Burleigh, M. (2000) *The Third Reich: A New History*, London: Macmillan.

Butler, M. (ed.) (1994) *The Narrative Fiction of Heinrich Böll*, Cambridge: Cambridge University Press.

Butz, P. (1993) *RAF: Terrorismus in Deutschland*, Munich: Knaur.

Byg, B. (1995) *Landscapes of Resistance*, Berkeley, CA: University of California Press.

Canovan, M. (1992) *Hannah Arendt: A Reinterpretation of Her Political Thought*, Cambridge: Cambridge University Press.

Carnap, C., Hahn, H. and Neurath, O. (1973) 'The Scientific Conception of the World: The Vienna Circle', in Neurath, M. and Cohen, R.S. (eds) *Empiricism and Sociology*, Dordrecht and Boston: Reidel, pp. 299–318.

Carr, J. (1985) *Helmut Schmidt: Helmsman of Germany*, London: Weidenfeld & Nicolson.

Carter, P. (1999) *Mies van der Rohe at Work*, London: Phaidon.

Celan, P. (1995) *Poems of Paul Celan*, trans. Michael Hamburger, London: Anvil Press Poetry.

Celan, P. (1996) *Selected Poems*, London: Penguin.

Celan, P. (1999) *Collected Prose*, trans. Rosemarie Waldrop, Manchester: Carcanet Press.

Childs, D. and Popplewell, R. (1996) *The Stasi: The East German Intelligence and Security Service*, Basingstoke: Macmillan.

Clemens, C. and Paterson, W.E. (eds) (1998) *The Kohl Chancellorship*, London and Portland, OR: F. Cass.

Clyne, M. (1995) *The German Language in a Changing Europe*, Cambridge: Cambridge University Press.

Cofalla, S. (ed.) (1997) *Hans Werner Richter: Briefe*, Munich and Vienna: Hanser.

Cohn-Bendit, D. and Schmid, T. (1992) *Heimat Babylon: Das Wagnis der mulikulturellen Demokratie*, Hamburg: Hoffmann und Campe.

Conradt, David P. *et al.* (eds) (2000) *Power Shift in Germany: The 1998 Election and the End of the Kohl Era*, New York and Oxford: Berghahn.

Cook, D. (1996) *The Culture Industry Revisited: Theodor W. Adorno on Mass Culture*, Lanham, MD: Rowman & Littlefield.

Cook, P. and Bernink, M. (eds) (1999) *The Cinema Book*, London: BFI Publishing.

Cope, J. (1996) *A Krautrocksampler: One Head's Guide to the Great Kosmische Musik – 1968 Onwards*, Calne: Head Heritage.

Crew, D.F. (ed.) (1994) *Nazism and German Society 1933–1945*, London and New York: Routledge.

Cronin, P. (2002) *Herzog on Herzog*, London: Faber and Faber.

DAAD (ed.) (2000a) *The German Academic Exchange Service (DAAD) 1925–2000: Mission, Timeline, Jubilee*, Bonn: LPG.

DAAD (ed.) (2000b) *Living and Studying in Germany: Hints and Information for Foreign Students*, Nürnberg: BW Bildung und Wissen.

DAAD (ed.) (2001–2) *Studies and Research in Germany: Scholarships and Funding for Foreign Students, Graduates and Academics*, Bonn: Köllen Druck.

Dahlhaus, C. and Eggebrecht, H.H. (eds) (1995) *Brockhaus-Riemann Musiklexikon*, Mainz: Piper-Schott.

Dalton, R.J. (1993) *The New German Votes: Unification and the Creation of the New Party System*, Oxford: Berg.

Damus, M. (1995) *Kunst in der BRD 1945–1990*, Reinbek: Rowohlt.

DeGroot, G.J. (1998) *Student Protest: The Sixties and After*, London and New York: Longman.

Dennis, M. (2000) *The Rise and Fall of the German Democratic Republic, 1945–1990*, Harlow: Pearson Education.

Deutsche Bundesbank, *Monatsbericht*, monthly.

Deutsche Bundesbank (ed.) (1998) *50 Jahre Deutsche Mark*, Munich: Verlag C.H. Beck.

Deutscher Industrie- und Handelstag publications.

Dirke, S. von (1997) *All Power to the Imagination! The West German Counter Culture from the Student Movement to the Greens*, Lincoln: University of Nebraska Press.

DIW-Wochenbericht.

Domarus, M. (1990) *Hitler: Speeches and Proclamations 1932–1945: The Chronicle of a Dictatorship*, 4 vols, trans. M.F. Gilbert, London: Tauris.

Eisner, L. (2002) *Fritz Lang*, Munich: Belleville.

Elsaesser, T. (1989) *New German Cinema*, New Brunswick, NJ: Rutgers University Press.

Elsaesser, T. (1996) *Fassbinder's Germany*, Amsterdam: Amsterdam University Press.

Emma (Jan.–Feb. 1997), special edition: '20 Jahre *Emma*'.

Emmerich, W. (1996) *Kleine Literaturgeschichte der DDR: Erweiterte Neuausgabe*, Leipzig: Gustav Kiepenheuer.

Emmerich, W. (2001) *Paul Celan*, Reinbek: Rowohlt.

Enzensberger, H.M. (1992) 'The great migration', in *Krauts!* (*Granta 42*, winter), Harmondsworth: Penguin.

Enzensberger, H.M. (1997) *Zig Zag: The Politics of Culture and Vice Versa*, New York: New Press.

Ermarth, M. (1993) *America and the Shaping of German Society, 1945–1955*, Providence: Berg.

Evans, M. and Lunn, K. (1997) *War and Memory in the Twentieth Century*, Oxford and New York: Berg.

Falkenstein, H. (1996) *Peter Weiss*, Berlin: Morgenbuch.

Farin, K. (2001) *generation-kick.de: Jugendsubkultur Heute*, Munich: Beck.

Faulstich, W. (1999) *Grundwissen Medien*, Munich: Fink.

Fest, J. (1970) *The Face of the Third Reich*, trans. M. Bullock, London: Penguin.

Fest, J. (1974) *Hitler*, trans. R. and C. Winston, London: Weidenfeld & Nicolson.

Fetz, G.A. (1997) *Martin Walser*, Stuttgart: Metzler.

Fiddler, A. (1994) *An Introduction to Elfriede Jelinek*, Oxford: Providence.

Figal, G. (1999) *Martin Heidegger zur Einführung*, 3rd edn, Hamburg: Junius.

Filmmuseum Potsdam (ed.) (1994) *Das zweite Leben der Filmstadt Babelsberg: DEFA-Spielfilme 1946–1992*, Berlin: Henschel.

Finney, G. (1999) *Christa Wolf*, New York: Twayne Publishers.

Fischer, L. (ed.) (1986) *Literatur in der Bundesrepublik Deutschland bis 1967*, Munich: Hanser.

Flug, M. (1992) *Treuhand-Poker: Die Mechanismen des Ausverkaufs*, Berlin: Ch. Links Verlag.

Frank, M. (2001) *Walter Ulbricht: Eine deutsche Biografie*, Berlin: Siedler.

Fricke, K.W. (1991) *MfS Intern. Macht, Strukturen, Auflösung der DDR Statssicherheit*, Cologne: Verlag Wissenschaft und Politik.

Fröhlich, E. (ed.) (1987) *Die Tagebücher von Joseph Goebbels: Sämtliche Fragmente, Teil 1: Aufzeichnungen 1924–1941*, München: Saur.

Fröhlich, E. (ed.) (1993–96) *Die Tagebücher von Joseph Goebbels: Teil 2: Diktate 1941–1945*, München: Saur.

Fuchs, P. (1997) *Kölner Karneval: Seine Bräuche, Seine Akteure, Seine Geschichte*, Cologne: Greven.

Fulbrook, M. (1999) *German National Identity After the Holocaust*, Cambridge: Polity Press.

Gaier, M. (1992) *Der Wiener Kreis mit Selbstzeugnissen und Bilddokumenten*, Reinbek: Rowohlt.

Gall, L. and Pohl, M. (eds) (1999) *Die Eisenbahn in Deutschland: Von den Anfängen bis zur Gegenwart*, Munich: C.H. Beck.

Gallup, S. (1987) *A History of the Salzburg Festival*, Topsfield, MA: Salem House.

Gaßner, H. (1994) *Elan Vital oder Das Auge des Eros: Kandinsky, Klee, Arp, Miro, Calder*, Wabern: Benteli.

Geary, D. (1993) *Hitler and Nazism*, London: Routledge.

Geary, D. (2000) *Hitler and Nazism*, 2nd edn, London: Routledge.

Gerhardt, M. (ed.) (1990) *Irmtraud Morgner: Texte, Daten, Bilder*, Darmstadt: Luchterhand.

Giles, S. and Livings, R. (eds) (1998) *Bertolt Brecht: Centenary Essays*, Amsterdam and Atlanta, GA: Rodopi.

Gilliam, B. (1994) *Music and Performance during the Weimar Republic*, Cambridge: Cambridge University Press.

Gillis, J.R. (ed.) (1994) *Commemorations: The Politics of National Identity*, Princeton, NJ: Princeton University Press.

Golub, J.L. (1991) *German Attitudes Toward Jews: What Recent Survey Data Reveal*, New York: The American Jewish Committee.

Golub, J.L. (1994) *Current German Attitudes Toward Jews and Other Minorities*, New York: The American Jewish Committee.

Gomringer, E. (ed.) (1972) *konkrete poesie: deutschsprachige autoren: Anthologie*, Stuttgart: Reclam.

Grambow, J. (1997) *Uwe Johnson*, Reinbek: Rowohlt.

Gregor, N. (ed.) (2000) *Nazism*, Oxford: Oxford University Press.

Grünbein, D., Lau, J., Schulze, I. and Tawada, Y. (eds) (2001) *Murnau – Manila – Minsk: 50 Jahre Goethe-Institut*, Munich: Beck.

Guignon, C. (ed.) (1993) *The Cambridge Companion to Heidegger*, Cambridge: Cambridge University Press.

Gunning, T. (2000) *The Films of Fritz Lang: Allegories of Vision and Modernity*, London: BFI Publishing.

Gysi, G. and Falkner, T. (eds) (1990) *Sturm aufs große Haus: Der Untergang der SED*, Berlin: Edition Fischerinsel.

Hafeneger, B. and Jansen, M.M. (2001) *Rechte Cliquen: Alltag einer neuen Jugendkultur*, Weinheim: Juventa.

Haffner, S. (1973) *Failure of a Revolution: Germany 1918/19*, trans. G. Rapp, London: Deutsch.

Hall, S. and du Gay, P. (eds) (1996) *Questions of Cultural Identity*, London: Sage.

Haller, R. (1993) *Neopositivismus: Eine historische Einführung in die Philosophie des Wiener Kreises*, Darmstadt: Wissenschaftliche Buchgesellschaft.

Hamelmann, B. (1989) *Helau und Heil Hitler: Alltagsgeschichte der Fasnacht 1919–1939 am Beispiel der Stadt Freiburg*, Eggingen: Edition Isele.

Hanesch, W. (2000) *Armut und Ungleichheit in Deutschland*, Reinbek: Rowohlt.

Hansen, W. (1999) *Das große Hausbuch der Volkslieder*, Munich: Orbis.

Hardach, G. (1987) 'The Marshall Plan in Germany, 1948–1952', *Journal of European Economic History*, 16, pp. 433–85.

Harpprecht, K. (1979) *East German Rising, Seventeenth June 1953*, Freiburg im Breisgau: Hyperion.

Haupt, J. (1980) *Heinrich Mann (Realien zur Literatur*, Sammlung Metzler, Bd. 189), Stuttgart: Metzler.

Hayman, R. (1983) *Brecht: A Biography*, New York: Oxford University Press.

Heidegger, M. (1962) *Being and Time*, trans. J. Macquarrie and E. Robinson, New York: Harper.

Heidegger, M. (1993) *Basic Writings: From 'Being and Time' (1927) to 'The Task of Thinking' (1964)*, ed. D.F. Krell, revised and expanded edn, London: Routledge.

Heimann, T. (1994), *DEFA, Künstler und SED-Kulturpolitik: zum Verhältnis von Kulturpolitik und Filmproduktion in der SBZ/DDR 1945 bis 1959*, Berlin: Vistas.

Heine, N. (1998) *Deutscher Weinführer*, Stuttgart: Ulmer.

Herbert, U. (2001) *Geschichte der Ausländerpolitik in Deutschland: Saisonarbeiter, Zwangsarbeiter, Gastarbeiter, Flüchtlinge*, Munich: Beck.

Herbst, A., Stephan, G.-R. and Winkler, J. (eds) (1997) *Die SED: Geschichte, Organisation, Politik: Ein Handbuch*, Berlin: Dietz.

Heydebrand, R. (ed.) (1998) *Kanon, Macht, Kultur: theoretische, historische und soziale Aspekte*, Stuttgart: Metzler.

Hilberg, R. (1985) *The Destruction of the European Jews*, New York: Holmes & Meier Publishing.

Hohendahl, P.U. (1995) *Prismatic Thought: Theodor W. Adorno*, Lincoln: University of Nebraska Press.

Hombach, B. (2000) *The Politics of the New Centre*, Cambridge and Malden, MA: Polity Press.

Honnef, K. (1990) *Kunst der Gegenwart*, Cologne: Taschen.

Horbelt, R. and Spindler, S. (2000) *Die deutsche Küche im 20. Jahrhundert*, Frankfurt: Eichborn.

Humphreys, P.J. (1994) *Media and Media Policy in Germany*, Oxford: Berg.

Jacobsen, W., Kaes, A. and Prinzler, H.H. (eds) (1993) *Geschichte des deutschen Films*, Stuttgart: Metzler.

Jahn, K-H. *et al.* (1994) 'Industrieliteratur in der Unterrichtspraxis', in *Der Deutschunterricht*, vol. 46, no. 3, pp. 71–80.

Jameson, F. (1990) *Late Marxism: Adorno, or the Persistence of the Dialectic*, New York: Verso.

Jandl, E. (1998) *Dingfest / Thingsure*, trans. Michael Hamburger, Dublin: Dedalus.

Jansen, P-E. (1999) *Zwischen Hoffnung und Notwendigkeit: Texte zu Herbert Marcuse*, Frankfurt: Neue Kritik.

Janz, M. (1995) *Elfriede Jelinek*, Stuttgart: Metzler.

Jarausch, K. and Siegrist, H. (eds) (1997) *Amerikanisierung und Sowjetisierung in Deutschland, 1945–1970*, Frankfurt: Campus.

Jarvis, S. (1998) *Adorno: A Critical Introduction*, London: Routledge.

Jay, M. (1984) *Adorno*, Cambridge, MA: Harvard University Press.

Jay, M. (1996) *The Dialectical Imagination*, new edn, Berkeley, CA: University of California Press.

Jencks, C. (ed.) (1992) *The Post-Modern Reader*, Academy: London.

Kaes, A., Jay, M. and Dimendberg, E. (eds) (1994) *The Weimar Sourcebook*, Berkeley, CA: University of California Press.

Kahn, C. (2000) *Ten Years of German Unification: One State, Two Peoples*, Westwood: Prager.

Kalb, J. (1998) *The Theatre of Heiner Müller*, Cambridge: Cambridge University Press.

Kammler, C. (1997) 'Kann uns nur noch ein Kanon retten?', *Der Deutschunterricht*, vol. 49, no. 4, pp. 97–9.

Kämper-Van den Boogaart, M. (1992) *Ästhetik des Scheiterns*, Stuttgart: Metzler.

Kappler, A. and Reichart, S. (eds) (1996) *Facts about Germany*, Frankfurt: Societäts-Verlag.

Kellner, J., Kurth, U. and Lippert, W. (eds) (1995) *1945 bis 1995: 50 Jahre Werbung in Deutschland*, Ingelheim am Rhein: Westermann Kommunikation.

Kershaw, I. (1999) *Hitler 1889–1936: Hubris*, London: Penguin.

Kershaw, I. (2000a) *Hitler 1936–1945: Nemesis*, London: Penguin.

Kershaw, I. (2000b) *The Nazi Dictatorship: Problems and Perspectives of Interpretation*, London: Arnold.

Kirchner, E.J. and Sperling, J. (eds) (1992) *The Federal Republic of Germany and NATO: 40 Years After*, New York: St Martin's Press.

KLG, Kritisches Lexikon der deutschsprachigen Gegenwartsliteratur, ed. Arnold, Heinz Ludwig, Munich: Edition text + kritik (loose leaves).

Kluge, M. (ed.) (1974ff.) *Hauptwerke der deutschen Literatur*, Munich: Kindler.

Koch, K. (1989) *West Germany Today*, London: Routledge.

Koch, P. (1989) *Willy Brandt: Eine politische Biographie*, Berlin: Ullstein.

Koepke, W. (1988) 'Max Frisch', in Elfe, Wolfgang D. and Hardin, James (eds) *Dictionary of Literary Biography*, vol. 69, Detroit: Gale, pp. 91–103.

Köhler, H. (1994) *Adenauer: eine politische Biographie*, Frankfurt: Propyläen.

Kolb, E. (1998) *The Weimar Republic*, trans. P.S. Falla, London: Routledge.

Kolinsky, E. (1995) *Women in 20th century Germany: A Reader*, Manchester: Manchester University Press.

Kolinsky, E. (ed.) (1996) *Turkish Culture in German Culture Today*, Oxford: Berghahn.

Kolinsky, E. (ed.) (1998) *Social Transformation and the Family in Post-Communist Germany*, Basingstoke: Macmillan.

König, W. (2000) *Geschichte der Konsumgesellschaft*, Stuttgart: Steiner.

Koopmann, H. (ed.) (1990) *Thomas-Mann-Handbuch*, Stuttgart: Kröner.

Krämer, M. (1996) *Der Volksaufstand vom 17. Juni 1953 und sein politisches Echo in der Bundesrepublik Deutschland*, Bochum: Brockmeyer.

Kraushaar, W. (2000) *1968 als Mythos, Chiffre und Zäsur*, Hamburg: Hamburger Edition.

Krawehl, E. (ed.) (1982) *Porträt einer Klasse: Arno Schmidt zum Gedenken*, Frankfurt: Fischer.

Krekow, S. *et al.* (1999) *HipHop Lexikon*, Berlin: Schwarzkopf.

Kreuzer, H. and Thomson, C.W. (eds) (1993–94) *Geschichte des Fernsehens in der Bundesrepublik Deutschland*, 5 vols, Munich: Fink.

Kuhnhardt, L. (1994) 'Multi-German Germany', *Daedalus,* vol. 123, no. 1, pp. 193–209.

Kulturbehörde Hamburg, Referat für Stadtteilkultur (1991) *Hauptsache Kultur: Bundesweiter Ratschlag zur Sozio- und Stadtteilkultur*, Hamburg: Döllig und Galitz.

Lau, K. (1996) 'The treatment of the German question in the Conference of the Länder Ministers for Culture' ('Die Behandlung der deutschen Frage in der Kultusministerkonferenz der Länder'), *Deutschland Archiv*, vol. 29, no. 5, pp. 766–9.

Lawson, R.H. (1991) *Understanding Elias Canetti*, Columbia: University of South Carolina Press.

Lees, C. (2000) *The Red-Green Coalition in Germany*, Manchester: Manchester University Press.

Leiby, R.A. (1999) *The Unification of Germany, 1989–1990*, Westport, CT: Greenwood.

Leisner, B. (2000) *'Ich würde es genauso wieder machen': Sophie Scholl*, Munich: Econ TB Verlag.

Lenning, W. (1962) *Gottfried Benn in Selbstzeugnissen und Bilddolkumentationen*, Reinbek: Rowohlt.

Lettau, R. (ed.) (1967) *Die Gruppe 47: Bericht, Kritik, Polemik: Ein Handbuch*, Neuwied and Berlin: Luchterhand.

Lindow, W. *et al.* (1998) *Niederdeutsche Grammatik*, Leer: Schuster.

Loschek, I. (1995) *Mode im 20. Jahrhundert: Eine Kulturgeschichte unserer Zeit*, Munich: Stiebner.

Lüdtke, A., Marßolek, I. and Saldern, A. (eds) (1996) *Amerikanisierung: Traum und Alptraum im Deutschland des 20. Jahrhunderts*, Stuttgart: Franz Steiner Verlag; Hamburg: Hamburger Edition HIS.

Lützeler, P-M. (1987) *Hermann Broch: Das dichterische Werk*, Tübingen: Niemeyer.

Martynkewicz, W. (1997) *Arno Schmidt*, 3rd edn, Reinbek: Rowohlt.

Mattson, M. (1996) *Franz Xaver Kroetz: The Construction of a Political Aesthetic*, Oxford: Berg.

McAdams, A.J. (1993) *Germany Divided: From the Wall to Reunification*, Princeton, NJ: Princeton University Press.

McCole, J. (1993) *Walter Benjamin and the Antinomies of Tradition*, Ithaca, NY: Cornell University Press.

Mestrup, H. (2000) *Die SED*, Rudolstadt: Hain.

Meulemann, H. (1996) *Werte und Wertewandel: Zur Identität einer geteilten und wiedervereinten Nation*, Weinheim: Juventa.

Meyers Grosses Universal-Lexikon (1981–86) Mannheim: Bibliographisches Institut.

Mileck, J. (2002) *Hermann Hesse: Dichter, Sucher, Bekenner*, Frankfurt: Suhrkamp.

Mitter, A. and Wolle, S. (1993) *Untergang auf Raten: Unbekannte Kapitel der DDR-Geschichte*, Munich: Bertelsmann.

Moos, D. *et al.* (1997) *Kulturelles Leben in der Bundesrepublik Deutschland*, Bonn: InterNationes.

Moreau, P. (1998) *Die PDS: Profil einer antidemokratischen Partei*, Grünwald: Atwerb.

Moser, D-R. *et al.* (eds) (1993) *Neues Handbuch der deutschsprachigen Gegenwartsliteratur seit 1945*, Munich: dtv.

Müller, J-W. (2000) *Another Country: German Intellectuals, Unification, and National Identity*, New Haven, CT and London: Yale University Press.

Müller-Enbergs, H., Wielgohs, J. and Hoffmann, D. (eds) (2000) *Wer war Wer in der DDR?* Berlin: Christoph Links Verlag.

Münz, R. *et al.* (1999) *Zuwanderung nach Deutschland Strukturen, Wirkungen, Perspektiven*, Frankfurt: Campus.

Murphy, R. (1999) *Theorizing the Avant-Garde: Modernism, Expressionism, and the Problem of Postmodernity*, Cambridge: Cambridge University Press.

Musil, R. (2001) *The Confusions of Young Törless*, London: Penguin.

Naumann, U. (2001) *'Ruhe git es nicht, bis zum Schluss': Klaus Mann*, Reinbek: Rowohlt.

Nicholls, A.J. (1991) *Weimar and the Rise of Hitler*, 3rd edn, London: Macmillan.

Nicholls, A.J. (1994) *Freedom With Responsibility: The Social Market Economy in Germany 1918–1963*, Oxford: Oxford University Press.

Nicholls, A.J. (1997) *The Bonn Republic: West German Democracy, 1945–1990*, London: Longman.

Niehoff, R. (2001) *Hans Henny Jahnn: Die Kunst der Überschreitung*, Munich: Seitz.

Niketta, R. and Volke, E. (1993) *Rock und Pop in Deutschland*, Essen: Klartext.

Noakes, J. and Pridham, G. (eds) (1983–98) *Nazism 1919–1945: A Documentary Reader*, 4 vols, Exeter: University of Exeter Press.

Nolan, M. (1994) *Visions of Modernity: American Business and the Modernization of Germany*, Oxford: Oxford University Press.

Novick, P. (2000) *The Holocaust in American Life*, Boston: Houghton Mifflin.

O'Conner, B. (ed.) (2000) *The Adorno Reader*, London: Blackwell.

OECD, *Germany*, annual.

Olszewska Heberle, M. (1996) *German Cooking*, New York: Berkeley Publishing Group.

Overy, R.J. (1995) *Why the Allies Won*, London: Jonathan Cape.

Owen Smith, E. (1994) *The German Economy*, London: Routledge.

Parker, R.A.C. (1989) *Struggle for Survival: The History of the Second World War*, Oxford: Oxford University Press.

Parkes, S. and White, J.J. (1999) *The Gruppe 47 Fifty Years on: A Re-appraisal of its Literary and Political Significance*, Amsterdam: Rodopi.

Paterson, W. and Spence, D. (eds) (2000) *German Unification*, Berlin: Blackwell.

Patterson, M. (1996) *German Theatre: A Bibliography from the Beginning to 1995*, New York: G.K. Hall.

Pelster, T. (1999) *Günter Grass*, Stuttgart: Reclam.

Pezold, K. *et al.* (1991) *Geschichte der deutschsprachigen Schweizer Literatur im 20. Jahrhundert*, Berlin: Volk und Wissen.

Pflaum, G. and Prinzler, H.H. (1993) *Cinema in the Federal Republic of Germany: The New German Film – Origins and Present Situation; With a Section on GDR Cinema; Handbook*, Bonn: InterNationes.

Plard, H. (1992) 'Ernst Jünger', in H.L. Arnold (ed.) *KLG, Kritisches Lexikon der deutschsprachigen Gegenwartsliteratur,* Munich: Edition text + kritik.

Poell, K. (1996) *Wilde Zeit: Von Teddyboys zu Technokids*, Mühlheim: Verlag an der Ruhr.

Poiger, U.G. (2000) *Jazz, Rock and Rebels: Cold War Politics and American Culture in a Divided Germany*, Berkeley, CA: University of California Press.

Preece, J. (2001) *The Life and Work of Günter Grass: Literature, History, Politics*, Basingstoke: Palgrave.

Pritchard, J. (1972) *Reichstag Fire: Ashes of Democracy*, New York: Ballantine Books.

Promies, W. (1986) '"Arbeiterdichtung" – Literatur der Arbeitswelt', in Fischer, Ludwig (ed.) *Literatur in der Bundesrepublik Deutschland bis 1967* (Hansers Sozialgeschichte der deutschen Literatur, 10), Munich: Hanser, pp. 403–19.

Puknus, H. (2002) *Rolf Hochhuth*, Reinbek: Rowohlt.

Raddatz, F. (1994) 'In mir zwei Welten', *Die Zeit*, 24 June, pp. 45–6.

Radevagen, T.T. (1993) 'Fernsehen: Ein Zeitalter wird besdichtigt oder Das Leben als Film im Kino- und Fernsehepos *Die zweite Heimat* von Edgar Reitz', *Film und Fernsehen*, vol. 3, pp. 34–41.

Raithel, T. and Strenge, I. (2000) 'Die Reichstagsbrandverordnung: Grundlegung der Diktatur mit den Instrumenten des Weimarer Ausnahmezustandes', *Vierteljahreshefte für Zeitgeschichte*, vol. 48, pp. 413–60.

Reed, J.A. (1987) *Germany and NATO*, Washington, DC: National Defense University Press.

Reed, T.J. (1996) *Thomas Mann: The Uses of Tradition*, Oxford: Clarendon Press.

Reichel, P. (1999) *Politik mit der Erinnerung: Gedächtnisorte im Streit um die national-sozialistische Vergangenheit*, Frankfurt: Fischer.

Bibliography

Reid, J.H. (1990) *Writing without Taboos: The New East German Literature*, New York: Berg.

Rogoff, I. (1991) *The Divided Heritage: Themes and Problems in German Modernism*, Cambridge: Cambridge University Press.

Rose, G. (1978) *The Melancholy Science: An Introduction to the Thought of Theodor W. Adorno*, New York: Columbia University Press.

Roth, R. and Rucht, D. (2000) *Jugendkulturen, Politik und Protest: Vom Widerstand zum Kommerz?* Leverkusen: Leske & Budrich.

Sachverständigenrat zur Begutachtung der gesamtwirtschaftlichen Entwicklung, *Jahresgutachten*, annual.

Sartre, J-P. (1948) *Qu'est-ce que la littérature?*, Paris: Gallimard.

Schäfer, H. (1998) *Telecommunications Law*, bilingual edition (German/English), with introduction, Cologne: Verlag Kommunikationsforum GmbH.

Scharf, T. (1994) *The German Greens: Challenging the Consensus*, Oxford: Berg.

Schlösser, H. (1992) 'Subjektivität und Autobiographie', in Briegleb, K. and Weigel, S. (eds) *Gegenwartsliteratur seit 1968* (Hansers Sozialgeschichte der deutschen Literatur, 12), Munich: Hanser, pp. 404–23.

Schmädecke, J. and Bahar, J. (1999) 'Der Reichstagsbrand in neuem Licht', *Historische Zeitschrift*, vol. 269, pp. 603–51.

Schmalz-Jacobsen, C. and Hansen, G. (eds) (1995) *Ethnische Minderheiten in der Bundesrepublik Deutschland*, Munich: Beck.

Schröter, K. (1978) *Alfred Döblin: Mit Selbstzeugnissen und Bilddokumenten*, Reinbek: Rowohlt.

Schulze, H. (1994) *Weimar: Deutschland 1917–1933*, Berlin: Siedler.

Schulze, M-S. (ed.) (1999) *Western Europe: Economic and Social Change since 1945*, London and New York: Longman.

Schwarz, H-P. (1995–97) *Konrad Adenauer: A German Politician and Statesman*, 2 vols, Providence, RI: Berghahn.

Seferens, H. (1998) *'Leute von übermorgen und von vorgestern': Ernst Jüngers Ikonographie der Gegenaufklärung und die Rechte nach 1945*, Bodenheim: Philo.

Seghers, A. (2000) *Wirkliche Leben in verlorenen Ländern*, 2 CDs, Frankfurt/Berlin-Potsdam.

Sellin, F. (2002) *Ich brech' die Herzen … Das Leben des Heinz Rühmann*, Reinbek: Rowohlt.

Sheppard, R. (1993) 'The Problematics of European Modernism', in Giles, S. (ed.) *Theorizing Modernism: Essays in Critical Theory*, London: Routledge, pp. 1–51.

Silbermann, A. (1982) *Sind wir Antisemiten?: Ausmaß und Wirkung eines sozialen Vorurteils in der Bundesrepublik Deutschland*, Cologne: Verlag Wissenschaft und Politik.

Silbermann, A. and Schoeps, J.H. (eds) (1986) *Antisemitismus nach dem Holocaust: Bestandsaufnahme und erscheinungsformen in deutschsprachigen Ländern*, Cologne: Verlag Wissenschaft und Politik.

Sinn, G. and Sinn, H-W. (1992) *Jumpstart: The Economic Unification of Germany*, Boston: MIT Press.

Sluga, H.D. (1993) *Heidegger's Crisis: Philosophy and Politics in Nazi Germany*, Cambridge, MA: Harvard University Press.

Solt, M.E. (1968) *Concrete Poetry: A World View*, Bloomington: Indiana University Press.

Spoerer, M. (2001) *Zwangsarbeit unter dem Hakenkreuz*, Stuttgart: DVA.

Spotts, F. (1994) *Bayreuth: A History of the Wagner Festival*, New Haven, CT: Yale University Press.

Staab, A. (1998) *National Identity in Eastern Germany: Inner Unification or Continued Separation?* London: Praeger.

Stadler, F. (1997) *Studien zum Wiener Kreis: Ursprung, Entwicklung und Wirkung des Logischen Empirismus im Kontext*, Frankfurt: Suhrkamp.

Statistisches Bundesamt, *Wirtschaft und Statistik*, monthly.

Statistisches Bundesamt, *Statistisches Jahrbuch*, annual.

Stein, W. (1993) *Der Grosse Kulturfahrplan*, Munich: Herbig.

Steiner, G. (1995) *Film Book Austria*, Vienna: Federal Chancellery/Federal Press Service.

Steiner, S. (ed.) (1996) *Federal Republic of Germany: Questions and Answers*, New York: German Information Center, pp. 83–100.

Stern, C. (1963) *Ulbricht: Eine politische Biographie*, Cologne: Kiepenheuer & Witsch.

Strate, U. (ed.) (1994) *Déjà vu: Moden 1950–90*, Heidelberg: Braus.

Sturm, E. (2000) *Und der Zukunft zugewandt? Eine Untersuchung zur 'Politikfähigkeit' der PDS*, Opladen: Leske & Budrich.

Sturzbecher, D. and Freytag, R. (2000) *Antisemitismus unter Jugendlichen: Fakten, Erklärungen, Unterrichtsbausteine*, Göttingen: Hogrefe.

Tafel, C. (1996) *Architectural Guide to Germany*, Basle: Birkhäuser.

Tebbutt, S. (ed.) (2001) *Sinti und Roma in der deutschsprachigen Gesellschaft und Literatur*, Frankfurt: Lang.

Thamer, H.U. (1994) *Verführung und Gewalt: Deutschland 1933–1945*, Berlin: Siedler.

Thomas, R. and Weidenfeld, W. (1999) 'Identität', in Weidenfeld, W. and Korte, K.R. (eds) *Handbuch zur deutschen Einheit 1949–1989–1999*, Frankfurt: Campus.

Thomson, P. and Sacks, G. (eds) (1994) *The Cambridge Companion to Brecht*, Cambridge: Cambridge University Press.

Thun, H.P. (1998) *Eine Einführung in das Bibliothekswesen der Bundesrepublik Deutschland*, Berlin: Deutsches Bibliotheksinstitut.

Tibi, B. (2000) *Der Islam und Deutschland: Muslime in Deutschland*, Stuttgart: DVA.

Timms, E. (1999) *Karl Kraus: Satiriker der Apokalypse*, Frankfurt: Suhrkamp.

Trevor-Roper, H. (ed.) (1978) *The Goebbels Diaries: The Last Days*, trans. R. Barry, London: Secker & Warburg.

Trompenaars, F. and Hampden-Turner, C. (1998) *Riding the Waves of Culture: Understanding Diversity in Global Business*, 2nd edn, New York: McGraw-Hill.

Unseld, S. (1973) *Hermann Hesse: Eine Werkgeschichte*, Frankfurt: Suhrkamp.

Urmoneit, A. (1991) *Ehe und Familie in Deutschland*, Munich: Nusser.

Von Wright, G.H. (1990) *Wittgenstein*, Frankfurt: Suhrkamp.

Vormweg, H. (2000) *Der andere Deutsche: Heinrich Böll – Eine Biographie*, Cologne: Kiepenheuer & Witsch.

Vossenkuhl, W. (1995) *Ludwig Wittgenstein*, Munich: Beck.

Wagener, H. (1985) *Siegfried Lenz*, Munich: Beck.

Wagnleitner, R. (1994) *Coca-Colonization and the Cold War: The Cultural Mission of the United States in Austria after the Second World War*, Chapel Hill: University of North Carolina Press.

Wallich, G. (1955) *Mainsprings of the German Revival*, New Haven, CT: Yale University Press.

Watanabe-O'Kelly, H. (ed.) (1997) *The Cambridge History of German Literature*, Cambridge, New York and Melbourne: Cambridge University Press.

Watson, A. (1992) *The Germans: Who Are They Now?*, London: Methuen, pp. 200–75.

Weber, C. (ed.) (2001) *A Heiner Müller Reader: Plays, Poetry and Prose*, Baltimore: Johns Hopkins University Press.

Weber, C. and Möller, R. (1999) *Mode und Modeschmuck 1920–1970 in Deutschland*, Stuttgart: Arnold.

Weidenfeld, W. and Korte, K.R. (eds) (1999) *Handbuch zur deutschen Einheit 1949–1989–1999*, Frankfurt: Campus.

Weinrich, H. (ed.) (1982) *Als Fremder in Deutschland: Berichte, Erzählungen, Gedichte von Ausländern*, Munich: dtv.

Weiss, C. (1986) 'Konkrete Poesie als Sprachkritik', in Fischer, L. (ed.) *Literatur in der Bundesrepublik Deutschland bis 1967* (Hansers Sozialgeschichte der Literatur, 10), Munich: Hanser, pp. 420–35.

Wenders, W. (1986) *Emotion Pictures: Essays und Filmkritiken 1968–1985*, Frankfurt: Verlag der Autoren.

Wenders, W. (1988) *Der Logik der Bilder*, Frankfurt: Verlag der Autoren.

Wenders, W. (1992) *The Act of Seeing: Texte und Gespräche*, Frankfurt: Verlag der Autoren.

Wendt, B.J. (1995) *Deutschland 1933–1945: Das Dritte Reich*, Hannover: Fackelträger.

Westgate, G. (2002) *Strategies Under Surveillance: Reading Irmtraud Morgner as a GDR Writer*, Amsterdam/New York: Rodopi.

White, A.D. (1996) *Max Frisch: The Reluctant Modernist*, Lewiston, NY: Mellen.

White, S. (ed.) (1995) *The Cambridge Companion to Habermas*, Cambridge: Cambridge University Press.

Whitton, K.S. (1990) *Dürrenmatt*, New York, Oxford and Munich: Berg.

Wildgen, W. (n.d.) *Niederdeutsch in Schule und Gesellschaft*, Bremen: Universität Bremen.

Wildt, M. (1996) *Vom kleinen Wohlstand: eine Konsumgeschichte der fünfziger Jahre*, Frankfurt: Fischer.

Willer, S. (2000) *Botho Strauss – Zur Einführung*, Hamburg: Junius.

Willett, J. (1998) *Brecht in Context: Comparative Approaches*, London: Methuen.

Willett, R. (1989) *The Americanization of Germany, 1945–1949*, New York: Routledge.

Wirtschaftsdienst.

Wirtschaftswoche, weekly.

Wirtschaft und Statistik, monthly.

Witte, B. (1985) *Walter Benjamin, mit Selbstzeugnissen und Bilddokumenten*, Reinbek: Rowohlt.

Wittmann, R. (1991) *Geschichte des Deutschen Buchhandels: Ein Überblick*, Munich: Beck.

Wittstock, U. (ed.) (1994) *Roman oder Leben: Postmoderne in der deutschen Literatur*, Leipzig: Reclam.

Wolffheim, E. (1989) *Hans Henny Jahnn*, Reinbek: Rowohlt.

Wood, J. (1999) *The Broken Estate: Essays on Literature and Belief*, London: Jonathan Cape.

Woyke, W. (1992) *Stichwort Wahlen: ein Ratgeber für Wähler und Kandidaten*, 7th edn, Opladen: Leske & Budrich.

Wright, V. (ed.) (1994) *Privatisation in Western Europe*, London: Pinter.

Yates, W.E. (1992) *Schnitzler, Hofmannsthal and the Austrian Theatre*, New Haven, CT: Yale University Press.

Yates, W.E. (1996) *Theatre in Vienna: A Critical History, 1776–1995*, Cambridge: Cambridge University Press.

Zimmer, A. (1996) *Vereine – Basiselement der Demokratie*, Opladen: Leske & Budrich.

Zinn, G. (2000) 'Germany's other Others: Teaching about Kurds, Roma, and Sinti in an Upper-Division Culture Class', *Die Unterrichtspraxis – Teaching German*, vol. 33, no. 2, pp. 106–12.

Zötsch, C. (1999) *Powergirls und Drachenmädchen: Weibliche Symbolwelten in Mythologie und Jugendkultur*, Münster: Unrast.